Mastering Systems Analysis and Design

Macmillan Master Series

Accounting
Advanced English Language
Advanced Pure Mathematics
Arabic
Banking
Basic Management
Biology
British Politics
Business Administration
Business Communication
C Programming
C++ Programming
Chemistry
COBOL Programming
Communication
Counselling Skills
Database Design
Desktop Publishing
Economic and Social History
Economics
Electrical Engineering
Electronic and Electrical Calculations
Electronics
English Grammar
English Language
English Literature
Fashion Styling
French
French 2
Geography
German

Global Information Systems
Internet
Italian
Italian 2
Java
Marketing
Mathematics
Microsoft Office
Microsoft Windows, Novell
    NetWare and UNIX
Modern British History
Modern European History
Modern World History
Networks
Pascal and Delphi Programming
Philosophy
Photography
Physics
Psychology
Shakespeare
Social Welfare
Sociology
Spanish
Spanish 2
Statistics
Systems Analysis and Design
Visual Basic
World Religions

Macmillan Master Series

Series Standing Order ISBN 0–333–69343–4
(outside North America only)

You can receive future titles in this series as they are published by placing a standing order. Please contact your bookseller or, in case of difficulty, write to us at the address below with your name and address, the title of the series and the ISBN quoted above.

Customer Services Department, Macmillan Distribution Ltd
Houndmills, Basingstoke, Hampshire RG21 6XS, England

Mastering

Systems Analysis and Design

Martin Hughes, BSc (Hons), CEng
Head of Computer Science
Anglia Polytechnic University
Cambridge

Series Editor
William J. Buchanan, BSc (Hons.), CEng, PhD
Senior Lecturer
School of Computing
Napier University
Edinburgh

palgrave
macmillan

To my wife Katharine, my children and my parents

First published 2000 by
MACMILLAN PRESS LTD
Houndmills, Basingstoke, Hampshire RG21 6XS
and London
Companies and representatives throughout the world

ISBN-13: 978-0-333-74803-9

A catalogue record for this book is available from the British Library.

This book is printed on paper suitable for recycling and made from fully managed and sustained forest sources.
Logging, pulping and manufacturing processes are expected to conform to the environmental regulations of the country of origin.

Typeset by W.Buchanan and J.Buchanan in Great Britain

Printed and bound in Great Britain by
CPI Antony Rowe, Chippenham and Eastbourne

Contents

Preface

The purpose of this book is to provide a practically-based introduction to the tools and techniques of structured computer systems analysis and design, suitable for use both by practitioners and students in all types of educational institutions. The notation and terminology used is compatible with the current version of the official UK government method, SSADM ver. 4.2+, but the content and delivery has been simplified to make it suitable as either a first text in the subject or as the basis for advanced practical work.
The most fundamental and powerful tools, as used in some form in all structured analysis and design methodologies, are described in depth. Structured methodologies, including SSADM, are designed to be 'scaleable' and this text demonstrates how to apply a reduced set of the many techniques available to produce a rigorous specification appropriate to the scale of the application. In addition, comments and advice on common skills and professional behaviour are included where appropriate throughout the text.

The book is divided into two logical parts, with the reference and descriptive text in Chapters 1 to 12 inclusive. These chapters contains all of the explanatory material and apply it to a consistent case study, the River Flow Meter System. Following that, in Chapter 13, all of the techniques learned previously are re-applied to a complete but separate case study, the Wooden Windows Sales System. In this way the activities of learning and practice could progress sequentially or in parallel. Each of these two logical parts is based on the practical application of the topic to the two different case studies, each of which is complete in itself but is small enough to be worked through in a term or a semester.

This structure and approach has the advantage that the different types of material and themes in this book are clearly separated and hence may be used in many different ways. This allows the book to be used to support the wide variety of courses in which this topic appears, with all of their diversity of delivery and content. Throughout this work, the reader is assumed to be the analyst completing the work, so the material refers to 'you' when it is advising how to actually tackle a task to proceed with the example under discussion, and 'we' when discussing alternatives which, in practice, would be chosen by consensus.

Martin Hughes, *Head of Computer Science, Anglia Polytechnic University, East Road, Cambridge, UK.*

Note from Series Editor

Structured Analysis and Design is an important area. I know this because of my involvement with software consultancy work. From this I found that the actual software developed was not the most important part of the project, and was not the thing that brought most praise (or any follow-up contracts). It was the documentation and the design, and most importantly of all it was speaking with people who would be using the software.

The development of a system is thus not just about developing the best technical solution, it's about all the extra bits that go into it: the documentation, the design, the time plans, the user interface, and so on. It is these parts that form the complete package, and it is these things that will define the overall quality of the system.

Seven tips I can pass on to any analyst or developer are:

- Always investigate every single part of a user specification, as there will always a small part of it that will actually take the longest time to complete.

- Always outline a hand-over test specification for any staged, or final, payments, so that both the developer and the user know what will be delivered, and on the guidelines that will define an acceptance.

- Always keep in contact with your clients, and keep them informed on any relaxations in the implementation, or problems with time scales. Most clients are willing to relax the specification or time scale, in order to complete a project. These changes will allow the client to modify their own time scales.

- Time is critical. Most things are technically possible; it is time that is the major factor in achieving them.

- Always know the most important parts of a specification, that is, what the user really wants from the system. From this, the main design can be formed. Most customers will allow a specification to be 'de-scoped', as long as it does not involve 'de-scoping' the main objectives of the system.

- Always produce top quality documentation. Most companies have had problems with lack of documentation from development contracts, and an analyst who produces top-quality documentation stands a much better chance to get further contracts.

- Learn from your mistakes. We all make mistakes. Admit to them, and learn from them (in life, too).

The Macmillan Mastering IT and Computing series is expanding rapidly and this book is another key foundation book in the whole series. Others include:

- Mastering Microsoft Windows, Novell NetWare and UNIX.
- Mastering Networks.
- Mastering Java.
- Mastering Pascal and Delphi.
- Mastering Visual Basic.
- Mastering C++.
- Mastering Microsoft Office.
- Mastering Database Design.
- Mastering the Internet.
- Mastering Global Information Systems.

William J. Buchanan, *Senior Lecturer, School of Computing,*
Napier University, Edinburgh, UK.

1 Introduction

1.1 Introduction

The purpose of this chapter is to introduce the concepts of systems analysis and design, and to answer some basic questions, such as: 'What is systems analysis and design?', 'Where does it occur in the development of a computer system?', 'Who does it?' and, 'Why are some people better at it than others?'.

We can start by simply stating that systems analysis and design, in the context of this book, is the term used to identify certain activities performed during the development of the software for computer systems. These and related activities have become increasingly studied and classified as the difficulties of producing large and complex computer software applications have become recognised.

Many of the initial topics within the subject are based on developing 'people skills' and rather lengthy definitions, which can seem irrelevant to those readers interested in the technicalities of computer software. For this reason the less technical aspects of the subject are all covered in this chapter as far as is possible, leaving the rest of the book free to focus on the application of the specific tools and techniques.

1.2 The system and development life cycle models

1.2.1 Definition of the 'system'

There are many definitions of the word 'system'. For example, a general definition from a typical dictionary could define a system in the following way. 'A system is group of related components that interact to perform a defined task.' Some examples of systems in the computer field are:

- A **computer system**, which is made up of the CPU, operating system and peripheral devices;
- An **information system**, which is made up of a database, all the related data entry, update, query and report programs and the associated manual and operating procedures; or
- The computer **operating system**, which is the software which allows the hardware to perform its basic operating functions.

For the purpose of this book, we will take the definition to be: any computer software project which is too large or complex for a single person to comprehend and implement alone in a reasonable period of time.

1

1.2.2 The system life cycle

The system life is the useful life of a system. It may be referred to as the project (or product) life. The length of the system life depends upon the nature and volatility of the business, as well as the software development tools used to generate the application programs. Often problems in using a system which has been developed lead to a requirement for modifications. In addition, natural changes in business and technology over the years will reduce the effectiveness of a system, no matter how well it initially fulfilled it purpose. As a result, the whole cycle of activities which were performed to implement the system in the first place may have to be repeated in order to modify it, and this can happen several times. Eventually, the basis of a system that has been changed or enhanced several times is no longer sound enough to allow it to be modified further, so a completely new system is implemented to replace it.

As an example, look at what is probably the most common piece of software in the world today, the micro-computer operating system. Many of these are up to version seven at the time of writing, having had a major release approximately every two years since they were first developed. Specialised application software, which is the end product of the process described in this book, is no different. In fact, it has been estimated that most of the software development effort of a system takes place after it has first been implemented.

It is possible to argue that each cycle of a system is really a system in its own, but we are now drifting into philosophical arguments, and all we wish to establish here is that at some point another system replaces the original systems function, and the whole process starts again, like the hours on a clock face, which is why we refer to it as a 'cycle'.

1.2.3 The system development activities

The system development activities are a series of stages or phases which take place in each iteration of the system life cycle and are the sequence of events followed to build the software to be used in a computer system. It requires mutual effort on the part of the people who want to use the system and the computer specialists, and is an iterative process, due to the fact that the customer is rarely completely satisfied with what is suggested initially. Modifications and enhancements are likely to be requested even during initial discussions as well after the system 'goes live' as mentioned above. These changes are often a continuous process until the full system goes through another cycle. For this reason many references books also call the development process a cycle in its own right. Certainly each of the individual activities tend to take more than one attempt before everyone agrees, or accepts a compromise, in order to make progress.

1.2.4 Methodologies and the development stages

A system development methodology formalises and codifies what must be accomplished during the system development activities. Each different methodology uses a related system life cycle model, which is an idealised way of viewing the process. These often divide the activities into phases, stages and tasks required to complete the development process. The methodology defines the precise objectives and the results required from each of the tasks before the next can commence. There are often standard layouts or specialised forms for the preparation of the documentation in each phase. The results tend to be in the form of paper products and these are assembled at major 'milestones' into specific documents. The production of the individual diagrams and forms are an intellectual activity, whilst the assembled documents communicate the findings to users and management so that the work may be scrutinised and either approved or modified.

Each methodology, together with the related system life cycle model, imposes a specific framework on the process of developing software which defines the sequence of tasks to be performed and the order in which they must be completed before it is safe to proceed to the next stage. There have been many different methodologies, each reflecting the current best practice at the time, but we will concentrate on only one. This is a 'compromise' model which is general enough to be compatible with most of the standard methods and yet detailed enough to allow us to work through the analysis and design of some typical 'case studies' in a realistic manner.

This model, as shown in Figure 1.1, shows one full system life cycle with the pre-development and post-development activities. The development activities themselves are divided into two major parts each with sub-parts.

Note that the actual coding plays a very small part in the total work. In fact the in-creasing 'computerisation' of software development attempts to go from the require-ments to the actual code production of the working system as automatically as possi-ble. Note also that the whole of Part I is labelled 'structured analysis and design' but that there are also activities, such as 'requirements analysis' which also use similar terms. There are not enough appropriate terms available, so some of them occur more than once which makes cross-reference between different methods very difficult. How-ever, the analysis and design activities are required throughout the initial part of the project, whatever word is used to describe the specific activity.

If the analysis and design activities are completed correctly, then the rest of the work, phase II, should be no more difficult than, say, performing a well-written piece of music. While this may demand great skill, what has to be done is clearly defined. This goal has never been fully achieved in computing, but to make the attempt is in line with much of current practice. Emphasising the importance of the analysis and the design tasks is an attempt to get as close to this ideal as possible, as any errors or omis-sions at this stage will be amplified later and become increasingly difficult to correct.

1.2.5 Basic techniques and notation

Just as engineers use blueprints and electronic engineers use circuit diagrams, so there are a variety of techniques to represent the technical details of the different stages of development. One of the major problems in the computer industry is that developments are taking place so fast that the techniques become out of date almost as fast as they are invented. New problem areas spawn new ways of representing solutions but people are often unwilling to abandon a practice if it works for them or there is no specific advantage to the new approach or method. Consequently there are many 'standards' often related to methodologies, each with particular advantages over its rivals. No methodology is accepted as being the world-wide common standard, but Structured Systems Analysis and Design Method (SSADM) is the standard for the analysis and design of computer software within government departments in the United Kingdom.

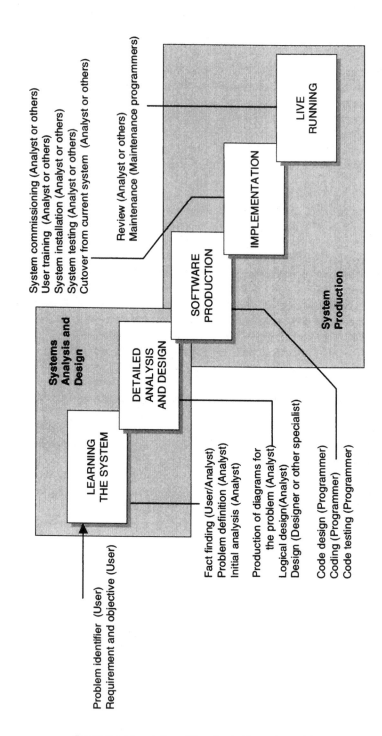

Figure 1.1 Description of the simple life cycle model

4   *Mastering systems analysis and design*

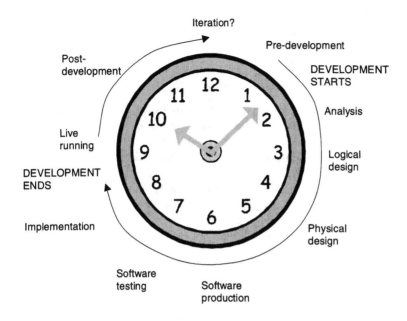

Figure 1.2 Diagram of the simple life cycle model

There are many representational forms and techniques which you may encounter when reading books on analysis and design, all of which are ways of depicting the results of the activities. With the general adoption of SSADM, these have been refined down to a handful of techniques. The major ones are:

- Data Flow Diagrams (DFD).
- Logical Data Structure Diagrams (LDS).
- Relational Data Analysis Tables (RDA).
- Jackson Structure Charts (based on JSP notation).

The majority of this book is concerned with providing practical advice and examples to help you learn to use the above techniques and hence to produce related diagrams. In addition you need to know when to produce them, and that depends upon the specific methodology being used. We are going to use the diagramming conventions of SSADM version 4 and broadly follow its life cycle model, without this being a specific book on that methodology. Once you have worked through the material in this book you will find it very easy to learn SSADM, in any version, or to apply analysis and design techniques in a practical situation. There is no need to worry that you will be taught bad habits or sloppy techniques. Everything in this book is correct in so far as it goes, but it is an introductory text, and in the same way that you do not learn to fly on a Jumbo jet, you need not learn your basic analysis and design skills in a methodology designed for complex large scale commercial projects.

1.3 Systems analysis and design in software development

Having set the scene by defining some terms and showing how they relate to one another, we can now discuss this material in more detail by stating precisely what we mean by some of the terms above.

1.3.1 Definitions of 'system analysis and design'

These are really two things, systems analysis and systems design, which are always spoken of in that order. Together they describe the examination of a problem and the creation of a solution to the problem.

Notice that there is no mention of computers so far. Many professionals from other disciplines object to the way the word 'Computer' is implicitly placed before this phrase, and they are quite correct. The flourishing software industry hijacked the terminology from earlier, related, technologies and the subsequent popularity of computing has led to the presumed association of the term with the topic. In this book, whenever we refer to 'systems analysis and design', we really mean 'computer systems analysis and design'. This means we are implicitly intending to generate a *computer* solution to the problem, if at all possible.

Systems analysis is the process of examining and learning about the current system, its problem and the user requirements, and defining an abstract solution. It is most effective when the current system is clearly defined, every view of it is available and previous solutions to similar problems are known to exist. **Systems design** is the process of turning the abstract (analysed) solution into a practical specification, suitable for implementation. Systems design itself is commonly split into logical and physical design. In practice it can be quite difficult to distinguish between the logical and the physical solutions, but in this book we will concentrate on the logical solution, as produced by the systems analysis in the form of a **'Systems specification'**. In order to understand what we mean by these terms, we need to go into more detail about the whole software development process.

1.3.2 Who does the systems analysis and design?

The individual who is responsible for the initial development of a system up to, and sometimes including, the design is the **systems analyst**. That person also often has overall management responsibility for the rest of the activities of the development. In these cases, or if it is a large system, the title given to the person in charge of the analysis is less well defined; Project Leader, Project Manager, Chief (Software) Engineer, Chief Programmer and Chief, or Senior, Designer have all been used. As with the stages of the life cycle the title of the person who performs the function is less important than the realisation that somebody is doing the analysis and design, even if only by default. From now on we refer to the systems analyst whenever we wish to identify the individual(s) performing that role.

Systems analysts are the architects, as well as the operational managers, of a computer software development. It is their job to identify the user's requirements, suggest proposed solutions, determine the technical and operational feasibility of these solutions, and to estimate the costs and resources required to implement them. They also turn these requirements into a set of specifications, which are the 'blueprint' for the required system. Analysts may also plan the database, and other data elements, and derive the manual and machine procedures and the detailed processing specifications for each data entry, update, query and report program within the system. In this latter case the systems generated are often referred to as information systems, the heart of which is a database held on a computer, or network of computers. Drawing a line between computer systems and information systems can be quite difficult as many modern computer systems rely on databases, and the result tends to be a matter of emphasis. Fortunately, the distinction need not trouble us as the general analysis and design skills described here apply equally to all systems in the early stages of development.

In today's environment, the systems analyst also may create a prototype of the system in consultation with the users, so that the final specifications include real examples of screens and reports that have been reviewed and agreed by the end user. Experienced systems analysts leave no doubt in users' minds as to the kind of system that is being proposed, and they should insist that users are responsible for their part of the system review and 'sign-off' every stage.

Systems analysts, therefore, require a good understanding of human nature, with a balanced mix of technical knowledge, analytical skills and occasionally application-specific knowledge. This last requirement leads some analysts to concentrate on one application area, with such titles as Business Systems Analysts, Information Systems Analysts, Scientific and Technical Systems Analysts, or even more specific Banking Systems Analysts being used. The tools and techniques they employ are identical, the only difference lies in the experience in dealing with particular groups of users, or in familiarity with the problems likely to be encountered in a particular specialist application.

1.3.3 The different skills required by analysts, designers and programmers

The roles performed by computer specialists can be grouped into three main categories: analyst, designer and programmer. In fact the boundaries are not that clear in practice, with many jobs expecting a combination of any two, or all three, aspects. We have already discussed the analyst's role and are implying that we can define programmers as the people who actually write the code which will be used within the system, which just leaves 'designers'. In order to see why these three jobs are so different it is necessary to examine the skills required to be effective in each of the three roles.

Systems analysts mainly deal with people! They must be able to:

- Listen patiently.
- Take good notes.
- Extract information without giving offence.
- Conceptualise computer systems.
- Document the systems using agreed standards.

On the other hand **programmers** deal with mainly computers! They must be able to:

- Understand the documentation.
- Produce working computer code.
- Test and implement computer systems.
- Document the programs for maintenance teams.

Somewhere between the pure analyst and programmer roles are the **Designers,** who communicate the abstract specifications produced by the analyst to the people who do the actual coding, the programmers, in precise computer terms but without actually writing the code. The design therefore has to be as syntactically correct as a programming language, without actually being C, Visual Basic or COBOL. The analyst's specification should also be as precise as the design but without going into the kind of constructs required to write modules or programs.

Design can be further split into two parts. The first part is **logical design**, which relates closely to the job of the analyst, in which a purely abstract solution to the problem is specified. The second part involves producing a **physical design** which includes actual file layouts and module specifications. These tend to be constrained by the actual hardware and operating system to be used, and relate closely to the job of the programmer. We can visualise the relationship between the different roles using Figure 1.3.

At one time the Analyst did all of the design. More recently it has become usual for the Analyst to do only the logical design, leaving Database Administrators or Programming Team Leaders to do the physical design. The exception is in very large projects where there may also be specific Designers doing both parts. In this book we will assume that the analysis and design jobs finish with the logical design.

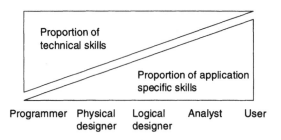

Figure 1.3 The roles of the analysts, designers and programmers

1.4   System documentation

Analysts and designers communicate with each other, and with the users and programmers, using standard documents for each phase of the project. Different methodologies specify slightly different documents and vary their content accordingly. In fact there are whole books written about the documentation required for computer systems. Despite this diversity, some generalisations about the documents, and their likely contents can be made. Those usually found are listed below.

- Project Initiation Documents (PID). These are anything which is produced, often by the user, to define the problem before development begins.
- Systems Proposal. A report produced by the systems analyst before in-depth analysis which is used to state what the proposed system should consist of in strategic

terms, and whether to start work in earnest. This is similar to a feasibility study in practice.

- Systems Specification. A document produced by the systems analyst between the logical design and the physical design activities and similar to the requirements specification. This document marks the change in activities to software development, where the products are aimed more at the computer specialist than the user.
- Functional Specification. A document produced between the physical design and coding which allows programmers to concentrate on coding possibly a small part of the application without reference to the user or the analyst.

These last two documents are also used as the formal reference for maintenance and support activities once the system is live. There are various intermediate documents, and this book uses the Business System Proposal, described later, as a convenient milestone between the end of the requirements analysis and the beginning of the logical design. This fits in with the philosophy of SSADM, without committing us to a full implementation of that methodology while we are still learning the basic tools and techniques. The exact position of these documents in the development activities is impossible to define in every case, but a general position in relation to the activities defined in Figure 1.1 is shown in Table 1.1.

Within these documents you will find the normal language contents of reports, and various diagrams and charts which are the result of tools and techniques specific to analysis and design used prior to that stage. A general familiarity with the skills of report writing is assumed in the reader, but the production of the specialist diagrams is the main topic covered in this book.

Table 1.1 Documents in the life cycle model

PART	ACTIVITIES	DOCUMENTATION (product of activities)	PRODUCED BY
Before the analysis starts	Performed by User before approaching Analyst	Project Initiation Documents	User
LEARNING THE SYSTEM	Fact-Finding & Problem definition	'Soft' system products (Described in Chapter 3)	Analyst
	Initial analysis	System Proposal	Analyst
DETAILED ANALYSIS & DESIGN	Production of diagrams for detail of solution	Business System Proposal (helps user choose solution)	Analyst
	Logical design	System Specification	Analyst
SYSTEM PRODUCTION starts around here	Physical design	Function Specification	Designer

1.5 Fundamental concepts of the systems approach

One of the problems particular to the subject is 'what are the skills and attributes which make a good analyst?' One way in which methodologies have been produced is to examine the work of successful analysts and try to document why their systems worked well when others, in apparently similar circumstances, did not.

There is a great deal of work going on in this area; see the related texts and specialist journals if you are interested in studying this topic further and want more details. This section will only introduce the basic ideas which are definitely required to complete the material within this book. It is worth stating though, if only once, that you need a fundamental belief in your ability to make computers work for you, rather than the other way around, before you start. Fortunately most people drawn to the profession already have that self-confidence.

1.5.1 The basic system model

Assuming that we have accepted that we can explain and understand the situations in question, then there is a fundamental way of looking at things which leads us naturally into analysing them. This is called the 'system model' and is depicted in its most basic form in Figure 1.4.

As you can see it consists of 'inputs' to a 'transformation' being turned into 'outputs'. We can use this in many ways. A fundamental computing example is the data processing model, as illustrated in Figure 1.5.

The definition of data processing is neatly encapsulated in the diagram. Data is unprocessed information, information is processed data, and data processing is the activity of transforming data into information! This may seem a bit of a cheat, but it illustrates our point very well.

That was a very simple example, though it has its uses, especially in answering some examination questions. A more technical example is the way in which we describe a television for instance. Its inputs are energy, in the form of electricity and a data source as UHF signals. It turns them both into vibrations in the air and photons to give us the sound and vision we associate with a television programme. We also get quite a bit of heat which normally we ignore, although cats, as an example of residents who have different priorities to humans, often regard televisions more as sources of warmth than entertainment. The system model illustrates our view of the system, as opposed to the cats or the customers whose views might be quite different. This concept is explored in greater depth later in the text when we discuss both soft system's methods, and data flow diagrams.

Figure 1.4 The basic system model

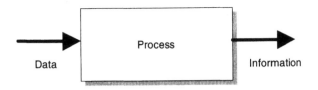

Figure 1.5 The data processing system model

1.5.2 The structured approach

The concept of structuring objects and ideas is not new or limited to systems analysis. In the Bible, Moses was advised that he should not attempt to run his whole tribe himself but appoint 'captains of thousands, captains of hundreds ... and of tens' (Figure 1.6). Samuel Colt and Henry Ford both used the concept of breaking large complicated objects down into well-defined sub-components in manufacturing processes. The hardware of computer systems has increasingly made use of the assembly of standard parts which can be replaced to produce a reliable working whole unit. In business, the staff and senior management are related by a company structure, which ideally they agree and adhere to. Hence the notion of structuring could be regarded as a coping strategy for handling large or complex systems.

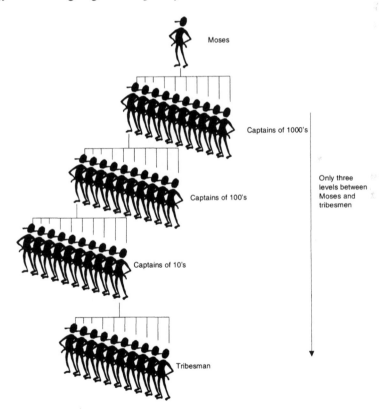

Figure 1.6 Moses' Tribes

1.5.3 Bottom-up and top-down approaches

There are two basic approaches to analysing a structure. One is to assemble the finished product from a large or reproducible number of small well-defined components, often called the LEGO© approach for obvious reasons. This is known technically as a bottom-up approach. The second is to start with the whole system and to break it down into smaller and smaller units, each of which has a defined place in the overall structure. This is the top-down approach and one that is extremely important in structured systems thinking.

The mistake of concentration on detail too soon is a little like rushing for a parking space in a very large and unfamiliar car park. We dash around looking for the object we are interested in, an empty parking space. When we find one, we park the car and run for the theatre or plane without a second thought. Some hours or days later we are faced with finding an anonymous vehicle in a massive site full of similar objects, often when we are, once again, in a tearing hurry – a very stressful experience. But fortunately these situations occur rarely in life and one such event is enough to convince most people of the need for care in similar situations. In analysis these circumstance are the norm and a systematic and structured approach is an accepted and popular way to tame a problem which is too large to hold in your head all at once. Indeed one of the first attributes recognised in a good Analyst was a willingness to take notes and keep good records. This is similar to the basic engineering technique of carefully keeping a logbook for each project.

The reason we are so interested in top-down methods is that we are usually starting, logically, at the 'top' of a system when we are analysing it. We are an outsider brought in to analyse someone else's system, and any attempt to concentrate on too much detail too quickly will inevitably lead to confusion. Unfortunately, it can happen that the top-down view is clearly different from the bottom-up view. For example, if we are dealing with a business system, we are often given the corporate view of the structure, and use it as a guide to do our analysis. Later on it may transpire that, for whatever reason, the actual staff in the business has a different model. Under these circumstances, the computer system can fail even if it is implemented perfectly. The techniques described in this book, especially the 'soft' methods in Chapter 3, may uncover such discrepancies in the user's business structure, and one of the jobs of the analyst may be to diplomatically draw attention to these problems in the next milestone document. Unless there is a need to illustrate a particular situation, however, we will assume that the applications in this book have no such problems.

1.5.4 Physical systems and logical models

This 'systems thinking' idea is basically rather simple, but is a tricky one to express. It is the difference between the actuality of the situation, and our conception of it which we use to model and examine what is happening. This is fundamentally a technical contrivance to allow us to ignore those aspects which do not aid in understanding, but whose presence detracts or distracts our thought processes. We have already introduced one technique for this with the 'system model' where we put together inputs and outputs in an established environment, e.g. a UHF signal. There is another dimension to the whole problem, that of choosing the correct level of complexity to model at the next stage.

The physical system we are examining is often a dynamic and complex one. We may look at a lawn and see it as a rather dull expanse of green – as 'boring as watching grass grow' is a common cliche. Closer inspection reveals a different picture, and from ground level there is a dramatic battle being fought between plants, insects and fungi. At a lower level still, there are rapidly changing levels of moisture and bacteria. Trying to model this is much too complex, so we choose a level appropriate to our interest and effectively take a snapshot in time of a representative area, say a square metre. We can then use this to look at only those aspects which interest us: nutrient levels, weed growth and so on. We may have counted the number and size of distribution of the blades of grass which we can then work on. Meanwhile the real patch carries on growing regardless of our model, using nutrients and generally behaving in precisely the way it wants.

In order to produce the proposed system you first have to produce a conceptual model of it on paper using the diagrams you will learn about in this book, and apply the user's requirements from the fact-finding to produce a conceptual model of the proposed system, which will be turned into a physical model at the later physical design stage. We can visualise these steps as in Figure 1.7.

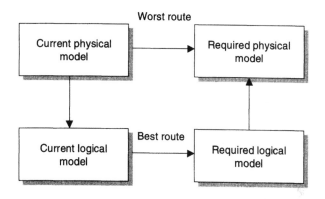

Figure 1.7 Going from the current to the proposed system

1.5.5 Overview of 'systems approach'

This chapter has amplified, albeit on an introductory level, how the people who make a success of analysis and design seem to think and the conceptual techniques that they appear to use. It involves trying to see situations as 'systems' which have a 'structure', using 'top-down' and 'bottom-up' methods of viewing them, and relating 'physical systems' to 'logical models' when necessary. Do bear in mind that the 'systems thinking' approach is a set of skills, just like the various techniques in the rest of the book. You do not have to 'believe in' them to make them work, just know about them and when it is appropriate to think in this way. The trick is to only use the various approaches when necessary, and abandon them when you are relaxing. It is easier for people who think like this all the time, but they can have other problems, such as over-analysing every situation in which they find themselves.

1.6 Summary of introductory structured methods

So far we have introduced the concepts of life cycle models and methodologies, defined the roles of the people who perform systems analysis and design, related these to the other activities in the development of computer systems and explained some of the underlying concepts used. Having done this we are now in a position to discuss the practicalities of these activities, such as what we do before the analysis starts and how to actually perform the tasks involved. The material becomes increasingly practical as we progress through the techniques covered in the rest of the chapters.

Many of the concepts introduced above will seem irrelevant or boring compared to the technical analysis and design. They are, in fact, fundamental and their significance will only become clear as you gain more experience. Rather than try to memorise all of these concepts now, move onto the technical work, but return and re-read this chapter two or three times as you work through the book. You should find that you gain more insight in each reading as you gain experience in the more practical elements of the work.

1.7 Exercises

In order to gain more practice at mastering the **overview of Systems Analysis and Design** you may now attempt the tutorial questions given next. As we progress through the work in later chapters, you will be in a position to complete the tasks within the relevant sections of Chapter 13 before proceeding to the following chapter if you wish to do so. However, as Chapter 1 describes the fundamental concepts and it has no related practical tasks in Chapter 13, what follows is essentially 'bookwork'.

1.7.1   Define systems analysis and design.

1.7.2   Where do systems analysis and design occur in the development of a computer system?

1.7.3   What titles are given to the people who perform the tasks associated with systems analysis and design?

1.7.4   What other jobs and tasks are required to implement computer systems?

1.7.5   Distinguish between top-down and bottom-up system methods.

1.7.6   Where do the activities associated with the production of the software lie in the development of a typical system?

1.7.7   Name three major techniques used in the development of a typical system.

1.7.8   Name three of the skills which must be mastered by a successful analyst, and contrast them with the skills required by a programmer.

1.7.9   Name three document milestones in the development of a typical system and briefly describe the purpose of each.

1.7.10   Use the system model diagram to illustrate a system of your choice, e.g. a health care system.

Basic Fact-Finding Techniques

2.1 Introduction to fact-finding techniques

At this point the analyst is at the beginning a new cycle of the life cycle model (LCM). The current system, and its users already exist for them to find out about, using the techniques described in Figure 2.1. This shows the increasingly specialised activities and skills as they relate to each part of the simple LCM.

The analyst needs to find out about the current system and the user requirements for the proposed system. 'Fact finding' is the first stage of the system development process and produces the fundamental inputs to the later processes. It is therefore vitally important to perform it correctly as the rule of 'garbage in, garbage out' is as true today as it ever was.

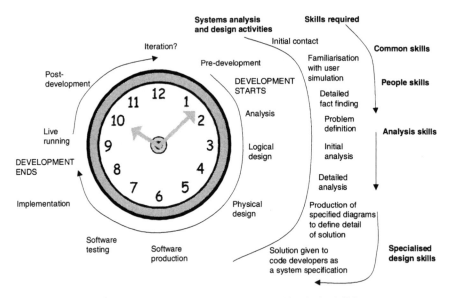

Figure 2.1 Overview of the analyst's position in the LCM

2.1.1 A summary of fact-finding techniques

Analysts need to master a range of techniques to gather the required information. The most important ones are: interviewing, questionnaires, reading, researching and observing. Of these the first is by far the most important. In it the analyst is personally involved, and consequently gains information at first hand via direct contact with the users and clients, who also get feedback and information. A great deal of communication is non-verbal. For example, a raised eyebrow or an ironic tone of voice can completely change the meaning of a sentence, and without personal contact this information is simply not available.

At the other extreme are questionnaires, in which the user is not only constrained to responding to the exact questions asked, but also to answering them in a manner predefined by the analyst. There is no opportunity for dynamic interchange or discussion, or to read non-verbal clues. The unreliability of information culled from questionnaires is legendary even for large samples. In a project where there are few users the analyst's chances of finding out what they need to know to implement a successful system are very slim indeed if they rely solely on questionnaires.

It is often possible to delegate or franchise the other fact finding techniques without detriment to the analysis process, but an otherwise excellent analyst who lacks fundamental interviewing skills will handicap themselves, the clients and the quality of the system. Observing is the only other technique which gives the same contact, and an experienced analyst does this whenever possible, whether they are interviewing or not. Because of this, this book concentrates mainly on interviewing skills and only briefly describes the other techniques.

2.2 Different types of current system

Following on from the view of the system development process being a cycle of events is the identification of the type of the current system that is being replaced. The analyst needs to know this in order to make the fact-finding effective. The first possibility is that there is no current system, but this situation is quite rare. Brand new companies do not just pop up from nowhere, they tend to grow from small companies where the procedures and processes expanded with the company. At some point a specialist, such as yourself, will be hired or contracted in, to implement a professionally produced system. Even if the analyst does happen to be called in at the very start of company, the customer will almost certainly have some system in mind to address their requirements, possibly one used by a rival company or a previous employer. So if you find yourself in this position, go through the fact-finding procedures as described below as though this system was actually available, rather than just being described by the user.

2.2.1 The current system is a manual system

This situation is where there is a manual or paper-based system which the company wishes to replace by an equivalent computer system. This is the general scenario used in the case studies within this book because it is the easiest way to introduce the analysis and design techniques, as learning how to represent a paper-based administrative system does not require any specialised computer knowledge. Once experience has been gained in translating such a system into a computerised one, then the specialist skills gained can be used in the other case.

2.2.2 The current system is a computer system

The alternative situation is where an existing computer system is to be replaced, either as a completely new system, or as a modification cycle as previously discussed. The fact finding in this case should be relatively easy, as the information required about the current system should already be available in the form of the analysis performed by the previous analysts. Even in this case, though, the analyst will still need to go through the user-related fact-finding activities described in this and the next chapter.

There are several problems special to the situation where the current system is already computerised. The first is that the analysis may have been performed using an out-of-date methodology, in which case the diagrams and notation should be documented either in an earlier standard reference work or the company's in-house standards. In this case the analyst will need to relate the documentation on the current system to the notation of the documents described later in this book,

The second problem is that the documentation on the current system may be incomplete or non-existent. Anyone who has worked in industry will probably recognise this possibility. The sad truth is that many computer systems were, and still are, documented either very badly or not at all. If you are studying at college and have completed programming assignments, ask yourself honestly if you documented your work as you went along well enough for someone else to complete it. The odds are that you did not, and neither did many of the people in industry that developed the systems you will be replacing. In this case the analyst can fall back on treating the current (computer) system as a manual system and do the fact-finding as described below.

2.2.3 Taking on the current system's data

The third problem is a special case of a major problem that all analysts must solve at some point, that of getting the data from the current system into the new system. There are whole books written about the various problems and strategies available, so the advice given here is very general.

This is often the last task done before live running, so why should we discuss it now? If the current system is a manual one then the data will eventually need to be typed in by hand, and the user easily recognises this need. However, if the current system is using a computer everyone may assume that the proposed system will use the current data 'automatically'. That may be possible, but it is often harder than one can imagine, and may be effectively impossible if the products or coding methods are incompatible. Be aware of the potential problem and get a solution onto the project plan and budget as soon as possible.

2.3 The types of information to be discovered in fact-finding

There are always two types of information that the analyst is trying to discover. One type is items of fact: the number of orders, the amount of stock, the distance between depots, and so on. The other involves value judgements on the part of the user: motivation for computerisation, expectations from the new system, areas in which costs should be cut, and so on.

The first type is difficult enough in most cases because the analyst is playing a kind of 'trivial pursuits' in a very specialised area. It is bad enough finding someone who can remember 'who won the Grand National in 1952', but that is trifling compared to 'what was the largest number of sales processed in any one day by a record department in this international chain store'. Unfortunately that is precisely the kind of information the analyst needs, but at least they are dealing with facts, and someone in the organisation should be able to find out or at least make a good guess.

The second kind of information is more problematical for two reasons. Firstly, the knowledge is only available in someone else's mind, and that involves getting them to explain it in terms that everyone understands. Secondly, people often genuinely do not know, or do not wish to tell, the reasons behind some decisions. Forcing them to 'explain' can irritate them enormously. This kind of communication is definitely two-way and requires sensitivity on the part of the analyst. Success may depend more on the analyst's abilities to understand than on the user's capacity to explain.

We can illustrate the problems involved by examining the two extremes of finding facts involving people's values. The best and surest way to get to know everything possible about a person is to spend as much time as possible together. There is only one thing better, from a communication point of view, than being an analyst married to the boss and already working in the company, and that is being the analyst and the user yourself! The truth of this scarcely needs explaining, and many professionals turn with relief and pleasure to using a computer to produce a solution for a personal project as relaxation after an exhausting day of doing precisely the same thing, but for someone else. The only difference is in the identity of the user!

2.4 Interview techniques

2.4.1 Overview of the aims of an interview

The aim of every analyst is to conduct successful and efficient interviews. Success in this context involves getting the information required whilst keeping on good terms with the user. At the same time the analyst cannot afford to waste resources or have more meetings than are necessary, as this puts the cost of the project up and possibly leads to missed deadlines.

2.4.2 When to use interviews

Interviewing the client or user is not always the most appropriate way of gaining information. There are cases when you want to use other methods but, for the reasons given in Section 2.2.1, an interview should be arranged wherever possible. This can become difficult if there are a large number of users scattered over great distances. In this case get the users to appoint a representative who can express the views of the majority, then just interview that person. If this approach is not possible for any reason, choose a co-operative user to interview and check the generality of their views by sending a questionnaire to a sample of the other users. This is a lengthy process, and the analyst will often have to chase up the responses. If the analyst is short of time, or really must have a response, then there is no alternative to arranging interviews.

2.5 Producing an interview plan

What is required is a compromise between the two extremes described above, one which neither relies on infinite time and knowledge, and is also not pre-defined or too closely constrained. The recommended method is to learn as much as possible by research and reading beforehand, attend the interview with a prepared list of questions, and leave time to respond to the information and seek clarification where necessary. Remember that communications should work both ways and the user should also have more information at the end of the process. An idealised system model of an interview is shown in the Figure 2.2.

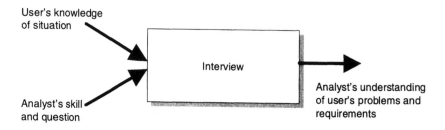

Figure 2.2 Idealised system model of an interview

This approach involves producing an 'interview plan' which allows the analyst to prepare as much as possible beforehand so as not to waste the time with the user. User availability is often very restricted and there is rarely enough time to discuss all the things required. Remember this when preparing for the interview and do as much as possible to use the time efficiently.

A good plan contains enough prompts to ensure that nothing is forgotten in the heat of the moment. It will most likely contain the following items:

- Basic facts about the interview.
- Standard questions which apply to any computerisation.
- Particular questions culled from the analyst's preparation.
- Reminders of timings and other matters required before finishing.

2.5.1 Basic facts about the interview

At the beginning of the plan put anything that has to be remembered immediately the interview begins or throughout the time with the user. It does no harm to put simple facts like the date, time and place of the interview. When dashing from the car to an unfamiliar venue, having one sheet of paper with all the facts on the top can be a real asset.

In the same way the name, title and position of the interviewee should be in a prominent position where the analyst can glance back at it. This is especially useful when there is more than one person to see. Getting someone's name or title wrong is a terrible way to start an interview. When the correct title is unknown, the best rule is not to use one at all. Alternatively stick exactly to what was in the letter or other information received.

Likewise it is worth putting any personal facts that are important to the person that can be used to re-establish contact after a successful previous meeting. The interview plan is best typed if possible just because it is easier to read. Remember that many people can read typescript upside-down so hand-write any personal comments, such as *'Careful, phobia about rabbits!'*.

A few words of friendly conversation before getting down to business is always useful as an ice-breaker but make sure it does not go on for too long. Comment (favourably) on the office view, the pictures on the wall, the clear instructions given (if on time) or, when desperate, on the weather. If this is the second meeting, a summary of what was agreed at the last meeting to refresh everyone's recollection is a good way to get started, after the friendly preamble.

Figure 2.3 gives a sample of a typical interview plan header.

```
2nd INTERVIEW - FLOW METER SYSTEM

2PM THURS 20TH MAY
ROOM 460 'J BLOCK', REGIONAL HQ, WASH ROAD,
WATERBOROUGH

MEETING WITH:
Gordon Bennett - Regional Flow Officer
Mr. Bennett, ask about recent holiday

Dr. Peter Cadd - Head of Regional Research Team
(Pete?), rowing in town boat next week

AGREED LAST MEETING (THURS. 6th MAY - Mr Bennett's
office)
General outline of the current Flow system.
Slight problems with some technical details.
Dr. Cadd to attend to go over the above and get his comments on
technical issues.

    ...............
    .....................
```

Figure 2.3 The flow meter system interview plan header

2.5.2 *Standard questions which apply to almost any computerisation*

For the first fact-finding meeting there are several questions that can be asked, in slight variations, whatever the system. Firstly, 'What are the reasons for considering computerisation?'. There seems to be a rule in interviews that states - the shorter the question the longer the answer. This is a short question and is likely to lead to a very long answer. Within the response are likely to be three pieces of information: what the user does not like about the current system, what the user expects to gain from the new system, and what they know about computers. All of the information tends to be condensed; typically the current system will be described as 'too slow' or 'too small'. Do not plough on with the next prepared question but follow up on any ambiguous statements. For example, 'Could you be a little more specific? In what ways is the system too slow at present?' Only when the exploration of the answer has been exhausted, or the user is getting restless, should the analyst move on to the next prepared question.

Make a note of any other information acquired and any unanswered questions as the interview progresses. The ability to do this whilst listening and responding is quite a skill in itself, by the way. Obviously the analyst should also cross-out any of the prepared questions which the user answers as part of the response to another question. This point applies to all the following questions, although a partial answer which allows the analyst to lead on, as in 'I was about to ask you about that. So you do not envisage .....?' can be useful.

Secondly, the analyst needs to find out how much impact the user expects the system to have on the present structure of the organisation. The response to this can range from 'none' to a description of how 2000 employees are going to be relocated or made redundant following a restructuring based on the system. Another general rule of computing is that either extreme should cause concern. If there are going to be no changes at all then why are the company computerising, and who is going to use or support the new equipment? It may be that this statement is correct and the users are merely modifying an existing system, using already trained staff in a prepared environment. On the other hand they may not be aware of all the implications of, say, computerising a manual system and it will be the analyst's job to alert them to all the problems connected with introducing computer equipment for the first time.

If massive structural changes are envisaged then the analyst needs to persuade the user to phase them in an efficient manner, securing and consolidating each stage before progressing to the next. Very few organisations can survive massive changes, involving more than 25% of the organisation, in these competitive days. An ideal answer to the question will give an overview of the company's functional structure along with a list of those areas likely to be affected. If the analyst does not get that information, then they should prompt the user for it.

If the analyst did not get answers to the three standard queries (what the user does not like about the current system, what the user expects to gain from the new system, and what they know about computers) then they should specifically ask those questions around this point.

Finally, money is always involved in some way in a company's decision to introduce a new system. This is a very complex area but the analyst should try to find out if any quantifiable expenditure or savings are envisaged. For example, 'make a 10% saving in production costs', 'save the salary of two clerks', 'increase productivity of current staff 20%' are all the kind statements they ideally want to hear. When relative terms are used, find out the definite figures for current production costs, the average salary or the current productivity.

A guide-line budget for implementing the system is always useful, but is often incredibly difficult to get. It is quite normal to find that the user will describe the system required and leave it to the analyst to suggest the possible cost before any figure is mentioned at all. This creates all kinds of difficulties as there are many examples of user estimates which are factors of hundreds or thousands apart from the final cost. Examples of such discrepancies are becoming more widely published but the analyst should be aware of the dangers. No one can possibly estimate the likely cost of the system until at least a strategic overview of the situation and requirements is available. Every analyst has a professional duty to make the user aware of the costs of the time to perform the initial study, the first rough estimates of the complexity and cost, and the more detailed information as it becomes available.

2.5.3 Specific questions produced from the preparation

As described above the analyst should do everything possible to gather information about the client before the first interview, and use that to produce a list of draft questions particular to the circumstances.

It is easy to overlook the obvious in this and believe that there is no information available, when it is published that the company is a privately owned manufacturing enterprise with its own sales force, or a large public company with an existing computer unit of their own. Each of these circumstances should prompt more questions. Are the sales and accounts departments essentially integrated? Is most of the work mail order? Do they deal with specific suppliers? and so on.

The purpose of this is to identify the function performed by each area within the organisation, their structure and managers, and their involvement in the analysis. This approach prompts some specific questions which can be used to gather information or to confirm the research about the company. Never underestimate the value of positive feedback and always try to establish the interpretation as facts. For example, the question, 'Am I correct in thinking that you never handle bad debts yourself and, therefore, there need be no provision for them in the new system?' may get the answer 'yes' or may draw out a change in working methods which would otherwise be missed.

TIMINGS

Be early, he is very punctual!!

Start time:	2.00pm	Introductions and Coffee?
	2.05pm	Basic Questions
	2.30pm	More detailed questions
>>>>	2.50pm	Sum up and next meeting
		Same time and place in 3 weeks? Be ready to leave by
End time:	3.00pm	*Do not let it over run like last time!!!!*

Remember to take: diary, project folder and spare paper

Figure 2.4 A typical timing section for the plan

2.5.4 Reminders of timings and other matters

Finally the interview plan should remind the analyst of any other matters, particularly the time available for each part of the interview. Do not assume that the whole hour, or whatever, can be spent asking questions and getting answers. Allow at least five minutes at the beginning to settle everyone down and create the correct atmosphere even if the interview starts on time. Leave at least ten minutes at the end to summarise what has been discussed, re-affirm any definite agreements made, and arrange an additional meeting if necessary. Allowing for all this should give an idea of the structure of the interview. Figure 2.4 shows an example typical timing section for the plan.

2.6 Practical advice during interviews

Preparing for, and conducting the interviews is only part of the picture. There are several other practical issues to consider during and after the event. Most of these are related to the EdExcel 'common skills' which may be explicitly taught, or which may have been learnt by experience. Chapter 1 identified the need for an analyst to be able to deal with people. The next section in this chapter describes what that means to you personally when you apply it in practice.

2.6.1 Listening and note taking in interviews

If you have studied in Higher Education you are probably quite good at note taking already. You should have learnt the essential skill of jotting down notes while still listening to the person speaking. If you cannot do this, try tape recording the interview, having first got the permission of the other person. Many students try this in role playing interviews in the Author's courses, and then find out how much work it is to try to separate out the facts afterwards. All the extraneous noises on the tape do not help because you cannot put professional quality lapel mikes on each of the speakers. Standing a 'Walkman' on a table is often very unsatisfactory – try it and see. You are also working without the clues the speaker's body language will give you and this information is often essential. That is why most people prefer to talk face to face rather than over the telephone for important communications.

Stopping the user in mid-sentence while the interviewer painfully inscribes their comments is not a professional image. One analyst, who was rather slow at note taking, provoked a caustic comment about it being 'quicker if he did not illuminate the capitals'. Not the kind of remark you want made about yourself. If you find note taking boring and think you do not need it, remember the old saying 'the weakest ink is more powerful than the strongest memory'.

Encourage the user to do most of the talking but look positive and occasionally say 'yes' or 'I see' so that they know that you are listening. Keep eye contact so that they know that you are following them, but avoid a basilisk stare. If you are shy or embarrassed you can often focus just to the side of, or above, their eyes. Do not overdo this, though, or they will think you are checking to see if they are wearing a wig. As one analyst told me when I was starting out, 'if in doubt just keep smiling and nodding'. However, if you have lost them look puzzled and frown slightly. Most people will pick that up and go over the point without you having to ask. Try to be both relaxed and attentive. Do not be discouraged if you find it difficult at first: good listening is a skill which is highly valued but rare.

2.6.2 After the interview

Take the earliest opportunity to go over the notes and turn them into a proper record. Every hour that elapses will increase the risk of you forgetting an essential point or not being able to understand an obscure comment which you scribbled in the margin. Leave time between interviews and other meetings so that you can do this and to allow for delays in starting and finishing. If you find yourself rushing from interview to interview and constantly writing up reports at midnight it is an indication that you need to seriously overhaul your personal organisational skills. There are many self help books and videos on this topic which have many good practical tips on self improvement in this area.

INTERVIEWING SKILLS

When in the role of an analyst listening and note taking needs to be discreet but continuous.

* Relax and help the interviewee to do the same.
* Try to listen and jot down notes at the same time.
* Try not to stop the user while you write.
* Make occasional encouraging noises and actions.
* Go over your notes as soon as possible after the interview.

Figure 2.5 Practical interviewing skills

2.7 Producing a problem/requirements list

2.7.1 Introduction

Whilst the fact finding is taking place you should be taking copious notes to use in the later analysis. What you are ideally aiming for is to produce a list of all of the requirements for the proposed system, plus a list of the problems identified in the current system to be avoided. The distinction between the two items can be fairly academic, which is why they are often referred to as a composite item, problem/requirements!

2.7.2 Types of requirement for the proposed system

Identifying the 'new' requirements is usually straightforward. The interviewee will often tell you exactly what they want from the new system that is not in the current system. The problem is that it is very easy to spend the whole time discussing all of the wonderful things the new system will do, and hence overlook the implicit requirements from the current system.

2.7.3 Requirements from the current system

What users often leave out are all of their requirements which are catered for in the current system which they assume you will carry forward into the new system. It is a combination of the user's failure to tell the analyst precisely what they are presently getting that they want to keep, together with the analyst's failure to find this out as a matter of course, which leads to so many system failures.

The rule is 'EVERYTHING THAT THE CURRENT SYSTEM DOES MUST BE DONE AT LEAST AS WELL IN THE NEW SYSTEM UNLESS IT IS IDENTIFIED AS A PROBLEM'.

2.7.4 Problems in the current system

The only exceptions to the 'carry the current system forward rule' occur when a new requirement modifies an existing feature, or when a current feature is identified as a 'problem'. Warning phases to listen out for are negative statements about the current features. 'We can find the customer name, but it takes too long', 'there is often a bottleneck as more people need to read the master index than there are copies available', and so on.

2.7.5 Gaining practice

Eventually you will be able to produce a draft problem/requirements list as you perform the fact-finding. This is by far the most efficient way. However, when gaining the requisite skills it is often easier to split the problem into two parts, note taking and analysis. To help with this an exact transcript of a project interview is given in section 2.9 below, with explanatory notes alongside. After gaining experience studying this example you should be in a better position to annotate their own notes, and eventually to analyse them as you go along.

2.8 Common skills in interviews

The interviewing process involves several Common Skills not included in other areas. Not only must these be passed for all EdExcel courses, but they are also essential for professional development. The topics given below are intended to guide you through some of the skills particular to this topic. The general approach is not to stop you being yourself, but help you avoid behaviour which may irritate the other parties involved, and hence distract from the fact-finding process. Like the advice in section 2.6, this material refers to issues personal to their behaviour as an individual. It therefore needs to be taken as well intentioned advice, not fixed rules or criticism.

2.8.1 General guidelines for improving common skills

Several points are worth noting before we continue. Firstly, most of the skills can be learnt but not taught and expertise only comes with practice. Do not be discouraged, therefore, if you realise that you are making mistakes. Try to be pleased that you have discovered a weakness and been given an opportunity to correct it. This is very important as most of the skills involved with interviewing are closely related to some aspects of personal behaviour and it takes a degree of maturity to admit to less than perfection in those areas.

Secondly, a book can only give advice and suggestions. You should take every opportunity to practise your skills in 'real life' situations. Be careful though, not to put close or valuable relationships at risk by constantly practising interviewing or analysis skills on your friends and family.

Thirdly, even if you have all the personal skills at your fingertips, and always enjoy good clear communications with everyone, remember that you still have to be analytical in your approach. Just getting on with people is not enough, you also have to produce accurate documentation.

2.8.2 Protocol in interviews

This is a very difficult field and one where you need to be guided by your instincts and current cultural standards. Some basic rules can be given to get you started; after that, experience and your native wit will get you through if you have the 'right stuff' for the job.

Firstly - be on time. Nothing gives a worse impression than turning up late. If you are going to be delayed then telephone ahead and let them know, even it is fifteen minutes before the meeting. If you are delayed apologise and then move on, do not keep referring to it. If they care they will remember, and if they do not then let them forget it. Either way concentrate on reversing a potentially negative first impression.

On the other hand if they are late do not make remarks about it. Accept their apology, if they offer one, with whatever good grace you can muster and get started on the first item on your notes. Resist the temptation to point out that you will have to drop half of your questions if you cannot have the allotted time. If you can afford the time, ask if you can also finish late to get through the work. Otherwise try to arrange another meeting as soon as possible.

Secondly, get their name and title right. Do not be over-familiar unless they encourage it. This particularly applies to using first names or shortening them. Be aware that standards differ enormously, even within the same company. The way of addressing people will vary depending on if you are speaking to the Head of Accounts or the Head of Security. You have to be a little careful, as continuing to refer to them as 'Mr. Smith' when everyone else is calling them 'Adam' may seem stiff and formal. Your manner can indicate friendliness without risking sounding like a 'spiv' and calling them 'Mart', 'Kathy' or 'Gray', when they referred to themselves as Martin, Katharine or Graham.

You can get through very long meetings without using names or titles at all when dealing with all-male groups, but the question of whether you use Miss, Mrs, and Ms. or just first names with females can cause problems. Fortunately if you are in doubt you can just ask – any reasonable person will tell you clearly what they want to be called.

2.8.3 Avoiding confrontation in interviews

Aggression and confrontation have no place in professional situations. The rule in this case is to avoid such types of situation at all costs. There are several simple rules you can follow which will reduce the likelihood of any such behaviour starting.

Avoid jokes or witticisms unless you know the people and situation well. Especially to be avoided are comments about sex, politics and religion. Humour is fine so long as it is not directed at individuals. You can even make fun of computers if you are lost for an amusing remark.

Similarly, avoid aggression, both your own and the client's. Do everything that you can to stop any competitiveness or antagonism starting. You simply cannot win in a confrontation where you are providing a service, and it is extremely unprofessional to try, so avoid these situations at all costs. That does not mean you should lie or avoid stating unpleasant facts so as not to upset the users. If these situations have to be faced concentrate on the issues involved, not the personalities.

If you do get faced with a seriously disturbed personality who turns every issue into a personal confrontation and every discussion into a diatribe against you and your company then the project is probably not going to succeed anyway. You must regard this as an emergency, so the normal rules do not apply. Say as little as possible and try to be as still and relaxed as you can. Aggression is contagious but so, fortunately, is calmness. If you have decided that you are never going to see the person again and can avoid reacting or defending yourself without getting upset, you may get out with your dignity and self-respect intact. It is just possible that your self-control will shame the other person into returning to professional behaviour and hence retrieve the situation.

2.8.4 Ending the interview

Finally, perfect the art of leaving gracefully. It is quite a difficult skill to bring a discussion to an end in good time, having allowed for summing up and arranging the next steps or meeting, without seeming brusque or unfriendly. This is one skill that you can try on your own friends without danger to the relationships.

If all the above sounds daunting do not be discouraged. You are probably quite good at most of these things already, or you would not be studying analysis. But they are now part of your professional skills and you should improve them wherever possible. If it sounds artificial or manipulative to practise 'getting on with people', remind yourself constantly that it is at least a constructive goal to aim for, and that the opposite is a handicap to your career.

Most of the skills described are ones that you continue to improve throughout your life; every time you think you have got as good as it is possible to get, you realise that there is another level to aim for, like opening Russian Dolls. After a while you will get used to this and it will increase your admiration for those people who are very good at jobs requiring these very demanding talents.

2.9 Summary of interviewing techniques

- Plan the interview carefully, do try to not 'busk it'.
- Learn as much as you can about the interviewee beforehand. Remember to communicate at the level of the person. Top management – Strategic Line management- Tactical Operational staff - Work and Duties.
- Arrange the time and place well before, and be on time.
- Select a good environment if you can.
- Listen more than talk.
- Take discreet notes as you go along.
- Try to interview only one person at a time.
- Control the interview - do not digress.
- Do not try to cover everything at one meeting.
- Avoid conflict and confrontation.
- Conclude positively with a summary of the topics covered.

2.10 The flow meter case study

In order to get started with the case study that we will use throughout the rest of the reference chapters of this book, we have to work through the fact finding for that scenario. The project initiation documents required to get started form the basis of the research and information that you would be given in this type of situation. The first is given in Figure 2.6 as a copy of the tender document from a mythical company which is responsible for the water and rivers in an imaginary country.

The second is a copy of the annotated organisation chart referred to in the transcript, and the third is a sample of the current reports.

WATERBOROUGH RIVERS AUTHORITY
TENDER REQUEST FOR PROPOSED FLOW METER COMPUTER SYSTEM

Waterborough Rivers Authority *is the largest of the Regional River Boards created under the new 'Privatisation of Utilities Act (1990)'. It is charged by the* **Western European Commission for Health, Pollution and the Environment** *(WECHPE) with monitoring the amount of surface water in the Waterborough Region. This area stretches from the Hummes to the Thaber and is divided into districts. Each district covers the catchment area of a tributary to a major river, and the stretch of that river up to the next tributary, or district boundary. A tributary includes ditches, brooks, creeks and streams together with all storm water retention, from puddles and ponds up to water meadows.*

The major task of each district manager is to monitor and record the rate of flow in the tributary. This task is presently performed manually in each district, with different local procedures. Under recent EEC legislation the regions are charged with maintaining a register of total weekly flows, and with allowing reasonable access to members of the public to recent records of these flows, a facility called Public Inspection of Water Flows (PIWF). This is in addition to the normal flow records which are held in perpetuity. A WEC-EEC grant scheme has been established to help Regional River Authorities implement this scheme.

The Directorate of Waterborough Rivers Authority has decided to exercise their option under Clause 54(y) of this legislation to hold their PIWF's centrally at their Regional Headquarters. The Directorate have also decided to commission an analysis of the centralised computerisation of flow recording, based on the manual method presently in use at the Bourn Brook District, with a view to subsequent computerisation.

Proposals for suitable systems are invited. For further information and to arrange for an initial interview please contact: Gordon Bennett, Regional Flow Officer, Room 460 'J Block', Waterborough Rivers Authority, Wash Road, Waterborough. Intention to submit a proposal should be registered by the......

Figure 2.6 Tender document

The following is a transcript of an actual interview by a team of students meeting with a lecturer who was role playing the part of Mr. Gordon Bennett, so it includes all the errors of grammar and fact that people typically make in the pressure of real interviews. Study it carefully as it contains the information required to perform the rest of the analysis of this system. Use it to try to determine what is **meant**, rather than what is **said**.

QUESTION
Is it true that you would like a computer system to record the water flows within the water authority?

ANSWER
'Yes and no, we have computer systems that record the water flow, but in fact what happens is that all of the computerisation takes place at the District level. At the Region, where we are now, I just get paper records.

Note that there are two distinct levels in the structure, District and Region.

Now that wasn't a problem until the EEC directive instructing us to provide PIWFs. We decided to take advantage of that opportunity and say that, as we have got computers all over the place, most of them are under utilised so let's use them for the PIWFs.

REQUIREMENT. Note to check whether there are computers at the Region.

I had better tell you right away that I am not an expert on computers. But I am told by the chaps who are, that it is a fairly simple matter to get the data.

Remember that any technical statements he makes are second-hand, and hence unreliable.

What we want to do is automate the whole process so that we get our PIWFs and the Regional Research Team get their data without it having to be re-typed or re-entered in any way.'

REQUIREMENT. Follow the reference to the RRT.

QUESTION
We are here to gather information about the current system and also the objectives and requirement of the new system, as you have requested the Proposal Document.

Not really a question! It was the 'tender document'!

ANSWER
'That's right, I'm the one who is in charge of the new system. And I am fairly new here. I have been put in place to make sure that the EEC regulations are complied with.'

Three useful pieces of information.
REQUIREMENT

QUESTION
This interview should not take more than 25 minutes. Would it be possible for you to fill-in this diagram of the organisation now or at a later date?

It is a good idea to set limits on the interview so that everyone can pace themselves. However, right at the start would have been better.

ANSWER

'I will have to fill it in now. Right. I work for the Technical Director. The Head of the Regional Research Team is called Pete. The Operations Manager you don't need to see. The person you do need to see is the District Manager of Bourn Brook. Other people agree that you should see Pete Cadd as he has got some information. Alan Cambridge is operating Bourn Brook. Jim Ladd is the District Flow Officer.'

(Annotates organisational chart handed to him) See the resulting chart in Figure 2.8.

QUESTION

How many Districts are there in this Region and how are the Districts divided?

ANSWER

'There are six. The operations people can explain better how the Districts are divided.'

QUESTION

Where is the centralised system going to be based?

ANSWER

'Regionally. Because the structure is based on operational considerations, the Districts look after their own areas, and between them that covers the whole of the Region. But we do not want to change the operational method which works at the moment.'

REQUIREMENT

REQUIREMENT

QUESTION

Do you have any documentation on the current system?

ANSWER

'All I get is the weekly reports from the Districts, which they each give me every month. I can give you a sample of one if you want it.'

See Figure 2.9

QUESTION

What is meant by reasonable access to the public of the weekly flows?

ANSWER

'We have to provide a list, so that they can come to the Regional office as long as they give notice and they can just look at a report. We have managed to get it down to the fact that it is a weekly average flow for the last year. Which is all they will see for each monitoring site. There are about five monitoring sites per District, which is about thirty in all. Basically we want to provide them, if they ask, with a list of 52 readings in the last year for each of those sites. Now we might bundle them together, depending on how you choose to print them. Perhaps by District, because we don't want to waste paper. It's a tricky area because they have not decided yet whether they can just walk in at any time and demand to see them or whether they have to make an appointment. We don't have to do this until the new system starts, so the first week will only show one week's data. We have to update it. We don't have to update it weekly at the Region, and we are allowed a certain amount of time, about six weeks.'

REQUIREMENT

REQUIREMENT
Notice how garbled the description is. He really wants a suggestion from you here.
PROBLEM

REQUIREMENT

QUESTION
Could you give us a brief on what is meant by the WEC-EEC grant scheme?

ANSWER

'Well basically they know that they have created a lot of work	*PROBLEM*
for us. So what they are going to do is to pay for the cost of	*REQUIREMENT*
your system, if it covers their regulations. According to Pete,	
the amount mentioned will only cover software development	*REQUIREMENT*
costs, so we must use the hardware that we have got already.'	

QUESTION
What hardware do you currently have?

ANSWER

'We tend to just have PC's, most of them are 3.5 inch disks.	
Some are five and a quarter inch but we are getting rid of	
those, and one of the technical chaps in charge told me that,	*REQUIREMENT*
because the equipment out on the river banks are 3.5 inch	
disks, it might be better to standardise on that. One person who	
may be able to help you is Pete who is the head of the Re-	*PROBLEM*
gional Research Team. He uses the data a lot for operational	
use, and because it is already on disk he gets very frustrated	*REQUIREMENT*
because all we get here are the paper records printed from the	
disks. If he wants any of the data he has to re-type it. So we	
thought that what you could do is to ensure that the data can be	
carried forward, validated, authorised and edited at the District	*PROBLEM*
level. This has to be done because sometimes it goes terribly	
wrong and they have to... I won't say make it up because that	*REQUIREMENT*
would be politically unwise of me, but they have to make sure	
that there are full records of data to the best of their knowl-	*PROBLEM*
edge. The District manager has to authorise it, and it is his	
authorisation that allows it to come to the Region. But what we	*REQUIREMENT*
are hoping for is that it comes to the Region in a form that	
allows us to just automatically print this report. At the moment	
we would have to get people to write the things out, and that	
take a long time. Another thing is that Pete Cadd is interested	
in the data because if he has got the data already on computer	
he can do a lot of calculating and modelling on it. He has told	
the Directors that he could do a lot more besides modelling, if	
he had the raw data rather than typing it in.'	

Figure 2.7 Interview transcripts - Gordon Bennett

There is considerably more information, as there is in any realistic application, but this is enough to get started. Further details will be given when required as the case study progresses.

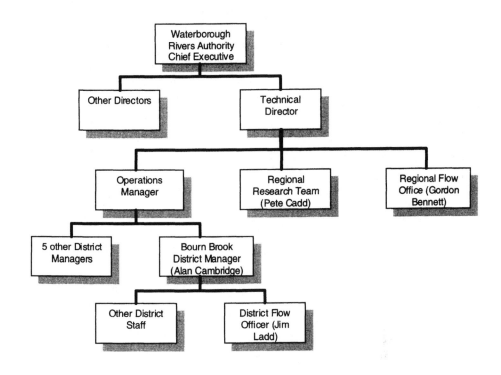

Figure 2.8 Waterborough management structure

```
Flow Meter report for
District                Bourn Brook
Week Beginning          22/06/98
Daily Aves
Meter    1      2      3      4      5      Temp C   Rainfall
Mon    12.67  13.01  14.20  15.06  15.55   26.00    0.57
Tue    12.48  13.25  13.36  14.01  14.87   26.80    0.55
Weds   12.41  12.52  13.64  14.26  15.52   27.63    0.55
Thu    11.68  12.69  13.66  14.31  15.41   28.03    0.54
Fri    11.33  11.80  12.07  12.23  12.61   26.98    0.51
Sat    11.28  11.70  12.38  13.20  13.63   25.12    0.12
Sun    10.70  11.47  11.79  12.49  12.86   25.90    0.35

Weekly
AveFlow 11.79  12.35  13.02  13.65  14.35

Prepared by: Jim Ladd
Authorised By: Alan Cambridge
On Date: 1/7/98
```

Figure 2.9 Sample monthly district reports

Figure 2.10 suggests contents for the FMS problem/ requirement list. For clarity in this simple scenario, each problem has been paired with the requirement which 'solves' it. Please note though that this it is not always possible in more complex situations, where you may get problems without requirements and vice versa. This approach also allows us to give a number to each pair for later reference.

Ref	Problem	Requirement
1	EEC have created a lot of work, and so are going to pay for the cost of your system, if it covers their regulations.	Must provide PIWFs, in such a way that the EEC regulations are complied with.
2	(According to Pete,) the amount mentioned will only cover software development costs,	Therefore, must use the existing hardware.
3	Still need to ensure that the data can be carried forward, validated, authorised and edited at the District level as at present.	Do not want to change the operational method which works at the moment (at the District level).
4	The Head of the Regional Research Team uses the data a lot for operational use, and gets frustrated because all he gets are the paper records printed from the disks.	Must automate the whole process so that Region gets PIWFs and the Regional Research Team get their data without it having to be re-typed.
5	Don't want to waste too much paper on public access records.	Regionally based central system
6	Making sure that there are full records of data to the best of their knowledge. The District manager has to authorise it, and it is his authorisation that allows it to come to the Region	A (paper) report is required to provide access to the public of the weekly average flow for the last year for each of the 30 monitoring sites.

Figure 2.10 The FMS problem/ requirement list

2.11 Other fact-finding methods

There are several other techniques, without which no reference book on systems analysis and design would be complete. They are mentioned briefly here but are not used directly within the case studies.

2.11.1 Questionnaires

We are all familiar with questionnaires - we are bombarded with them, from political opinion polls to quality assurance surveys in college. Most of us have dual standards regarding them. If we design one ourselves we think that only an idiot could misunderstand the meaning. On the other hand, when we are completing one, every flaw and ambiguity is painfully obvious.

The simple truth is that questionnaires are very difficult to design well and, if we are using them to elicit information, we are essentially ignorant of the answers. If we knew the answers then we would not need a questionnaire! When designing a questionnaire, we have to essentially try to cover every possible answer, when we do not know the range of responses. Whole books have been written on the subject and a browse through a library will find examples for further study. My personal favourite reference is the 'Yes Prime Minister' episode on disarmament where Sir Humprey demonstrates that it is possible to elicit any response you want by designing the questionnaire appropriately.

The other major difficulty is that people just do not respond to questionnaires unless you make it as easy for them as possible. A self-addressed envelope is essential, even within a company. Prepaid postage, for users outside the company, is a must. An accompanying letter explaining just why it is in the users interest to respond is a very good idea. Even so, companies that compose questionnaires and rely on the information, go to extraordinary lengths to persuade the respondents to complete them. Free entry to prize draws for cars and holidays are commonplace, but without the incentive of another person actually present with a poised pencil, busy people can always find something else to do. The only solution is to explain clearly why it would be a personal disaster if the user did not respond, and then to make the questionnaire as clear and simple to fill in as possible. If you do all that and get 70% responses then you can count the questionnaire a success. If you keep these difficulties firmly in mind you cannot go far wrong.

2.11.2 Research and reading

There is very little advice that can be given, other than to state that you should do as much of this as you can find the time for. Treat everything connected with computers, human communications and business matters as part of a life-long learning process. Keep notes and records of anything you find interesting and references to sources of information. Go over the notes and re-classify them from time to time, throwing out obviously irrelevant material and breaking the growing amount of relevant content into clear sections. In this way you will build up a fund of useful knowledge and good skills at accessing available sources. Then when you need to build up the background before an interview you will probably go straight to the information you want.

2.11.3 Optional exercise

Choose a local or national company that is involved in computerisation. Search the press and trade papers for references to the company, its personnel and trade policies. You may find this easier than you think as companies revel in the free publicity such press coverage gives. If you get stuck, get some back copies of COMPUTING or COMPUTER WEEKLY and search for references to local companies. Then look in the local papers or ask in the public library for information about the companies. Also try the College's Careers office where company recruitment material is often held.

2.12 A summary of the fact-finding activities

A few lasts words of advice before we get into the technicalities. We are assuming that some current system is in place and working reasonably well, and that the motive for starting the analysis is to gain the advantages of computerisation. However, if the current system is a shambles then beware. Users may think that computerising a poor system will in itself sort out their problems. In fact all that results is a poor computerised system. That is enough theory to get started on more practical techniques, as covered in the rest of the book.

2.13 Exercises

In order to gain more practice at **Finding out about the current system** you may now attempt the tutorial questions given below. Once you are confident of your skills in this topic you are in a position to complete the tasks within Section 13.2 if you wish to do so, before proceeding to the next chapter.

These tasks specifically cover:

13.2.1   Preparing For An Interview.
13.2.9   The Formal User Interviews
13.2.16 Producing An Initial Problem Requirements List

2.13.1   What name is given to the process of learning about the user requirements, and where does it lie in the development of a typical system?

2.13.2   Briefly describe two relevant techniques used by the analyst at this stage in the development of a typical system, and state the circumstances where each would be used.

2.13.3   What activity associated with the system's data is common to all types of system implementation, and why is it often overlooked?

2.13.4   What two 'inputs' are required to an interview process to produce the analyst's understanding of the user's requirements or problems?

2.13.5   Which three 'standard questions' apply to almost any interview relating to computerisation?

2.13.6   What information on each area within an organisation must an analyst identify during the interview process, and what should an analyst do as soon as possible after an interview?

2.13.7   What type of requirements from the current system is often overlooked by the analyst?

2.13.8 List four basic rules that, if followed, give the best chance of an interview proceeding smoothly.

2.13.9 Identify the four tasks that Gordon Bennet suggests should be completed on the river flow data at the Districts before it is sent to the Region.

2.13.10 Complete the 'optional exercise' in Section 2.11.3, and list the attributes required by employers associated with the jobs that interest you. Compare this list with the skills listed in Section 1.3.3 and the common skills in Section 2.8. Honestly, compare these with your own personal attributes (ask a close friend to confirm your self-image if you are unsure), and identify those areas where you need to improve your skills to eventually get your ideal job.

3 | Soft Systems Tools and Techniques

3.1 Introduction

We are have learned so far about the general concepts of a system and how to do basic fact finding, along with some common skills to allow us to behave in a professional manner. The next step would seem to be to start our analysis in earnest, and this is what many people did when computing first began. However, it became increasingly obvious as computer development became a major activity that there were many things being taken for granted in launching into analysis, whatever the methodology, and that this approach could lead to inefficient or inappropriate solutions. It became clear that the best course was to pause and to take stock of the situation before producing methodology specific products, which came to be called 'hard' analysis as they were constrained by the actual methodology being used. It was proposed by researchers, such as Peter Checkland, that the choice of methodology had built into it many decisions that should be reviewed before progressing, and that there were general features common to all systems that should be identified and recorded at this stage. These techniques have become known as 'soft' systems methods as they can be applied generally and are capable of use in a flexible way. A brief overview of this approach is given in this chapter, but the serious reader is advised to consult the books dedicated specifically to soft system methods and theory.

3.2 The environment of the system

The first thing to do is to try to make sense of the parts of the system that are not directly associated with the people involved. People tend to complicate situations so it is worth deciding which aspects are independent of individual views and opinions first.

3.2.1 Identifying the supporting environment

Obviously we cannot take an item such as a television in isolation. It depends upon a whole infrastructure that enables us to plug in a socket in the home to get electricity or buy suitable batteries. We also need an industrialised society that can build the sophisticated electronics and other components used in the set, and the ability to film and transmit programmes by the broadcasting companies.

These external conditions are important but clutter up our thinking. As discussed earlier, what is useful about the system model is that it allows us to isolate one, perhaps very general process and define it in terms of its particular inputs and outputs. Within that closed, or bounded, world we can ignore everything else and concentrate just upon what we have to do to turn those special inputs into the outputs. Lots of domestic appliances use electricity, but only a television turns UHF signals into sound and vision.

The power of this general model is such that we can often overlook the obvious factors, such as the reliance of the average domestic television on a precise and reliable electricity source, until that source fails. A decision to ignore the electricity source is fine so long as it is a conscious decision. The problem comes when we do our analysis sloppily and fail to see how important that is.

For example, in the mid-1980s one system involved using microcomputers in remote laboratories to enter and locally analyse chemical data, which were then transmitted via a telephone link to an existing central computer system. Microcomputers were new then, but the system was very successful. However, one particular site experienced continual bizarre problems for no apparent reason. After a great deal of puzzling and several visits it transpired that this site had a very powerful automatically switched pumping station close by, which had been installed by another group, and which was playing havoc with the voltage levels. This was causing the computers to corrupt disks, blow memory chips and generally behave in an unpredictable fashion. The installation of a battery isolation system completely obviated the problems and, as far as is known, the system is still working quite successfully. In this isolated case the availability of a suitable power source was an erroneous assumption.

3.2.2 What can we take for granted?

The importance of listing the environmental factors which we can then 'take for granted' is an important step in producing our 'computer' system model, and has got very little to do with the system development as such. We have already mentioned the electricity supply but special circumstances demand special solutions. Computers and other electrical equipment now exists which can be used in hazardous situations where the smallest spark may be lethal, which do not emit radio frequencies within certain wavebands, or which can withstand temperatures and vibrations which would destroy the average personal equipment (or person). The point is that you should list all of the possible factors and check to see if you can discount them. If so, you can proceed with your simplified model, if not you must include the factors that matter.

As an exercise draw a system model (see Figure 1.4) of an electricity generating station. Ten years ago this would have been a relatively simple diagram such as the one given in Figure 3.1.

The increasing awareness of environmental factors has made it abundantly clear that the diagram should really look more like the more complex one below depicting 'waste products'. These may be low-grade heat, smoke, nuclear waste, coal dust or whatever. We can label them very generally in our initial systems model, which is non-fuel specific. In order to go into more detail we need to apply the previous concept of structuring, by expanding the initial model, once we are sure that it is correct for our purposes.

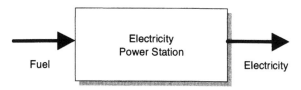

Figure 3.1 Original system view of an electricity generating station

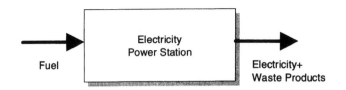

Figure 3.2 Contemporary system view of an electricity generating station

3.2.3 Rich pictures

The most basic task to perform as you are learning about a system is to try to sketch it. This is a well-known educational technique and there are various excellent books which describe ways to start expressing yourself pictorially even if you are not an artist. 'Stick' people and labelled arrows can be very expressive and are very useful for conveying understanding even to untrained users. In fact, several of the figures given up to now could be considered to be rich pictures describing aspects of the analysis process. As we have been describing analysis and design, and the activities required, a good way to illustrate the use of rich pictures is to look at Figure 3.5 which gives an overview of the river flow meter system, the case study being used to illustrate the techniques described in Chapters 2 to 12.

The objects you can include in these diagrams are not constrained in any way. Do not try to produce a major work of art or a professional poster at the first attempt. The two essential points are that the diagram should be simple to produce by the analyst, and also that it should be easy to understand by anyone else. Even if you are a totally incompetent artist, you can use computer presentation graphics packages with standard objects to produce something quite acceptable.

3.3 Identifying the people involved

The next soft technique is to ensure that you have found all the people and correctly identified their function in relation to the system. There are several standard roles to look for when initially performing this task; you can go into greater detail during the 'hard' fact-finding. The essential roles to look for are the current users, the owner of the proposed system, and the users of the proposed system. We will call the latter 'customers' to distinguish them from the current users.

3.3.1 The current users and the customers

The first party to identify is the actual user or users of the current system. They will be your source of operational information, or how the current system really works, which may sometimes be quite different from the management's belief of how it should work. Usually closely related to the current users are the potential users of the proposed system. They are your customers, the people who must be directly satisfied that you have done a good job when the project is finished.

The Analyst

Everyone else

Figure 3.3 The analyst and the other people

One group of these is often a subset or superset of the other. For example there may be fifty financial clerks who use the current financial system. It may be proposed that the new system will only need twenty of these to complete the same amount of work. On the other hand it may be proposed that all the financial clerks be re-deployed to other work and the line managers use the system directly to perform all of the tasks currently performed by specialist clerks. Ideally you should get permission to talk to a representative body of those who will be using both the old and the new system.

Each scenario presents special difficulties. But by skilful examination of the different views of the people involved you can often predict and allow for these difficulties long before you start your detailed analysis and before the design is more than just a line on the project plan.

3.3.2 The owner of the system

This is the individual or group who has the power to scrap the system. This may sound very dramatic but it is the only solid criteria you can use. Note that we have not distinguished between the present and proposed systems. It may be that there are two owners, one for the present system and one for the proposed system, but that is unlikely. Either way you, the analyst, are mainly concerned with the proposed system, as this will be the 'baby' which you have to nurture and rear. The owner can, potentially, stop this process at any point, even before a line of code is written or a single interview has taken place.

There is always someone in the position of owner. Your contact with them may be direct or indirect. It may be that you have to deal with an intermediary or you may be fortunate enough to have direct access to the individual owner or the chairman of the owning group. If you can arrange at least some access this will be extremely valuable. A few moments of real communication with the owner is worth hours of discussion with everyone else.

In the end it is the owner who must be satisfied with the product. The customers may report satisfaction or problems to them as employees, user groups or both. Make no mistake; there will always be some problems. They may seem trivial and irrelevant to you, but be serious difficulties to the users. The person who will ultimately decide which is which, and what to do, is the owner.

This raises a special problem when the owner is also the customer. In this case you must expect that any problem will be treated as a major one. If you know this in advance you can make allowances for the extra cost, and take the opportunity to establish a link between facilities and cost in the final system. This is not to imply that problems by non-owner users can be treated in a cavalier fashion. All problems should be assigned their proper priority and dealt with accordingly. If a link between facilities and cost is established early in the project then the owner can decide where the available resources should be spent.

3.3.3 Other players

Strictly speaking the only people who should be involved are the analyst(s), the users or customers and the owner. There are often other people on the periphery, shown in Figure 3.4, and they are hard to identify and classify, especially when you are being introduced to the system. Remember we have not even started the development yet, we are just thinking about the general problems.

The role of the other players may become clearer as you progress and the good analyst notes the presence of apparent bystanders. Anyone who you meet may be involved with the system and if you cannot identify their role specifically, you need to be sensitive to their possible associations to the others, without of course becoming paranoid.

The other players may change roles during the course of the development, and you may find yourself with a new owner. Being a professional you will have already left open the possibility of good relationship with this person. There is nothing dishonest or deceitful about this. Enemies are a luxury few can afford, and analysts leading a system development, never. Keep on good terms with all the other players, and if you cannot manage that, do not react emotionally to provocation or become involved in confrontations even with irritating apparent bystanders.

This is hardest when dealing with the most dangerous peripheral group, the local experts. They could be the company's Computer Services Department who may have been by-passed by the management when bringing in your company as consultants, or they may be the brother of the owner who owns a micro-computer. Either way you will stand or fall, not on your technical abilities (although you should be able to use those to earn, not demand, respect) but on your inter-personal skills with these other people.

Figure 3.4 The analyst and the others (identified)

The Analyst

The Owner

Current users

The other players

The customers

Current users who are also customers

We are gradually slipping into the material for next part of the section, but let us consider one final example of role changing before we finish. One very large and complex system was running though a rather intricate implementation process in the mid-1970's. The manager of the user department was struggling with this extremely stressful situation, which regretfully proved too much for his health at a crucial stage just before implementation. The owners were faced with the apparently impossible task of replacing a key employee at a transition point, where the new person needed to be knowledgeable about both the pre- and post computerisation procedures at every level. To their credit they realised that there was only one person for the job and promptly made the Senior Analyst an offer he could not refuse. The implementation problems disappeared and the system went into life running with an ease that seemed unachievable.

The general lesson to be learnt from that experience is this - the more all of the people involved know about, and are committed to the system, the smoother will be the transition.

3.4   The root definition

When you are towards the end of the fact-finding, and have completed the soft methods, there is one final check to see if you have really mastered the system. This involves writing a short definition of the fundamental characteristics of what we are trying to achieve in this particular system. By 'short' we mean one sentence if possible. It is more difficult than you may imagine, and is similar to the exercise that businesses and institutions go through when they write their 'mission statements'. If you are studying at a university or college, look in the handbook and find the mission statement. It will probably be at the beginning or outlined in the Vice-Chancellor, or Principal's, introduction. The most influential people in the institution will have argued over that statement for hours or weeks.

You should now reproduce this process by writing a 'root definition' for the river flow meter system, as you understand it. To test your work, and understanding, show it to any of the people involved with yourself in learning this system. If you have to explain it at all, then it is needs improving. The definition and the terminology involved should exactly encapsulate the goal of the system using terms that are immediately understandable to the people involved.

It must be made clear that you are writing a sentence, not an essay that summarises the spirit of what is to be achieved. You may have to go to two, or at most three sentences, but ideally what they add should be implicit in the root definition and when the 'one sentence' goal is defined, they should offer to remove their modifications.

Of course you may not get agreement from some individuals because they personally are opposed to the actual goals of the system. If you establish that that is the case, then you can proceed so long as it is not the 'owner' of the system. If it is, then your are in real trouble, and success may be impossible.

3.5   The river flow meter case study – soft system products

To gain practice at applying the soft system techniques described above, they can now be applied to the river flow meter system, and the case study being used to illustrate all the practical techniques as they are introduced. This has the dual advantages of demonstrating the techniques and of filling in some of the essential details required to apply the more rigorous methods required in later chapters. In practice, the analysts would produce this work themselves and discuss them with the owner and users to get feedback before proceeding. The rich picture of the river flow meter system is provided as an example and to give some information for you to attempt to provide the other soft system products described above.

A model answer to the questions regarding the identity of the people and the root definition is given in Figure 3.6 for you to check your attempts against.

3.6   More soft system practice using the river flow meter system

One of the major difficulties in dealing with users is in getting them to define, or sometimes even mention, things that they have known for so long that they take them for granted. If you were able to use the soft system methods described in this chapter to get feedback from the current users, in this case Jim Ladd and his boss, it should become clear that there are several other pieces of information that did not emerge during the fact finding interview with the Regional Flow Officer.

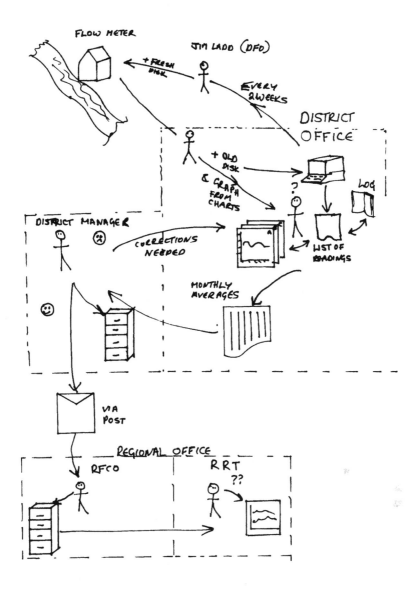

Figure 3.5 Rich picture of the river flow meter system

For example, Jim Ladd knows where all the meters are in his District. This may sound obvious, but if someone else had to go around instead of him, they would need a map and a set of locations. In addition, he may keep all sorts of other information on each meter. Typically a user such as this will have some record, such as a card on each item, for example as in the figure below. They may have had this information for so long that they will not even refer to it unless asked what sounds like an obvious question, such as 'How would anyone else know where the meters are, and when you last visited them, if you went on a long holiday?'. Hopefully the answer would come back of the form, 'Oh, there is a record card for each meter'.

The 'Owner' is really the Waterborough Rivers Authority Directorate, but they are represented by Gordon Bennett, who should be treated as the Owner.

The current 'users' are the District Flow Officers, who are also the primary 'customers', along with the District Managers. If you were continuing the fact finding for real, the only user you would be likely to get access to is Jim Ladd, and possibly his manager, Alan Cambridge.

The only 'other players' identified are the Regional Research Team who may become users if they access the data in the system. This type of situation is quite common but care must be taken not to compromise the goals of the primary users to include other players who may wish to become users.

ROOT DEFINITION
To produce a computerised river flow meter system using existing equipment and based on the current Bourn Brook procedures. The system to be suitable for use throughout the Region, to provide PIWFs reports with no additional effort, and allow access to raw meter data for modelling purposes.

Figure 3.6 Sample soft system products for the river flow meter system

Meter:	x
Location:	Bourn brook, upstream of Biba Gaga
Grid Ref:	TN1234
Type:	W-clump weir
Last serviced:	1/3/94

Figure 3.7 A sample meter record card

Some of these things may only become obvious if you actually accompany Jim on a visit, which is a form of observation. Let us say that, watching him do the work it also becomes apparent that the 'log', as shown in the rich picture, is actually a weather diary. We will assume that he records the temperature and rainfall in the District for each day, as these affect the amount of surface water and are an added check on the reading. At this point the analyst needs to know if any of this information is to be added to the proposed system, or whether it is just used manually and hence is transparent to the system.

From this point on, we will assume that the weather data and the meter cards are required, but that any other information, such as the pen charts, are purely physical and never directly affect the data in the system. We will need this extra information later, but for the moment it is filed away with the other products from the fact finding.

We also need to be a little clearer about the exact form of the data within this system. There are several levels of river flow meter reading within this system:

- The raw 15-minute data from the river flow meter disks (see Figure 3.8).
- The daily average readings which Jim Ladd calculates from the raw data.
- The weekly average readings which Jim Ladd calculates from the daily averages.

The latter two items are the ones which are included on the reports which the District Flow Officer authorises and sends to the Regional headquarters when he is happy with the figures. The fact that they are sent every month merely confuses the issue, as what is actually sent is a set of weekly reports covering the period since data was last sent. This is fortunate, as weeks are always seven days, whereas different months have a different number of days and can be the bane of the report designer's life.

For this example, we will assume that samples of the raw data and the 'Authorisation Report' are as shown in the figures below, as this is the information given in the fact-finding interviews. These reports will also appear later when we use them for the more rigorous analysis later in the book. Remember though, that if you do not unearth this information, which is the purpose of using the soft system methods, you will be working from incomplete information later in your analysis. Figure 2.9, in the previous chapter, is the other main report.

12.67	12.84	13.23	12.95	13.14	13.70	13.50	13.19	13.27	13.44	13.20	13.53
13.77	14.07	13.43	13.27	13.46	13.20	13.61	14.24	13.83	13.32	13.97	14.26
14.35	14.57	14.77	15.43	15.17	15.76	15.91	16.27	15.70	15.75	15.57	15.39
15.35	15.77	15.71	15.34	14.74	14.79	14.76	14.69	14.02	14.16	14.69	14.22
13.74	13.74	14.40	13.72	14.21	14.73	14.75	14.58	15.18	15.51	14.87	14.89
14.75	15.44	16.08	16.28	15.89	16.67	16.82	17.09	16.82	17.36	17.77	17.36
17.31	16.60	17.23	17.24	17.44	17.61	17.25	17.77	18.34	19.12	19.04	19.77

Figure 3.8 Raw 15-minute river flow meter data as it appears when listed from the disk

3.7   Exercises

In order to gain more practice at **Producing a 'Soft' system overview of the current system** you may now attempt the tutorial questions given below. Once you are confident of your skills in this topic you are in a position to complete the tasks within Section 13.3 if you wish to do so, before proceeding to the next chapter.

3.7.1   Choose any area in which you are interested and are familiar with and which could be thought of as a system. Attempt to illustrate this in the form of a rich picture. Explain your drawing to a friend and listen carefully to their comments. Try not to be defensive or aggressive if they criticise your work or are unsympathetic to your point of view. Try to modify your picture to take their views into account.

3.7.2   In the example you chose in Q3.1 try to see the situation only as a 'system' by identifying the inputs, outputs and transformations involved. Illustrate the result of this as a system diagram, as in Figure 3.2.

3.7.3   In the example you chose in Example 3.7.1 try to identify the people involved. If possible assign them the roles identified in Section 3.3. If this is not possible in your example, repeat Exercises 3.7.1, and 3.7.2 with another example which is more suitable for this exercise.

3.7.4   In the example you chose in Exercise 3.7.1 try to write a root definition of the situation, as described in Section 3.4.

3.7.5   Modify the rich picture of the river flow meter system (Figure 3.5) to show how the situation would appear if all of the work on the river flow data were to be centralised at the regional office. Would the root definition change if this were the case?

Modelling System Processes

4.1   Introduction

At this point in the analysis we must make an attempt to communicate our understanding of the system as it currently operates. If we use structured analysis methods, the implicit model within SSADM, there are two elements to be covered, the processes and the data. In the chapter we introduce the most common structured method which analysts use for depicting processes: data flow diagrams, followed by the related forms which document the diagrams.

Data flow diagrams (DFDs), first proposed by Gane and Sarson, are a powerful and flexible way of communicating the processing elements of a computer system. DFDs are now one of the major tools used in structured analysis methods and have taken over the role of Flow Charts and Flow Diagrams except in certain specialist applications. Consequently, it is extremely important to master their use.

DFDs can be used for slightly different purposes at several points in the life cycle, as described in detail later in the book when we discuss more advanced techniques. However, for the moment we will just concentrate on learning the basic techniques.

In most of the diagrams in this book the notation used will be as defined in the current SSADM standards (version 4.2+ at the time of writing). However, you should be aware that there are many ways in which DFDs can be drawn, in exactly the same way that different maps can have different symbols. Just as each map uses a uniform format for its contents, you must be consistent in your conventions when documenting DFDs during each project.

DFDs are easily structured and each process may be expanded, or exploded into another data flow diagram. The notion of 'structuring' was introduced in Section 1.5.2 and this concept must be understood before attempting to progress through the material in this section. Each system may require many layers of DFDs to represent it, and the number of layers is a good indication of the complexity of the system. The first DFD has a special name, the context diagram. After that we use numbers, so the first diagram exploded from the context diagram is called the 'Level 1' DFD. There is one context and one level 1 diagram per system. After that the number of data flow diagrams depends upon the complexity of the system.

4.2   Getting started drawing DFDs

There are only four basic objects used in the construction of a logical data flow diagram. The SSADM representation of these is shown in Figure 4.1.

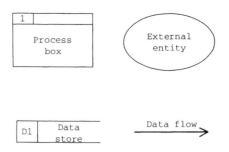

Figure 4.1 The four basic objects used in the construction of a logical data flow diagram

A complete DFD for even a simple system can be extremely complex. This may result in a bewildering network of data flows. This should be avoided by careful structuring, by labelling all the objects and by duplicating External Entities and Data Stores to avoid crossing data flows. The Data Flows and Processes must be unique and cannot be duplicated, although the same name is often used for different data flows. Figure 4.2 gives the conventions used within SSADM for labelling external entities and data stores in DFDs. The extra lines are used for showing that duplication exists.

4.2.1 Data flows and external entities

When we first start our analysis, unless it is of a very trivial system, it is difficult to decide what is part of the system and what is not. During the fact-finding exercise many objects will have been identified. These are the entities associated with the system, and the analysis, documentation and modelling of them is contained in the data modelling chapters. However, they also occur as the starting point for the data flow diagram drawing.

We may have found a whole collection of entities and the first and most essential step is to decide which lie within the system, which lie outside of it, and which are data flows. This is not always a simple process, but by continually examining the entities and trying to place them correctly in a simple context diagram we can start to make decisions which will allow us to produce an initial document. Do not expect to get it right first time. It is important to use the procedure to create a draft diagram, examine and if possible discuss it, and then modify it.

This process should be repeated until the first diagram is a correct representation of the system. For this reason paper and pencil are the best tools to use. Try to avoid the temptation to use computer packages at this stage, unless they are specialist CASE tools, otherwise you may spend a long time producing a very neat, incorrect, diagram and be unwilling to modify it if you discover an error. The first objects encountered when drawing the initial DFD are the external entities, the data flows into and out of the system, and the system itself.

Figure 4.2 The conventions used within SSADM for labelling objects

4.2.2 Identifying and placing entities in a context diagram

External entities are objects, people, institutions or other systems that are related to the system under analysis, but are not an integral part of it. This is a difficult concept to describe but is quite simple to recognise once the basic idea has been grasped. For example, most of us recognise our friends and can distinguish them from other people without any effort. The difficulty comes when we try to exactly define what we mean by the term 'friend'. The same is true for analysis in general but, fortunately, the situation is simplified when we are applying the technique to computer systems analysis.

The external entities first occur when we try to draw a context diagram, and they permeate the analysis and design from then on. Using the Systems Approach, described in Section 1.5, external entities become the fundamental source of all our inputs and the final destination for all our outputs. As such the correct and complete identification of the external entities of a system is an essential first step in the analysis process. The details of what they actually contribute and receive can be filled in later.

The correct identification of the simpler external entities is often quite straightforward. We start with a simplified data flow diagram (context diagram) and attempt to identify all data flows into and out of the proposed system or existing system. We use a data flow diagram so as not to mix up our analysis with the (messy) reality, which was represented in the rich picture.

If we have an ordering system then we generally have an external entity 'customer' who sends us the orders. The customer may also take delivery of the goods and pay for them, although this is not always the case.

There are several simple checks to see if we have missed out an external entity. All our data flows into the System should originate from somewhere identifiable, and all our outputs must terminate somewhere. The output reports are the part most often overlooked, and typically the inexperienced analyst will get well into the Design knowing that they need to produce, for example, a management report, without ever clearly showing this on the context diagram. This is particularly problematical if, as is often the case, the actual purpose of the system is to provide management information and the Owner of the system (see Section 3.3.2) is not shown anywhere.

The fundamental object in the diagram is of course the data flow, hence the name of the diagram. Using the System Model approach it can be seen that we are interested in transforming the 'inputs' into the 'required outputs'. The process of analysis can be expressed as the identification of these outputs and hence, using this systems approach, defining the transformations to be applied to the relevant inputs to achieve the required results. Nothing may leave the system unless it has entered it as an input, or has been calculated or transformed from the inputs.

At the highest level of analysis we may identify these data flows as general entities: Customer Order, Monthly Report or Invoice. Later on we must check that the data required to produce each individual item leaving the system actually enters it, and identify the source of the data within these general entities. For the moment it is sufficient to allocate the entities we identified during fact finding.

The source and destination of each of the data flows is now correctly identified as an external entity, also known as a 'Terminator' in some older reference books. They have also been described as a data 'source' or a data 'sink' in American textbooks to help the student visualise their purpose. If something enters or leaves the system we must identify the corresponding external entity. Sometimes, if we know about a data input or report, we can deduce the existence of the external entity which contributes or receives it.

4.3 Drawing a set of general data flow diagrams

4.3.1 The context diagram

We draw the first diagram of the system by combining the data flows and the external entities and show a representation of our system, with no internal detail. This is known as the context diagram and sets the boundaries for the rest of the analysis. We can use a context diagram to show the existing system or the proposed system, and as they may look very similar, clear labelling is important. The system itself is often shown as a 'cloud' at this point to show that we are hazy about the actual processes involved, although SSADM uses a large, blank 'process' box to represent the system.

Let us say, however, that the bill requires the current date to be printed on it. It is not enough just to assume this will be magically provided, we must define the source. It may be that the operator types the date in when the equipment is switched on or, more commonly nowadays, the hardware has an in-built clock/calendar and the proposed system must read the date from it. If this is the case we would draw the context diagram to show this, with a separate external entity.

Note that in this case the 'system' is the software, which we are designing, and not the hardware which we use to run the program when it is complete. The example chosen, the computer 'calendar' is deliberately in the grey area where we can see that it is part of the total package (often called the system) which we will provide, but that one element provides an essential input. It must, therefore, be separately identified to aid in the understanding by another reader. If you are ever in doubt about whether to put something in like this, always aim on the side of over-explaining.

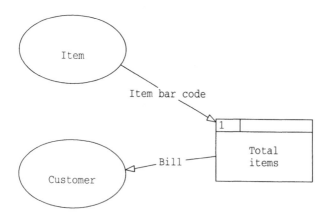

Figure 4.3 A point of sale system context diagram

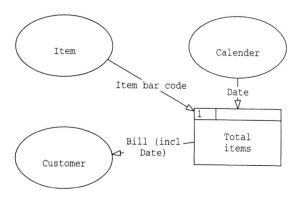

Figure 4.4 A point of sale system with calendar input

It can seem odd to label an automatic clock or calendar as 'external' when it seems an integral part of the computer. It is, however, a sub-system in its own right which contributes data and which we rely on to work correctly. Should the battery fail we soon notice its existence, and our reliance on it. Up to that point, though, it is easy to take its contribution for granted. Although this is a special case it illustrates the importance of identifying the source of all the inputs. A much more complex context diagram is shown in the figure below. This illustrates a company which arranges tours for groups by placing co-ordinated bookings with hotels, airlines and coach operators.

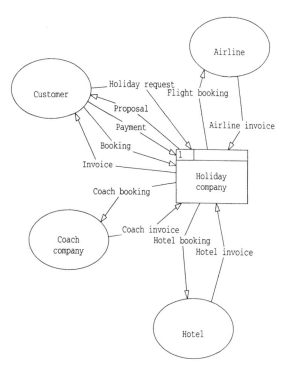

Figure 4.5 The context diagram for a holiday tour company

Obviously, any other people who are dealt with, local tour operators for instance, would have to be included if they were discovered as the analysis progressed. It is extremely important that all diagrams are updated whenever errors or omissions are uncovered. The context diagram is easily overlooked when making changes later in the development process, and yet it is the first document most analysts look for nowadays when modifying or updating a system. Try as hard as you can to get the context diagram right. If it is incorrect then everything that follows will be wrong as well.

4.3.2 Introduction to processes and data stores

Once we are happy with our (sketched) context diagram we can now start to add some internal detail to the system. In order to do this we must trace the data flows inside the system and invent Processes and Data Stores as necessary. Before we do, it is important to master some conventions about DFDs. Data is considered to flow instantly and all data is expected to be available for use by processes the moment it is required. If there is any noticeable t ime delay then a Data Store must be used to store the data. If all this sounds complex then an example from another field may help to clarify matters (Figure 4.6).

The received signal has both sound and vision contained within a carrier signal specific to a particular channel. To fill in more detail we could specify that the 'system' processes all the signals it receives to select the channel it is tuned to at the time, and to remove the specific carrier signal leaving only the combination of the audio and the visual data. This combined signal is then passed forward to two different processes, one of which separates out the vision element and displays it as pictures on the screen, and the other which separates out the soundtrack element and amplifies that to the speakers. If we were to draw this out using DFD notation it would look like Figure 4.7.

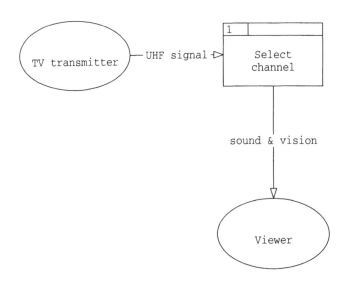

Figure 4.6 A television receiver DFD

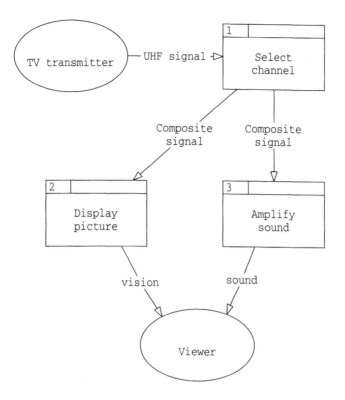

Figure 4.7 A television receiver DFD 'exploded'

Note how the 'composite signal' carries all the elements simultaneously to two processes to output the sound and vision together to the viewer(s). In the same way a data flow can be an input simultaneously into two (or more) processes. All the information it carries will be available as inputs, unless it is split by another process first. If the processes which transform the two types of signals could not accept both of them at once, the diagram would have to be drawn differently, as shown in Figure 4.8.

Anyone who has detailed knowledge of this subject will know that this is a rudimentary description of what is really a very complex process. But by using a data flow diagram we can concentrate on the functionality of the process without worrying about the technicalities. It is important to remember, however, that the techniques described are intended to produce a deliberate simplification at this stage of analysis. This is usually necessary because the initial data flow diagram is really being used in an innovative situation, to design a system from scratch, in this example to re-invent the Television via a top-down process. When in doubt it is better to move in many simple steps than leap into complexity too quickly and lose the thread of what is being attempted. For the general student a good technique to use is to draw these diagrams as though you are trying to explain the concept to a rather intelligent six-year-old child, taking each stage at a time. The information at each level must, of course, be correct! There is a fundamental difference between clear elementary descriptions which we are trying to achieve, and fantasy, which we are trying to avoid.

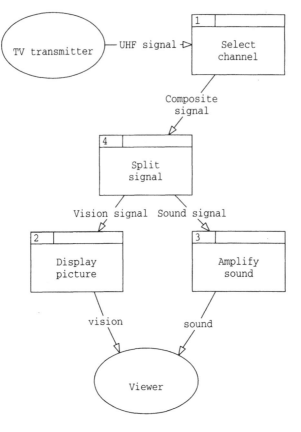

Figure 4.8 A television receiver DFD 'exploded' with split signals.

The DFD drawn above could be used as a simple block diagram of a TV, and interested students could look up a circuit diagram in any reference book on electronics to see how it would look if we had attempted to put all the details on one page. We are, however, only interested here in explaining the DFD conventions.

One last related example allows the inclusion of a data store. If the functionality of a TV is used to select a channel and then store the picture on tape, then we have a logical view of a VCR. The system for playing back the tape through a TV relates this to the previous TV example. The combined processes can be drawn as one system as shown in Figure 4.9. In this example, the video tape is represented by a data store.

4.4　Filling in the details

Up to this point, we were implicitly showing how to start creating a more detailed data flow diagram in the previous set of diagrams. To illustrate this further, we must abandon the TV/video example and return to a more usual data processing scenario, such as the holiday company described in the 'context diagram', Figure 4.5. Using the input data flows it is possible to trace the top level of detail into the system. We can only take our analysis so far because, whilst we can easily generate the next DFD below the context diagram on paper, we should be trying to represent the system we investigated in fact finding, and we do not have enough information here, as it has not been provided. We really need the results of a detailed investigation, as in the flow meter system.

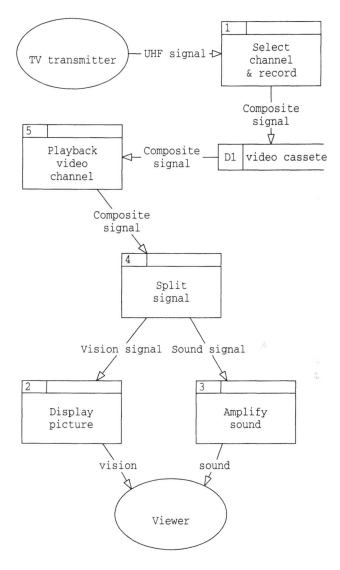

Figure 4.9 TV and VCR (as one system) DFD

4.5 Summary of the rules for drawing data flow diagrams

There are as many ways of drawing DFDs as there are analysts and lecturers! As in mental arithmetic, everyone has their own favourite method, often for very good reasons, and there is no one right way. The various standards of SSADM, of which version 4.2+ is the latest at the time of writing, have given increasingly detailed objects and advice on how to use them. However, the range of problems is so wide that, even closely following the rules shown below, two analysts documenting the same problem can easily produce data flow diagrams which appear to be very different, even if their purpose is identical. The method described below has proved successful for many practitioners as it is simple to follow, covers most cases and reinforces the fundamental concepts of top-down analysis. However, do not be afraid to modify it if you find a procedure which is easier for you to use.

1. Identify the External Entities.
2. Identify the inputs and outputs of the system (dataflows). Ignore dataflows which are the result of errors or exceptions at this point.
3. Draw the context diagram.
4. Using the context diagram as a guide, take each input in turn from each external entity. Trace its flow through the system. Invent processes and data stores as required.
    Hint: In the first DFD (level 1) try to keep both to the absolute minimum to aid the clarity of the structure.
5. Resolve any unconnected data flows. Check that each process has all its necessary inputs and outputs.

The above rules cover the context and level 1 DFDs. The next two rules explain how to add more detail, which will be covered later, but are included here for completeness.

6. Take each process in turn and 'explode' it on a separate diagram to give more detail using steps 4. & 5. Each time you do this you are creating another level. So each of the process boxes in the level 1 DFD 'explodes' to a separate level 2 DFD, and so on. (See 'Exploding the Objects in a DFD' for a full description of this process.)
7. Stop when you find yourself requiring 'IF..THEN..' constructs in order to continue. (By this time you are close to designing the code, which requires other techniques, such as JSP or Step-wise refinement.)

Try to take great care in drawing the diagrams. Remember that the analyst trying to make sense of your documentation in six months' time may be you!

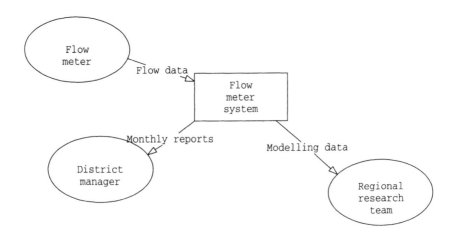

Figure 4.10 The current river flow meter system context diagram.

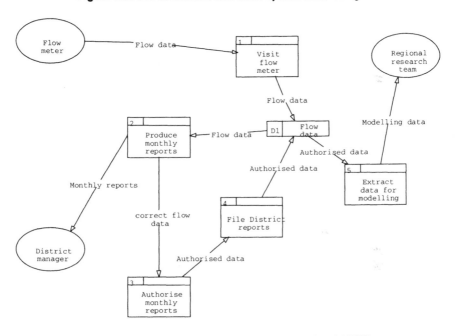

Figure 4.11 The current river flow meter system level 1 DFD

4.6 The river flow meter case study (top-level DFDs)

As we progress through the text we need less and less explanation as the diagrams should 'speak for themselves'. This section contains the diagrams showing the analysis to this point for the river flow meter system: these are the top-level current data flow diagrams.

4.7 The supporting forms for data flow diagrams

There are several special forms which must be completed to document the set of data flow diagrams to current professional standards, such as those defined in SSADM. When taken in total this process is often referred to as data flow modelling to distinguish it from the sub-process of data flow diagram production. There are a great many special forms in a fully documented system, but we will describe the use of three of the most common of these which we need to follow the simplified method used in this text. These common forms are:

- Function Summary Form.
- Function Definition Form.
- User/Function Matrix Form.

The practical use of the forms is best demonstrated via an example. As we have already shown how to produce the DFDs for the river flow meter system, it makes sense to go through the tasks required to produce the rest of the documentation of the processes for the current system using the forms for the river flow meter system as an example.

Below are samples of the forms as they should look when you have completed them. To save space, and to make it easier for you to check your work against the samples, only the first two forms have been completed in full. The contents of key paragraphs for the remaining forms are given in the table that follows the next two examples.

4.7.1 The forms for the Current Logical Flow Meter System DFD

As can be seen from the example on the next page, the top part of the form defines its position in the life cycle model. Having defined the form as a Function Summary Form in the header, the next line prompts the analyst to state whether they are modelling the current or required system. The system name, author of the form and the date it was completed is on the next line, along with a page number. This form is often the first of a set which includes the function definition forms, and it is good practice, once all the forms are complete, to enter the number of sheets in the complete pack so it is easy to see if one has been removed. As there are five level one functions, there will be six supporting forms, or seven if we include a User/Function Matrix Form in the documentation of this system at this stage. This process of constantly cross-checking the detail to ensure correctness and completeness can be irritating to some people. However, it is this level of documentation required to ensure that the job has been done properly, and it is a requirement for most of the professional documentation standard awards which many companies aspire to gain.

4.7.2 Function summary form

The body of the form follows as three columns, Ref(erence), Function Name and Comments. The first column should hold the reference number of the process on the level one DFD being documented. In this example, these have only one digit to show that they are level one processes. It may be worth clarifying the terminology at this point. Strictly speaking, only functions should be included on this form. Functions are processes that cannot be 'exploded' into other processes on a DFD. They are marked with an '*', which means that they will eventually be implemented as a piece of code, and the sum of the functions comprise the programming work which must be done to implement the system.

Function Summary Form				
Current System **yes**		Required System		
System **Flow**	Author **MJH**	Date **2/3/93**	Page **1** of **7**	
Description				
Summary of the high-level functions performed in the current logical system				
Ref	**Function Name**		**Comments**	
1	Visit Flow Meters		5 meters per District	
2	Produce Monthly Reports		The Reports are a diary and a graph	
3	Authorise Monthly Reports and send to Regional HQ		Send unsatisfactory reports back to the DFO for re-editing	
4	Check & File District Reports			
5	Use Central file of District reports for Modelling		Not much we can do about this. The new system needs to be accessible in same ad hoc way	
Sample Function Summary Form. PISAD-FS1. Version 1.				

At this point, however, we are only modelling the current level one DFD, so we can treat all of the processes as though they were high-level functions. We can then use our common sense to turn the descriptions in the fact-finding into actual tasks completed within these as actual functions and describe them on the form. The alternative is to explode the processes down to the function level, which is what we do later in Chapter 7, but this can be hard work and does not help our understanding with an essentially manual system so we are sticking to level 1 processes for the moment.

Comments are always tricky things to deal with. The best way to use them is to put in a brief note of anything that will remind you why you are doing something, such as quantities or explanations that will make the processes easier to understand. Remember that the purpose of these forms is to put down that information that cannot be included on the diagram itself.

4.7.3 Function definition forms

The next task is to fill in a Function Definition Form for each of the entries on the Function summary form. The Header information is filled in as in the previous form, and the name and reference should be identical to the corresponding values on the entry for the function being documented.

Function Definition Form				
Current System **Yes**		Required System		
System **Flow**	Author **MJH**	Date **3/3/98**		Page **2** of **7**
Function Name - **Visit Flow Meters**				Function Ref. **1**
Type Manual/Clerical **Manual**		Initiated By - **DFO**		
User Roles - **District Flow Officer**				
Function Description 1. Visit each of the five meters every 2 or 3 weeks. 2. Perform simple maintenance and note major problems for reporting. 3. Replace pen chart paper and floppy disk. 4. Wind up pen chart recorder and check ink				
Error Handling				
DFD Processes **1**				
Events				
I/O Descriptions **See 'Flow.Dat' file layout**				
I/O Structures				
Requirements Catalogue Reference - **No change to these procedures.**				
Volumes **5 charts and 5 disks per visit**				
Related Functions **see 2**				
Enquiries - **N/A**				
Common Processing - **N/A**				
Dialogue Name - **N/A**				
Service Level Requirements Service Level - **N/A**				
Description	Target Value	Range		Comments
Sample Function Definition Form. PISAD-ED1. Version 1.				

The next two lines refer to the type task in the current system, and identifies the person who completes it. As the DFO decides himself when to visit a river flow meter, that person is referred to twice, but if his boss told him when visits should be made, the 'initiated by' box could contain, for example, DM for District Manager.

After this header there is a large box in which the information about the tasks performed in this process should be entered. This is where the analyst turns their rough notes from the fact finding into a professional record for posterity. Remember that when the system is re-written or modified, maybe in several years' time, this information may be all that is available to the person doing the work. By this time, it is possible that the staff who provided the original information have left or retired, so that the fact finding could not be done again. Even if it could, good notes at this time will save time and money later, so always try to be put down all the relevant facts as clearly as possible.

The rest of the form includes fields for entering detailed information required in the implementation of large systems, and some of them refer to work which is beyond the scope of this book. The error handling, though, is of particular interest. When we draw the DFDs we make the, unrealistic, assumption that there will be no problems and only draw the processes required to work in an ideal situation. In practice, there will be many error and exception conditions described by the current users and these can be documented here. It is quite an advanced skill to write brief but accurate descriptions of what may have been quite complex explanations, but that is what analysts get paid so much money for doing, so long as they do it well. You can always refer to separate documents if the error handling processes are really too complex to describe in a few words, but it is worth making the attempt to summarise what you have learned if at all possible.

Normally you should fill in separate forms for each of the functions but, in order to save space, the contents of the essential fields on the forms for the remaining four processes are summarised in the table below.

Form	Function Description	Error Handling
Page 3 of 7	Produce Monthly Reports 1.a) Validate the data against previous readings and up/downstream readings 1.b) Draw draft report and compare to pen chart. 2. Compare anomalies to the 'weather log'. 3. Edit data using personal judgement where necessary. 4. Draw up neat report for District Manager.	Use pen charts if possible or use up/down stream readings. Otherwise use weather log and personal judgement, i.e. guess!
Page 4 of 7	Authorise Monthly Reports and send to Regional HQ Note :- needs computerising for non-technical user	Discuss unsatisfactory readings with DFO and request re-edits until satisfactory.
Page 5 of 7	Check & File District Reports Note :- no change needed. (That's all at the moment!)	Chase up late District Reports.
Page 6 of 7	Use Central file of District reports for Modelling.	N/A

4.7.4 User/function matrix form

This form lists all of the tasks identified on the previous forms. It also defines who does which task by an entry in a box connecting the row (tasks) to the columns (users). This matrix form allows greater detail in defining user roles where more than one person uses, or contributes to the completion of a defined task. Notice that the rows are made up of the most detailed tasks, or functions, listed in the previous forms.' between the two tables.

User/Function Matrix Form												
Current System **YES**						Required System						
System **FLOW SYSTEM** Author **MJH** Date **2/3/93** Page **7** of **7**												
User	A	B	C	D	E	F	G	H	I	J	K
A DISTRICT FLOW OFFICER B DISTRICT MANAGER C REGIONAL RESEARCH TEAM FUNCTION											
1 Collect river flow disk and pen chart	✓										
2 Load fresh disk and pen chart paper	✓										
3 Validate readings against previous reading	✓										
4 Internally validate readings	✓										
5 Validate readings between river flow meters	✓										
6 Compare anomalous readings with weather diary	✓										
7 Edit readings as necessary	✓										
8 Record new readings	✓										
9 Produce monthly reports	✓										
10 Check readings and reports		✓									
11 Request changes to unsatisfactory readings		✓									
12 Authorise satisfactory results		✓									
13 Use data for modelling			✓								

Sample User/Function Matrix Form. PISAD-UF1. Version 1.

4.8   Summary of the process modelling for the current system

In Section 1.8.4 we described how the analyst moves from the real (physical) world via logical models to the required system. The distinction between the current physical and the current logical system can be a fine one. In fact, in some information systems there are no differences at all, which cuts down the analyst's workload. Some analysts perform the change from physical to logical 'in their heads' by never including any physical objects in their data flow diagrams in the first place. The increased use of Soft Systems Methods has helped in this approach as this makes it possible to include all of the transfers and movements in physical objects in the rich Picture, and then only draw the (logical) data flow transfers on the first DFD produced. For this reason, as this is an introductory text, we have assumed that the current physical and the current logical DFDs are identical. Be aware, however, that more advanced texts may cover the distinction between the two in considerable detail.

To summarise, when modelling the current system, you normally need only analyse down to level 1 processes and then fill in a Function Summary form. You can then fill in a Function Description form for each of the level 1 processes and finish by completing a User/Function Matrix form. After that it is worth looking at the level 1 data flow diagram to ensure that none of the processes need exploding. Use your common sense and be sure, if you decide to just rely on the reduced documentation as suggested, that you are not just rationalising laziness. If you are satisfied that the correct level of documentation is now available, proceed to the next stage. But, be prepared to come back and do more work on the current logical processes if you realise that it will help with your analysis of the required system as described in the later chapters in this book.

4.9 Exercises

In order to gain more practice at **Modelling the current system processes** you may now attempt the tutorial questions given below. Once you are confident of your skills in this topic you are in a position to complete the tasks within section 13.4 if you wish to do so, before proceeding to the next chapter.

These tasks specifically cover:

13.4.1   Producing the Current Context Diagram
13.4.8   Producing the Level 1 Data Flow Diagram
13.4.10 Producing the Current Logical Data Flow documents

4.9.1   In Figure 4.12 there are several simple errors which break the rules of drawing DFDs Change the diagram to correct these errors.

4.9.2   In Figure 4.12, draw the corresponding context diagram for the system represented.

4.9.3   In the diagram in Exercise 4.9.2, imagine that the fact finding stated that 'process1' consists of: validating the input data, calculating and storing the total value, and preparing the items for later processing. Produce the corresponding level 2 DFD derived from the previous question and this information.

4.9.4   In Figure 4.13 there are several more subtle errors which imply problems with the system represented by the DFDs. Change the diagram to correct these errors.

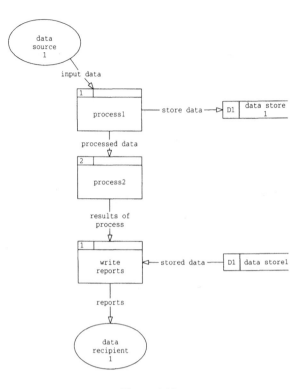

Figure 4.12

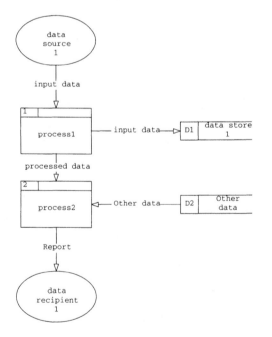

Figure 4.13

Logical Data Structures

5.1 Entity relationships - an introduction

One of the most commonly used techniques in analysis is to employ some method to represent and model the relationship between the various data items, or entities, discovered during the process. Whilst the analysis of relationships is a constant human activity, and we are all fascinated to discover that the person sitting next to us in the airport bus is a friend of someone we know or a second cousin twice removed, finding a consistent way to represent general relationships is quite difficult. SSADM has a standard notation for showing the relationships between entities and, as previously, it is the form which will consistently be adopted here. However, there are many other notations, which are standard to other methodologies, to perform the same task, and these may be encountered in other texts.

5.2 Basic definitions

The basic definitions are:

- **Entity**. An item of interest to the system under consideration, but is not a process or activity. This term includes both internal entities, which eventually become data items, and External Entities which are objects associated with the system. (See also 'External Entities' in the DFD Section). Typical examples include the documents and reports carrying data (INVOICE, ORDER), the people involved (CUSTOMER, ACCOUNT MANAGER), and items concerned with providing or receiving data (METERS, SATELLITES).
- **Attribute**. Entities are made up of attributes as records are made up of fields or, as a non-computer example, houses are made up of rooms. The entity ORDER may have the attributes: Order Number, Order Date, Customer Name, Customer Number and so on. Sometimes it is difficult to tell whether an item is an entity in its own right, or an attribute of another entity. The modelling process should take care of these decisions and sometimes we have to keep changing our minds and re-drawing the diagram until we are happy that it accurately represents the relationships in the particular system which we are currently analysing.
- **Relationship**. A way of defining association between entities.

5.2.1 Types of relationship

Entities do not exist in isolation, and every entity is, in some way, related to the others in a given system. An INVOICE will be the result of an ORDER, and the two entities (INVOICE and ORDER) will have a defined RELATIONSHIP specific to the way they are dealt with in that system. The relationship is an association between the entities unique to a particular system. We have to find names for the relationships and these can tax our ingenuity occasionally. An INVOICE 'is the result of' an ORDER. Or even more pedantically, an INVOICE 'is the result of a delivered' ORDER. When performing the fact-finding activities the analysts should make a note of the terminology adopted by the User, as this will enable them to name the relationships appropriately for that system.

We classify the relationships by three factors: the degree or order, the contingency or optionality, and the exclusivity. If all this sounds daunting do not worry, the first classification, degree, is by far the most important and is easily mastered.

5.3   Degree of relationship

5.3.1 One-to-one relationships

When we draw a relationship between two entities the main thing we are trying to represent is the degree, or order as some books call it, of the relationship. The simplest is the one-to one relationship. When two people are married under English law (that may sound over-pedantic but there is a reason for the qualification) they are have a special relationship to one another. A man can only be legally married to one woman at a time, and a woman to one man. This is a very good example of a one-to-one relationship. The 'at a time' qualification is very important and we may find that we rely on that term many times during analysis in the real world.

We represent the entities by rectangles and the relationship by a plain line as shown in Figure 5.1. Wherever possible we name the relationship, and this is often like the verb in a sentence. The Man is married to the Woman. So the relationship can be labelled 'is married to'. In this case the sentence works equally well when reversed. The Woman is married to the Man. This is why we only require one label for this particular relationship.

Figure 5.1 Man-woman relation

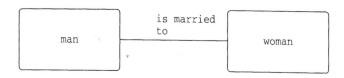

Figure 5.2 Man-woman relation labelled

Sometimes we are lucky enough to have special names for the entities when they are part of a relationship. In this case a married man is called a Husband and a married woman is called a Wife. If we have such names it is better to use them unless we require the more general name to form some other relationship.

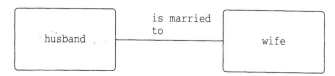

Figure 5.3 Husband- wife relation

By now some of you will be thinking, 'Surely a person can be married more than once'. This is quite true but, as stated previously, they can only have one legal spouse at a time. Notice how precise the terminology is in speaking about marriage. Because it is important to Society, which is the system which creates the environment for this relationship, then there are many precise terms to describe the entities involved. Societies often have a lot of terms for things which are important to them. For example, there are many words for sand in Arabic languages and for snow in Eskimo. When we encounter functioning Data Processing Systems we often find that there are many words for the entities which are important within them.

One exercise to confirm this, if you are studying at a college, is to talk to the Admissions Tutor about the various names given to the different types of offers given to Students before they are enrolled. You may think that there are Students, and everyone else, but this is rarely so to people dealing with enrolling, teaching and examining as a full-time occupation.

For another exercise, try to think of other one-to-one relationships that you have encountered. There aren't really that many, so be careful. If we ever have to write down a one-to-one relationship we refer to it as '1:1'.

5.3.2 One-to-many relationships

So much for the simple relationships. Let us continue with examples drawn from human kinship, as they are very general and familiar to most of us. Let us say that our couple have a child or children. To represent the relationship between one of the parents and the children we can draw a similar diagram to the previous ones but this time we put a 'trident' or 'crow's foot' at the CHILD end of the line.

There are several points to note regarding this diagram. Firstly, we have stuck to MAN as the entity name for the male parent, no sexism intended. We can use the term FATHER here as any man who has children is automatically a 'father'. For those of you who are wondering about adoption, separation, re-marriage, illegitimacy and so on, we are representing here the NATURAL FATHER of the CHILD and the diagram is accurate for that relationship regardless of any other complications humans manage to introduce!

Figure 5.4 Man-child relation

Secondly, we now have trouble labelling the relationship as it is not symmetrical, as in marriage. There are two alternatives which are shown in Figure 5.5.

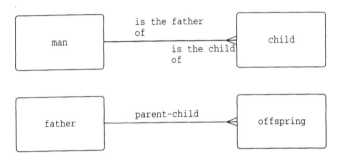

Figure 5.5 Man-child relation labelled

One way is to label each end of the relationship with the specific description. So the relationship of the MAN to his CHILD is: the MAN 'is the father of' the CHILD, and the relationship of the CHILD to the MAN is: the CHILD 'is the child of' the MAN. A simpler, if less precise, way is to label the relationship by the name of the two entities involved, in this case FATHER-CHILD. A more general name would be PARENT-CHILD and this is such a typical example that it is often used to label one-to-many relationships when they occur in practice, especially in database systems.

Thirdly, we should take care to note that the entity names are singular. This is usually the case. We denote plurality by putting the 'many' end against the required entity and by that we are indicating that, while a man may have many children (ie none, one, two or more) a child can only ever have one natural father. The 'one' is fixed and immutable for normal human beings. What gives the 'many' at the CHILD end is the possibility of a man having many children, even if some individuals do not.

As this last point is one that many people accept until they attempt to draw a diagram themselves, and then get confused, a little over-explanation is in order. If we register customers and then accept orders from them, we have a situation where a customer may place many orders, but each order is placed by only one customer. Therefore we would draw the relationship as in Figure 5.6.

This is how we draw the relationship because it is possible for each customer to place many orders, even though some may only place one and we never hear from them again, and some may never order anything. The firm may have special names for these, possibly not polite ones, but if they do not, we have to lump the one-off customer with the regular buyer as far as the chart is concerned.

70   *Mastering systems analysis and design*

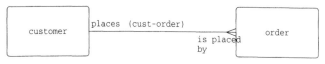

Figure 5.6 Customer-order relation

Some practitioners make it a point of pride to avoid using names twice. In the earlier example, PARENT-CHILD relationship, it could be argued that the entity MAN is too restrictive. It could equally well be that the entity should be named PARENT to go with the name of the relationship. Again one could say that CHILD is not general enough. SON or DAUGHTER would be too restrictive as we would need two entities and some way of connecting them to the FATHER or MOTHER. But children grow up and still have the same basis for a relationship with each of their parents. We could substitute OFFSPRING for CHILD without restricting the relationship to a particular sex or time.

The point is that Entity-Relationship Diagrams are there to be argued about. They are a way for an analyst to externalise their understanding of the connections between the items they have discovered during their fact-finding activities. By drawing them as shown, these concepts become available to other analysts, and perhaps even users, and hence open to discussion. One has to be prepared to defend one's interpretation of the entities and their Relationships, whilst being open to suggestions and different ideas.

If we ever have to write down, as opposed to draw, a one-to-many relationship it is usually called '1:N'.

As an exercise draw and label the relationship between the female and her offspring. Do it now, without looking back, as a check that you have fully understood the material so far. You should only take a minute, at most. Do not turn draft entity-relationship diagrams into works of art! When you have tried this, compare your diagram with Figure 5.5 to see if you have got everything correct. Is this the crow's-foot at the CHILD end? Have you labelled the relationship in some way?

5.4   A simple logical data structure diagram

Before we go on to the last degree of relationship there is one slight complication which it is worth introducing. So far we have considered the connections between two entities at a time. We call these 'Binary Relationships' and they are the best way of concentrating on the smallest meaningful amount of information to make sure we have really got it right. Having, somewhat awkwardly, drawn the relationship between an individual child and each of its parents in turn we can put the three entities MAN, WOMAN and CHILD together in one diagram. When we put more than two entities together, along with their relationships, we call the result various names depending on the purpose and the methodology. It may be called a Logical Data Structure, often abbreviated to LDS. Or it may be referred to as a Data Model Diagram, shortened to DMD. Some references also use the term 'Entity Model' and later when designing the database, the Logical Data Model (LDM). Whatever these diagrams are called they tend to use one notation, and the one introduced here will suffice for all of them.

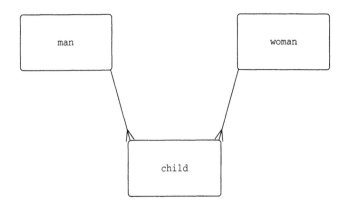

Figure 5.7 Man-woman-child relation

As usual there is more to this diagram than would appear at a glance. Firstly, it is a convention that the one-to-many relationships should be drawn with the 'one' end higher than the 'many' if at all possible. This makes the diagram easier to read, especially if the readers are familiar with the convention. Secondly, note that there is no direct relationship drawn between the MAN and the WOMAN. This is because they are linked by their joint relationship to an individual CHILD. This type of linking is often called a 'revealed' relationship.

It is worth labouring the point that when we draw LDS diagrams such as the above it should be understood that we are referring to three classes of entity, MAN, WOMAN and CHILD, and each entity represents a multitude of actual occurrences. There can be a thousand, or a million, men, a similar number of women, and five, or two point four, times that number of children. All we are saying with the diagram is that for every CHILD we find there is, somewhere, one MAN who is the father and one WOMAN who is the mother; that for every MAN we find it is possible for him to have 'some' children, where some is none, one, or more, not necessarily with the same WOMAN. Also the diagram shows that every WOMAN can have some children, not necessarily by the same MAN. We can be more specific, but before we are we need another degree of relationship.

5.4.1 Many-to many relationships

This is the commonest form of 'un-analysed' relationship and represents the case where many of one thing is related to many of another. For example, an orchestra can play in many venues, and a venue can also be host to many orchestras.

Note that the 'crow's feet' appear at both ends of the connecting line showing the many-to-many degree of the relationship, and that we still stick to the convention that ORCHESTRA and VENUE are singular in the entity boxes.

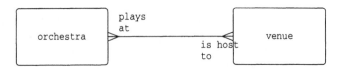

Figure 5.8 Orchestra-venue relation

If we ever have to write down a many-to-many relationship it is usually referred to as 'M:N'.

One purpose of entity or data analysis is to reduce relatively unhelpful forms to more simple forms by finding the connecting revealed relationships. In the case of many-to-many these almost invariably take the form of two one-to-many relationships. In fact we have already come across one. The first logical data structure diagram we produced, in Figure 5.7, was a simplification of the many-to-many relationship shown in Figure 5.9.

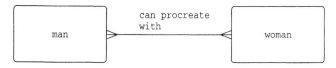

Figure 5.9 Man-woman relation revisited

This shows that it is possible for a man to produce offspring with many women, and vice-versa. We are not making suggestions or moral judgements, merely noting that it is possible.

One additional notation is possible with many-to-many relationships, and that is to label the relationship with the exact number if it is known. If we use our previous example of a family unit once more, but have the general entity PARENT to represent the father and the mother, then a child has many (more than one) parent and a set of parents can have lots (one, two or more, up to an undefined number) of children. In this case we have to put 'crow's feet' at each end of the relationship line but qualify the many-to-many with '2:N'.

Figure 5.10 Parent-child relation

As a final example of human marriage possibilities there exists somewhere in human culture the full range of possibilities from a one-to-one, two types of one-to-many, and a many-to-many form of marriage.

As an exercise use your knowledge or imagination to draw these four forms of relationship and look up their correct names in a good dictionary or encyclopaedia.

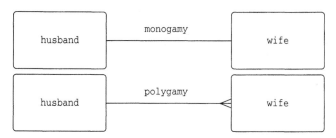

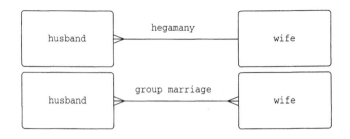

Figure 5.11 Four types of marriage relation

In addition we should try to find the revealed relationship and entity which resolves the problem of our Venues and Orchestras. If you find it difficult, try to think of an occasion where there is a definite venue and orchestra.

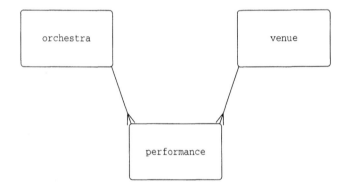

Figure 5.12 Orchestra-performance-venue relation

5.5   Contingent and optional relationships

So far the types of relationship we have examined have been 'mandatory' relationships. This means that both entities participate in the relationship, and this was implied by the solid line between the entities involved. We have actually been rather lax about this so far, to introduce the material. Sometimes it is 'optional' for one or both entities to take part in a relationship. If this applies to both parties then it is called an optional, or sometimes a 'fully optional' relationship. Taking our one-to-one form of Marriage (which by now you should have found is called monogamy) between a MAN and a WOMAN, the relationship is optional. The reason being that a MAN is still a MAN whether he is married or not. The same is true of a WOMAN. We draw this type of relationship with a dotted line at the optional end, and a solid line at the mandatory end. An alternative notation is to put a dot, or small circle on the line where it is optional.

However if we change the name of the entities to HUSBAND and WIFE we must use a solid line, as explained earlier.

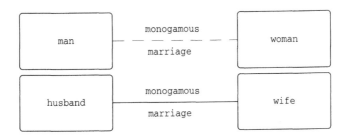

Figure 5.13 Optionality

There are more restrictions on this notation in SSADM than in any other methodology. These constraints are very limiting to the general understanding of the concept, in that only one entity in a relationship may be shown as optional, even if they both are. For the moment we are going to ignore this restriction in order to fully introduce the ideas of data modelling. Once the reader understands these, applying them in any methodology is considerably easier.

Notice how important the terminology used to describe the entities becomes when we add this extra complexity. Remember that so far we are only discussing general examples with which we are all familiar, in order to establish the rules. When we move into 'live' systems the names used to describe the entities become open to the interpretation of the users. Take, for example, the illustration in Figure 5.14.

Figure 5.14 Bus example

The diagram is depicting an example of a bus, which can have many passengers. However, a bus is always a bus, whether it is carrying passengers or not. It can be stationary, in the garage, or even on the back of a lorry, but it is still a bus. As usual, it is the people who are complicating the issue. They have to get onto a bus to become passengers in this context. We could argue that someone standing in a queue is a passenger, even if only a prospective one. It would depend on the view of the bus company whether this is allowable or not. At some point, perhaps when they actually get on the bus, or when they buy a ticket they become a passenger, and not before. Their existence is 'contingent' upon their relationship with a bus. In fact many transport and service companies refer to their bona fide customers as 'ticket holders'!

There are a great many examples of this kind, University to Student, Player to Football Team, Member to Club and so on. As an exercise draw out these relationships and discuss them with other people. Make sure you choose other students if possible. Having an analytical discussion on a topic not of mutual interest can be a good way of losing friends. Check carefully that you have the dotted line, or contingent marker, at the correct end of the relationship. It is easy to reverse it and lots of practice is the only sure way to remember how to draw it correctly.

Another way to gain practice is to re-draw the relationships between Parents and Children that we used to introduce the concept of degree of relationship. You can use the contingent relationship to denote no relationship if the degree is below one, i.e. in FATHER-CHILD there must be a CHILD for the MAN to be called a 'Father'. I will leave you to worry about whether it is self-evident that the CHILD cannot exist without a FATHER, or whether it should be shown explicitly on the diagram!

Be careful not to get bogged down in this analysis. It can seem very easy at first but sometimes the more you think about it, the harder it gets. If this happens, do something else for a while and come back to the problem with a fresh mind. Do not just give up.

Beware also of introducing a time element into the relationships. There is no diagrammatic representation for permanence or otherwise of relationships. Entity Life Histories use the concept of time, and they are discussed in a separate section of this book.

5.6   Exclusivity of relationships

The last type of representation we shall introduce here is the method used to show exclusivity of relationships. This is the way we show that an entity may be involved in two more relationships, but only one can be valid for each instance. To represent this we draw either one large arc, or series of small arcs through the relationship line nearest the entity which is being restricted to a single relationship.

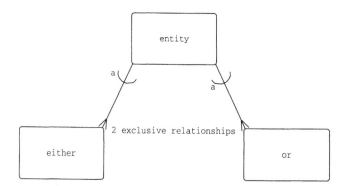

Figure 5.15 Exclusivity notation

We can use this concept to represent one facet of human existence, re-drawing our MAN-WOMAN-CHILD Logical data structure Diagram. You may have felt that it was unsatisfactory that we stopped with the child – after all, every man and woman was a child at some time. The diagram as originally drawn shows only one generation. With the help of an exclusive relationship we can now draw the options that a CHILD 'grows up to be' a MAN or a WOMAN.

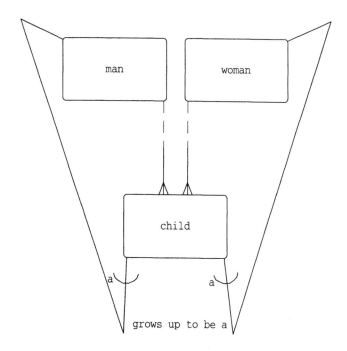

Figure 5.16 Exclusivity example

To take a different type of example, students are either 'Full-time' at an Institution (this is a deliberately vague term due to the changes taking place in Higher Education) or 'Part-time' but are rarely both at the same time. If they are both full-time and part-time, they typically have to be registered separately as both. This example is particularly interesting as there are two relationships between only two entities and there is a contingency on which relationship the student may have with the Institution. Unless the person is registered at an Institution they are a not usually considered to be a Student.

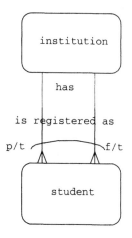

Figure 5.17 Institute-student relation

This same type of situation occurs in many other ways. For instance hospitals classify their 'active' patients as being registered as current In-patients or Out-Patients. Use the diagram above to help you draw this situation.

5.7   The river flow meter system logical data structure diagram

In order to fully appreciate how to apply the rules described above we will now work through the process of analysing the relationships in the case study, which we have been using throughout this section, the River flow Meter System.

Study the material available on the River flow System. Specifically you should read carefully over the interview notes in the paragraphs in the fact finding 'interviews', in Section 2.11 again. These paragraphs are in two-column form, with the interview material on the left-hand side, and an explanation and analysis on the right. Try reading the left-hand side only first and make an attempt at the logical data structure diagram for the river flow meter system. If necessary read the explanation as well. Then compare your reasoning with the development of the diagram below. You can, of course, just read the material without making an attempt first, but you will get much more out of the exercise if you make an attempt on your own, however inaccurate your attempt may be. Before we start, printed below is a solution to the Hospital problem asked after Figure 5.17.

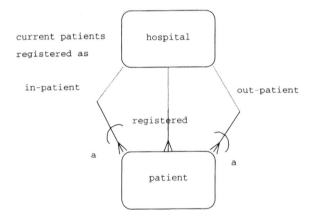

Figure 5.18 Hospital-patient relation (solution)

5.7.1   The river flow entities

Most students identify RIVER FLOW READING as an entity more or less immediately. Often they get stuck there, but a bit of encouragement and prompting brings out another group of possible candidates. Remembering that 'an entity is anything associated with the system' and 'unknown entities usually have relationships with existing known entities' often helps. The river flow readings are recorded by the RIVER

FLOW METER onto a PEN CHART and the DAILY AVERAGE RIVER FLOW is written to a RIVER FLOW METER DISC. Each of these are things associated with the system and hence are possible entities. The way we find out whether they are really entities is to try to model them in a set of entity relationships, which lead eventually to a logical data structure diagram.

How does a RIVER FLOW READING relate, if at all, to the other candidates? To find out we take each entity in turn and examine its relationship to the entity which we are currently considering.

Each RIVER FLOW READING belongs to a single RIVER FLOW METER, but the RIVER FLOW METER can have many RIVER FLOW READINGS, a 1:N relationship. In the same way RIVER FLOW READINGS are shown on a PEN CHART and used to calculate DAILY AVERAGE RIVER FLOWS. There are a different number of readings on each of these, but it is normally more than one, so the relationships are both 1:N. This information is shown on Figure 5.19.

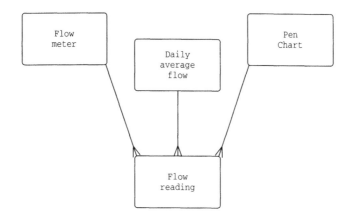

Figure 5.19 River flow entity diagram 1

So far we have used the RIVER FLOW READING as the central point of our modelling, but now we need to consider whether the 'new' entities our modelling has revealed to us have any connections with other entities. The RIVER FLOW METER DISC holds the DAILY AVERAGE RIVER FLOWS for the period in which it was used, and each DAILY AVERAGE RIVER FLOW will become a REPORT ENTRY in a MONTHLY REPORT and a MONTHLY GRAPH. We can add this information to update our model, as shown below. At the same time we could explicitly state that each RIVER FLOW METER DISC has associated with it a unique PEN CHART by adding the 1:1 relationship between them (Figure 5.20).

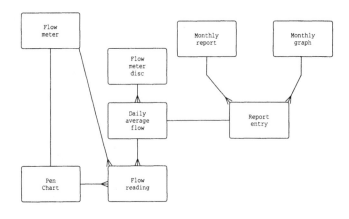

Figure 5.20 River flow entity diagram 2

An alternative way of representing this information would be to ignore the REPORT ENTRY as an entity and merely show a direct relationship between the DAILY AVERAGE RIVER FLOW, MONTHLY REPORT and MONTHLY GRAPH as shown below. However, whilst this would not be wrong it would not allow us to show the direct relationship between the DAILY AVERAGE RIVER FLOW and each ENTRY drawn on the two reports, which are now clearly different ways of representing the same value. This definite distinction has the added value of also showing another analyst that these values are related to the lines drawn on the PEN CHART, but are produced by a different means (Figure 5.21).

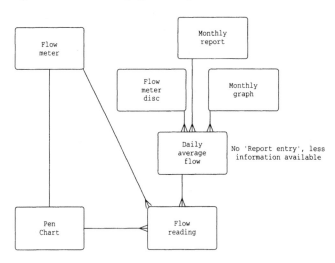

Figure 5.21 River flow entity diagram 3

Another advantage of drawing the logical data structure diagram as shown in Figure 5.21, as opposed to Figure 5.20, is that we can add the relationships between the RIVER FLOW METER and its MONTHLY REPORTS and MONTHLY GRAPHS in a relatively neat way that lets us draw most of the 1:N relationships downwards, as mentioned earlier.

This gives us a fairly complete logical data structure of the current River flow System. We have built this up from its fundamental elements, in other words by 'Bottom up' methods. But this is not a complete logical data structure diagram of the current River flow system. The reason for this is that we have stopped at the point where all of the likely data and reports for each river flow meter have been shown (remember DATA is plural). This is logical and makes sense from a programmer's point of view. Nevertheless, other entities exist which are associated with the system and we are limiting the picture, from an analytical viewpoint, by not including them. This would be a subtle but extremely dangerous mistake to make at this point because we are looking at only part of the whole picture and hence limiting any subsequent analysis to this restricted view.

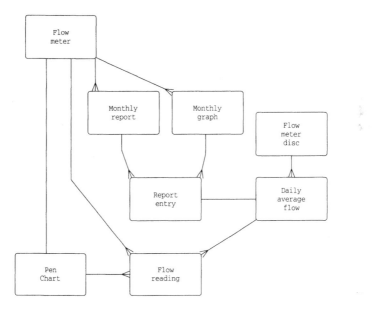

Figure 5.22 River flow entity diagram 4

The entities which are missing are the ones which seem too obvious to be included. If we had drawn the context diagram first, however, we would find them as the external entities to the system. (See the section on Data Flow Diagrams). They are the District Flow Officer, the District Manager, the Regional Research Team, and the Regional Flow Officer - the people associated with the system. How are we to include them in a logical data structure diagram? We know that there is one of each of them, but we need some entities or relationships to link them together. One possibility is their work relationships.

Figure 5.23 River flow entity diagram 5

This is reasonable but concentrates solely on the work relationships of the individual, which would be acceptable within a model of the required system, later in the life cycle. At this stage (we are assuming that we are still producing the first ever set of entity-relationships for this system) we need a very general representation, and Figure 5.23 gives none of the organisational structure information to an analyst trying to view the whole situation. The key to this is in the words within the titles of the personnel: Region and District. The organisation covers a Region, and has only one Regional Research Team and one Regional Flow Officer. There are many (more than one), Districts each of which has only one District Manager and one District Flow Officer. These are hard facts which we have ascertained by our reading and interviews. There is no need to disguise, interpret, or otherwise obscure them. The best approach is the simplest at this stage and that is to 'draw it exactly as it is'.

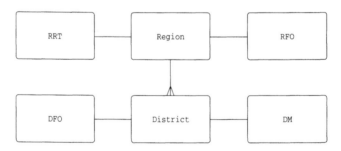

Figure 5.24 River flow entity diagram 6

We now have two reasonably satisfactory sets of entity relationship diagrams, one of which (Figure 5.22) represents the data elements within the current system, and the other (Figure 5.24) which clearly shows the relationship between the organisation entities directly associated with the system. As a matter of interest the former may change in the Logical Data Structure Diagram of the required system, but the latter should not! You are probably wondering by now why entities such as RIVER FLOW METER DISC are in capitals within this text, but District Manager is not. This is not an absolute requirement but it satisfies my sense of logic to refer to entities which are objects, meaning physical things that can be handled, in capital letters, to distinguish them from people and organisations units. If this confuses you, or you do not like that particular method, just ignore it.

All that is required now, to complete our logical data structure diagram exercise, is to find a way to put the two partial diagrams together. The key element in Figure 5.22 is the RIVER FLOW METER, which seems to control everything below it in the diagram. Remember that this entity is a representative of all the actual RIVER FLOW METERS in the Authority. Each RIVER FLOW METER is located within a District and that is how we can link the two structures. A District has many RIVER FLOW METERS. Add that relationship, and we have finished the first part of the task.

What remains now to be done is to add contingency to the diagram. We have to examine each pair of related entities, or binary relationships, to see if either or both entities can exist without the other. We change the line to a dotted one if it can exist and leave it as a solid line if it cannot.

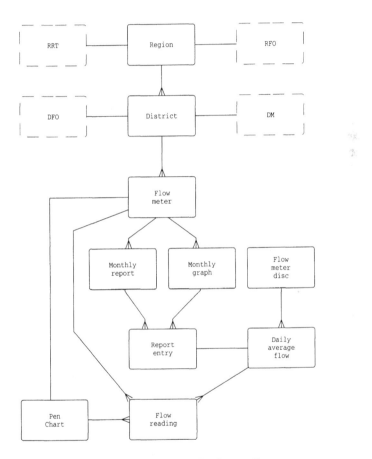

Figure 5.25 River flow entity diagram 7

You should try this as an exercise before looking at the solution. Some of the decisions seem arbitrary so if in doubt leave the line solid. For instance is a Region still a Region if it has no Districts? It is hard to say for sure. The 'powers that be' could easily restructure the Authority so that the Region it covers is no longer sub-divided, or introduce twenty smaller units called areas. In the same way, while a District Manager must have a District to be a Manager of, if for some reason that post was removed, the District would not necessarily disappear. You can spend an awful lot of time worrying about decisions like these, which are not going to affect the system you produce in any noticeable way, and it is often better to leave them as they stand. When examining the actual objects which may eventually become data items in your required Logical Data Structure one has to be much more pedantic. In other words concentrate your efforts on the parts of the Logical Data Structure which were originally in Figure 5.22, and do not worry too much about the part that comes from Figure 5.24

The first of these problems refers to the relation between Districts and RIVER FLOW METERS. If in doubt we ask ourselves the key question both ways and, hopefully, the answer is obvious. If we removed all of the RIVER FLOW METERS from a District, would it still be a District. The answer is of course, yes, so the line from District half way to RIVER FLOW METER can be a dashed one.

In the case of the RIVER FLOW METERS we reach our first difficulty. A RIVER FLOW METER is still the same object in a box in the factory so surely it can exist alone. This is the kind or reasoning which confuses many students. The point is to look at it from the view of the system. Until it is actually installed in a brook or river this entity is not producing RIVER FLOW READINGS and is therefore not a RIVER FLOW METER from the system's point of view. Hence its existence, in this context, depends upon its being installed within the District and is contingent on that. There may even be spare meters in a Depot at Headquarters, waiting to be installed, but we show that the system is not expecting data from them by drawing a solid line from the entity RIVER FLOW METER.

The same type of arguments apply throughout the production of any initial data model. A piece of graph paper is just that, until it has a line drawn on it. That line represents data which must have come from a RIVER FLOW METER. Remove the RIVER FLOW METER and the data must disappear, and with it the line and hence the MONTHLY GRAPH. So we can deduce that the existence of a MONTHLY GRAPH is contingent on the existence of the RIVER FLOW METER, whilst the converse is not true. Most of the reasoning is of this form, and having examined each relationship we can now re-draw the logical data structure diagram with contingency shown (Figure 5.26).

5.7.2 Summary of logical data structures

This has been a fairly lengthy discussion but has now completely introduced the topic as a top-down technique. What we have done is to start with whatever entities are obviously available to us and construct a conceptual picture of how they relate to each other. There is another approach covered under 'Relational Data Analysis' in Chapter 10 when more advanced techniques are discussed.

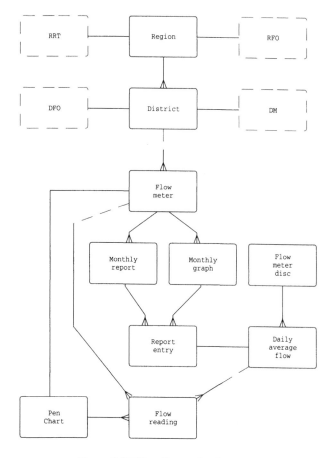

Figure 5.26 River flow entity diagram 8

5.8 Exercises

In order to gain more practice at **Analysing the current system data** you may now attempt the tutorial questions given below. Once you are confident of your skills in this topic you are in a position to complete the tasks within section 13.5 if you wish to do so, before proceeding to the next chapter.

These tasks specifically cover:

13.5.1   Producing the Current Logical Data Structure

5.8.1   Draw the diagram to illustrate the following entities and their relationship to one another. Remember that we are only modelling the relationship at a given time, not over their whole life. You could try suggesting modified entity names that could be used in a database to make that clearer.

i)   Car, Owner
ii) GP, Patient
iii) Post-code, House
iv) Line, Page
v)   Booking, Flight

5.8.2   Draw the logical data structure diagram to describe the following entities and their relationships.

i)   An open fire can be a gas fire, an electric fire, or a coal fire.
ii) A private motor vehicle can be a motor cycle, a car or a van. A car can be a saloon or an estate car. (There are many more possibilities, but we are limiting them to make a point.)
iii) A Public house may have overnight accommodation or not, and it may have a pool table, or not.

5.8.3   Draw the logical data structure diagram to describe the following entities and their relationships:

A University may be offering many Course(s), and may be made up of many Department(s).
A University Course must be run by one University, and may be taken by many Student(s).
A University Department must be funded by one University, and may be made up of many Lecturer(s).
A Lecturer must be employed by one Department, and a Student must be registered on one Course.

5.8.4   Modify the diagram such that a student must be registered either as an Undergraduate or as a Postgraduate.

5.8.5   Draw the logical data structure diagram to describe the following entities and their relationships.

A Firm may be employing many Employee(s)
An Employee must be employed by one Firm, and may be the manager of many Employee(s), and must be managed by one Employee.

5.8.6   A house must be made up of many Rooms. Each Room may must be contained in one House and:

1) may be a one Bedroom
2) may be a one Living room
3) may be a one Bathroom
4) may be a one Kitchen

5.8.7   Describe how the diagram in Figure 5.27 differs from the answer to Exercise 5.8.6. What extra information does it contain, and what does it not tell the reader?

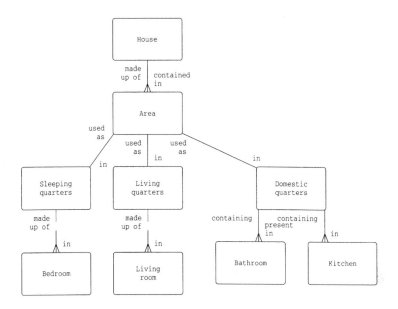

Figure 5.27 Exercise 5.8.7

6 | Proceeding with the Development

6.1   Introduction

At this point in the life cycle model, the current system has been completely modelled using both soft and structured techniques. The Analyst is now in a position to start work on the required system, but before doing that it is essential that the documented work to date be collected and presented to the user. In Chapter 1, the necessity of involving the User in all the decisions was emphasised, and the need for proper documentation milestones was described. This is the first of the 'milestone' documents as described in Section 1.4. This book is concentrating mainly on teaching the practical application of the tools and techniques of structured systems analysis and design, so only a brief coverage will be given of these documents. In practice each document may be as long as this book, duplicating many of the diagrams shown, with supporting forms and descriptions. To save space here, previously produced material will be referenced to avoid duplicating the figures and diagrams already given in previous chapters.

6.2   The proposal document

There is no single specific definition of what should or should not be included in a proposal document. The Analyst(s) look to the purpose of the document, and ask themselves if the contents are necessary and sufficient to fulfil that purpose. Unfortunately the purpose can vary with circumstances or between organisations. As far as a typical small project is concerned the purpose is to demonstrate that the project team has:

- Understood the objective(s) of the proposed system.
- Identified all the major functions of the present system.
- Determined the major functions of the required system.
- Produced an estimate of timescale, resources and cost.

The proposal document should contain enough material to convince the reader that all these objectives have been accomplished, without the document becoming a system specification. It should also be written and structured well enough to communicate that understanding easily and efficiently.

The following contents list is offered as a pro-forma. It can be used as a basis for your proposal, but feel free to add or subtract sections if you think your system has different needs.

a) A clear strategic definition of the proposed system requirements.
b) Overview of the present system.
   i) Description
   ii) Diagram (level 1 DFD or Rich picture)
   iii) Identification of current reports.
   iv) Identification of major current tasks.
c) Overview of the proposed system
   i) Description
   ii) Diagram (level 1 DFD or Rich picture)
   iii) Identification of new reports.
   iv) Identification of new tasks.
d) Broad timescales and costs (if they are available).
   i) Estimates of the system requirements if they are available.
   ii) Estimates of the software requirements if they are available.

Figure 6.1 Suggested contents for a system proposal

6.3 Preparing the river flow meter system proposal

The work for the proposal has mainly been completed by preparing the products in the previous chapters. All that is required now is to assemble these products into a document and add any additional text required to turn the result into a professional report. The easiest way to achieve this is to work through the suggested contents given in Figure 6.1, and specify where the material comes from.

6.3.1 Clear strategic definition of the proposed system

You should be able to use the root definition from Figure 3.6 for this item. The crucial word here is 'strategic', so avoid the temptation to go into any more detail than is absolutely required. Remember that this document may form the basis by which the system you deliver is judged to be adequate or not, so do not make or imply promises that cannot be kept.

6.3.2 Overview of the present system

Again this is fairly straightforward if all the previous work has been completed. The description can be assembled from the soft system products related to the people, suitably edited to remove any identification of their soft system roles, e.g. owner, other player, and so on. A suggested text is given in the figure below, but feel free to prepare your own if prefer. Note that the person we have decided is the owner is identified by name and title, but everyone else has only a title. The reason for this is that most of the individuals holding the posts may change during the life of the system without affecting the functionality, but if the owner changes then 'all bets are off'.

The diagram of the current system can be either the level 1 DFD given in Figure 4.11, or the rich picture given in Figure 3.5. The current system reports are as shown in Figure 2.9. When preparing proposals it is always useful to include actual examples to put the information you are using on record. Should anything go wrong at a later date, for example a field missing from the proposed report, you and the user can go back to this document to establish whether the information in dispute was available to you at this point.

The major current tasks are the:

- DFO visits each of the District's river flow meters every two weeks.
- DFO changes the data disks and charts in the pen recorders at each visit.
- DFO produces draft river flow reports for the DM every month.
- DM requests modifications to be made to the reports by the DFO if necessary.
- DMs authorise satisfactory reports and send them to the RFO at regional HQ.
- RFO files the monthly reports from all of the DMs.
- RRT occasionally use the data in the filed reports to model flows in river and changes to associated structures.

The current Waterborough Rivers Authority river flow meter system is a mixed computer and manual system, used by the Authority to calculate and record the groundwater flow within the Waterborough Region. Mr. Gordon Bennett, the Regional Flow Officer (RFO), has the overall responsibility for the management of the system.

The operational running of the system is performed by the District Flow Officers (DFOs) who produce monthly reports. The District Managers (DMs) authorise these reports locally before sending them to the Regional Headquarters. The Regional Research Team (RRT) access the data in the system to perform river flow modelling, the results of which are used to advise the Authority Directorate of the likely outcome of changes affecting the use or flow of water in the rivers.

Figure 6.2 Suggested description of the current system

6.3.3   Overview of the proposed system

The description can be produced by paraphrasing information from the fact-finding interviews with Mr. Bennet in Section 2.7. What we produce is more likely to be acceptable if we use his terminology when possible. A suggested text is given in Figure 6.3, but feel free to prepare your own if prefer.

Note that we have carefully avoided saying how we are going to perform these tasks, such as transfer the data to the region. That is a design consideration, and while we may have a range of options in mind, it would be foolish to commit to one at this stage. The diagram will have to be the rich picture if we have not already used it, as we have not produced the data flow diagrams for the proposed system yet.

The proposed river flow meter system is intended for use by the Waterborough Rivers Authority to calculate and record the groundwater flow within the Region. The intention is that the system should be fully computerised, and based on the current procedures used at the Bourn Brook District. The operational running of the system will be performed by the current District Flow Officers at each district using the data from their own meters. The new system will use the existing equipment to produce monthly reports for their District Managers to authorise before digital forms of these reports are sent to the regional headquarters. No changes to the current operation of the river flow meters themselves is planned at this stage, nor is extra computer equipment likely to be required.

The overall responsibility for the management of the proposed system will lie with Mr. Gordon Bennett, the Regional Flow Officer. In addition, the Regional Research Team will have access to the data in the HQ computerised system to perform river flow modelling calculations, although the actual processes involved are outside of the proposed system. The only addition to the current functionality of the system is the production of the PIWFs required to allow the public to view the river flow data.

Figure 6.3 Suggested description of the proposed system

The only new reports identified so far are the PIWF reports identified in the fact-finding so we may as well propose a layout for this report, as described below, to get the user's agreement to it if possible. There may be other working reports to allow the operators to use the system, but they should emerge during the design process and we do not wish to commit ourselves to more than is necessary at this stage. There are no new tasks as such. Some of the current manual tasks may be computerised, but the comments above regarding the reports also apply here.

6.3.4 Broad timescales and costs

A rough estimate of the system requirements has already been implied in the products, so no additional information is needed in this case. The same comments apply to the software requirements

We do not have enough information in this case study at this point to make any sensible estimates regarding costs and timescales. The only professional thing to include in the proposal is a clear statement that this is the case, and not try to invent figures if they do not exist.

6.4 More proposal practice using the River Flow Meter system

In addition to the above products, we can also insert draft layouts for any new or modified reports for the required system which are not included in the current system at this point. For example, we can propose keeping the District Flow Authorisation Report, as shown in Figure 2.9, exactly the same. However, that commits the proposed system to holding the daily weather data somewhere on the computer. In addition we can use this opportunity to suggest and agree a layout for the PIWF reports requested by the user. Do ensure that any new reports are agreed at this point, as their content and layout is required for the more rigorous design that follows. Should a new report, with data which is incompatible with the proposal, be slipped into the process later in the design, it is certain to cause serious problems at the implementation stage.

In order to progress, we will assume that this layout is agreed by the user.

DRAFT PIWF
ROOM 460 'J BLOCK', REGIONAL HQ, WASH ROAD,
WATERBOROUGH

Average flow readings for all meters in Bourn Brook District (in litres per second). 1998

WK	Week-begin	Meter 1	Meter 2	Meter 3	Meter 4	Meter 5
1	05/01/98	12.67	14.63	20.11	25.08	28.98
2	12/01/98	12.94	14.12	20.36	25.91	28.51
3	19/01/98	12.99	13.92	20.37	26.47	27.09
4	26/01/98	13.33	14.54	21.20	27.52	28.25
5	02/02/98	13.32	14.21	20.24	26.97	28.22
6	09/02/98	10.42	12.49	16.26	29.33	32.50
7	16/02/98	9.96	12.40	16.98	28.72	31.93
8	23/02/98	9.81	12.61	16.15	28.03	31.62
	etc.	10.26	12.98	15.60	28.62	30.54
	up to date	...	....	....	.....	....

Figure 6.4 Suggested draft layout for the PIWF report

6.5 Exercises

In order to gain more practice at **Assembling a document proposing how to proceed** you may now attempt the tutorial questions given below. Once you are confident of your skills in this topic you are in a position to complete the tasks within Section 13.6 if you wish to do so, before proceeding to the next chapter.

These tasks specifically cover:

13.6.1   Producing the Initial Proposal (Feasibility) Report

6.5.1   Study the detail in Section 6.4 and suggest the changes required to the system to include the weather data as on the original report.

6.5.2   Following on from Section 6.4, imagine that the User decided that they may want all of the functions to be centralised at the regional headquarters. Write a simple proposal to suggest how this could be achieved.

7 Using Processes to Develop the Required Logical System

7.1 Introduction

Section 1.5.4 explained how analysts move from the real, or physical, world using conceptual models in order to perform their analysis and produce a new physical solution to the user's problem and requirements. There is no easy way to do this, as the final system must incorporate several fundamentally different ways of looking at any non-trivial situation. As human beings it is difficult for us to deal with more than one aspect at once. This means that we often have to start with one view of the system, say the processes, and then check this against the data view, making minor adjustments until we have a solution which is compatible with both. In practice this means building the best initial model of the proposed system, knowing that it is incorrect, and being prepared to change it or even start again. This may sound obvious, but people get very attached to their work once they have produced it and can become defensive, hanging on to a model of the system long after it is clear that another view is incompatible with it. This 'siege mentality' is best overcome by accepting that the first model is almost certainly wrong and being prepared to change anything in it wherever possible.

7.1.1 Modifying data flow model to produce an initial version of the system

One way to produce the initial model is to use the data flow products described in Chapter 4 as the starting point. In this, a diagramming tool to represent the processes in the current system was introduced, and two simple DFDs, the context and level 1 diagrams, were produced to represent the current logical system. The forms that are used to document these diagrams were also described. These are often neglected, as computer practitioners seem to dislike filling in forms even more than most people. However, it is important that these forms are completed for two reasons. Firstly, the diagrams alone cannot give sufficient detail of what is intended by the analyst. For example, the error and exception conditions are often left out to make the diagrams clearer. Secondly, we can use the forms in a simple way to move onto the analysis of the required system. This is the process described in this chapter and, as we are moving increasingly into practical work, the simplest way to describe the use of each new technique is to use the case study as an example. In other words, we are going to produce a paper model of the proposed system processes, totally based on the current system processes, and, as we know that is not what is wanted, it should not be too painful to the make any changes required to produce the required logical model.

Please note that, as the analysis and design work progresses, it becomes increasingly practically based which is why the use of case studies is so important. There are limits to the value of verbal descriptions when we are learning these topics, and simple relevant examples are often a good way of demonstrating the use of these techniques.

7.2 Producing the River flow meter system processes

At this point in the simplified life cycle model that we are using within this book, the analyst's next task is to start to produce the data flow model for the required system. As described above this can start from the current logical data flow diagrams together with their corresponding forms. One way to explain this process is to continue with the extended worked example we have been using so far, and carry on with the practical application on the forms introduced at the end of Chapter 4. There we produced just two of the diagrams, and then generated the supporting forms, but a simple way to progress is to reverse this procedure and use the forms to help us produce more detailed diagrams as an initial guess at the required system. The most useful form to start with is the user/function matrix form, which we reproduce below to save you looking back.

User/Function Matrix Form											
Current System **YES**							Required System				
System **RIVER FLOW SYSTEM** Author **MJH** Date **2/3/93** Page **7** of **7**											
User A DISTRICT FLOW OFFICER B DISTRICT MANAGER C REGIONAL RESEARCH TEAM FUNCTION	A	B	C	D	E	F	G	H	I	J	K
1 Collect river flow disk and pen chart	×										
2 Load fresh disk and pen chart paper	×										
3 Validate readings against previous reading	×										
4 Internally validate readings	×										
5 Validate readings between river flow meters	×										
6 Compare anomalous readings with weather diary	×										
7 Edit readings as necessary	×										
8 Record new readings	×										
9 Produce monthly reports	×										
10 Check readings and reports		×									
11 Request changes to unsatisfactory readings		×									
12 Authorise satisfactory results		×									
13 Use data for modelling			×								

Sample User/Function Matrix Form. PISAD-UF1. Version 1.

7.2.1 A first pass at producing the required system

A first pass at producing the required logical system is to examine the forms for the current logical system in conjunction with the requirements list, as shown in Figure 2.10, and hence to modify the current system documentation 'on the fly' to comply with the user wishes expressed there. This can be basically a copying forward and editing process in the case of simple transitional systems. Where a complete re-write or change of practice is involved, much greater effort is needed. The trick is to be thorough without putting in such enormous effort that whatever is produced has to be the solution because all the analyst's time and patience have been exhausted.

The river flow meter system being used here as a case study contains aspects of both these conditions. Requirements 2 and 3 show that there should be no real change to the operation at the District level, so the system is relatively straightforward from this point of view. The same people will be completing more or less the same work. All that is required is that certain aspects of these tasks should be automated at the District level, using the existing computer equipment. But a completely new, if relatively simple, computerised system must be installed at the Regional Headquarters, fed by the data from the District systems. Our 'Business System Option' is therefore defined for us (this will be expanded in a later chapter). Requirement 2 states that no extra equipment should be purchased but use made of the existing desktop microcomputers, and therefore most of the available technical options are defined for us as well.

Note this carefully! It is a continual source of amazement that, despite the interviewers labouring the above point, when this example is used for student group work, at least one group will usually produce a proposal for a complex networked system to resolve a problem which could easily be solved by posting one floppy disk per month! In fairness, it can be very easy to do this if you do not think about the options and requirements clearly, and the Author has seen similar inefficiencies committed in actual practice. A paraphrase of Occam's Razor is a help in these cases: when faced with several alternative systems, implement the simplest! You can often introduce a more complex alternative later as an expensive 'enhancement', but if you later remove a costly facility because it is not being used, it will be seen by the user as a failure on your part.

7.2.2 Identifying the new processes

Even though the District system is remaining essentially the same, there is a considerable change in the way in which the actual functions are performed. The quickest way to identify these changes is to modify the user-function matrix, adding any new functions and mark those existing tasks which the user has indicated should be computerised. The table below is essentially the table for the current system modified to include the new tasks. The functions are marked with an 'x' if they are manual or unchanged, and with a 'C' if they are to be computerised. In the latter case, the 'user' column is an indication of who will be responsible for using that function in the computerised system. By the way, we do not know how many pages there will be until we fill in all of the other forms, so that is left blank for the moment.

Comparing this form with its previous version, it can be seen that many of the physical tasks performed by the District Officer are unchanged. All that has been done is to indicate that the paper-based calculations are to be computerised (if possible) and the references to paper records, such as the 'diary', have been updated to say 'data'. These indicate intentions at this point, rather than fixed decisions. The reference to 'monthly reports' has been clarified. The reports are produced every month, hence the user's terminology, but each actual report has only one week's data as can be seen in Figure 2.9 on the example report. A set of reports is required to cover the period since they were last produced.

User/Function Relation Matrix Form												
Current System					Required System **YES**							
System **RIVER FLOW**	Author **MJH**			Date **2/3/93**			Page of					

USER	A	B	C	D	E	F	G	H	I	J	K
A DISTRICT FLOW OFFICER B DISTRICT MANAGER C REGIONAL FLOW MANAGER D REGIONAL RESEARCH TEAM											
FUNCTION											
1 Collect river flow disk and pen chart	×										
2 Load fresh disk and pen chart paper	×										
3 Validate readings against previous reading	C										
4 Internally validate readings	C										
5 Validate readings between river flow meters	C										
6 Compare anomalous readings with weather diary	×										
7 Edit readings as necessary	C										
8 Enter new readings into system (database)	C										
9 Produce weekly reports (each month)	C										
10 Check diary and reports		×									
11 Request changes to unsatisfactory readings		×									
12 Authorise satisfactory data and reports		C									
13 Send data and reports to Regional HQ		×									
14 Read reports and store data from Districts into central database.			× C								
15 Use data for modelling				C							
16 Produce PIWFs			C								
17											

Sample User/Function Matrix Form. PISAD-UF1. Version 1.

7.2.3 Drawing the required system data flow diagrams

Using this as a basis for DFD-type analysis, it can be seen that the data stores are likely to be the disks and databases holding the river flow data, with the fundamental data inputs being the values of the river level readings. We can use this information and the above table to produce a context diagram of the required system. As there are no new inputs this diagram is relatively unchanged from the previous version except adding for the PIWF reports as a new output. Another, more subtle change is that the 'Monthly reports' are shown as both an input and an output. This is because the system has to cope with the District Manager rejecting a report by asking for changes to it. The detailed mechanism to implement this procedure is not defined at this level, but if we allow a generally named input on the context diagram, then allowance has been made for some data to enter the system.

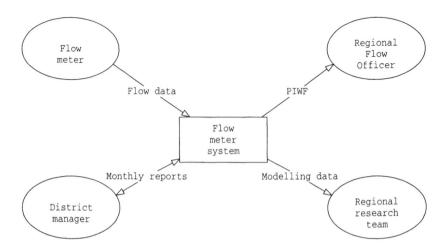

Figure 7.1 Context diagram of the required system

Following the inputs as described in the main body of the text (see the 'Basic Rules for Drawing Data Flow Diagrams' in Chapter 4) we can expand this into a level 1 data flow diagram. This is a fairly easy process if we have completed the matrix as above. The trick here is not to go into too much detail. This can be avoided by finding a general process name for all the contiguous tasks performed by the same person. As we are now producing the required (computerised) system model, the manual processes can be left out completely unless they actually affect the data in some way. This was why, in Chapter 4, only the top two DFDs for the current system were drawn. By leaving out the manual processes as far as possible, a lot of redundant effort is avoided, as manual activities are much easier to depict in rich pictures rather than DFDs.

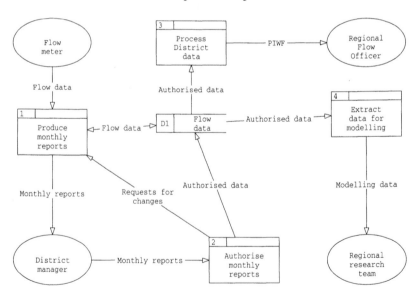

Figure 7.2 Level 1 DFD of the required system

This is similar to the current system DFD, shown in Figure 4.11, because we drew a fairly general picture where all the activities of the District Flow Officer to do with visiting the river flow meters were in one level 1 process. This has been removed as suggested above, and all the data processing functions are a single process. All the tasks of the District Manager also go into another level 1 process, as do the tasks of the Regional Flow Officer. We have noted the existence of the Regional Research Team with another process for completeness. At this stage we are still not sure whether these roles will change or even continue to exist in the required system but we include them just to be on the safe side.

The real changes come when we expand the detail of the level 1 processes and this time there will be no alternative to exploding the processes down to a sufficient level of detail where program or module design can be produced. This is because the work from now on is our own creation. Before this stage, during the fact-finding and the current system analysis, we were concerned with trying to communicate our understanding of the current system. This was essential to get feedback from the user before starting the process of producing the required system, the present task. Previously, the users were the experts, and the analysts were going through a learning process during fact finding. As the work progresses into the definition of the required system, only the analysts really know the proposed solution, and the understanding everyone else gains depends upon how well the analysts explain their proposed solution. Note that it is still really only a proposal until the systems specification has been accepted by the users and the project management team, and how well they view the quality of the proposal will depend upon how well it is documented.

This can be an expensive and time-consuming task. But if there are any flaws or misunderstandings, it is cheaper and less painful for them to be discovered at this point rather than later when the system is being implemented, or even worse during live running. This can only be achieved by a complete and clear documentation of our 'proposed' required system before we proceed. Persuading the users to adopt a system which has not been fully researched is not only unprofessional, it is a guarantee of failure in the long term.

So it is important to at least convince ourselves that the proposed system has been clearly defined and any potential problems identified. Note that this is a similar aim to that of the original proposal or feasibility study, but here the detail is much finer. To achieve this we can either explode the processes as described in Chapter 4 previously, and then fill out the Function Definition Forms, or vice versa. Whichever approach you think will be most effective can be adopted, but you must end up with both the diagrams and the forms to complete the documentation for each level of the data flow diagrams, but based on the diagrams for the required system.

7.2.4 Using forms to produce the required logical system

In the river flow meter system we are more or less translating from a manual to computer system at the District level so it is reasonable to do the forms first and then the data flow diagrams. For the Regional system we can reverse the process and produce the diagrams first, to help us visualise the new structure. As the two parts are effectively two sub-systems it is reasonable to approach each in the way that suits them best, and it is a convenient way to demonstrate both methods. We can start by getting the simplest part out of the way, i.e. copying forward and modifying the forms from the current system.

Function Summary Form				
Current System		Required System **yes**		
System **River flow**	Author **MJH**	Date **2/3/93**		Page **1** of **6**
Description **Summary of the functions in the required logical system**				

Ref	Function Name		Comments
1	Produce Monthly Reports		Each Report covers one week only (This should be fully automated)
2	Authorise Monthly Reports and send to Regional HQ		Send unsatisfactory reports back to the DFO for re-editing (No change in procedure, option in 2 for Authorisation?)
3	Accept & Process District data to produce PIWFs.		New process required.
4	Ad hoc extraction required to use Central file for modelling.		New process, needs to be accessible in same way as current method

Sample Function Summary Form. PISAD-FS1. Version 1.

As described previously we should now complete a Function Definition form for each of the functions identified above. This would normally require an additional four forms, so to save space we will summarise the essential fields of the forms in a table. Look back to the form we completed previously if you wish to see how each form would appear if we were documenting the system as completely as in a real system.

Function Definition	Function Description	Error Handling
Form 2 of 6	Produce Monthly Reports 1.a) Validate the data against previous readings and up/downstream readings 1.b) Produce draft report and compare to pen chart. 2. Compare anomalies to the 'weather diary'. 3. Edit data using personal judgement where necessary. 4. Draw up draft report for District Manager.	Use pen charts if possible or use up/down stream readings. Otherwise use weather diary and personal judgement, i.e. guess!
Form 3 of 6	Authorise Monthly Reports and send to Regional HQ Note :- needs computerising for non-technical user	Discuss unsatisfactory readings with DFO and request re-edits.
Form 4 of 6	Accept & Process District data to produce PIWFs. Check & File District Reports	Chase up late District Reports.
Form 5 of 6	Ad hoc extraction required to use Central file for modelling.	N/A

The user/function relation matrix form shown previously can now be seen as being page 6 of 6.

7.2.5 Expanding the required logical DFDs

Using these forms and the level DFD, the work of drawing the exploded, level 2 DFDs, is relatively straightforward. The set of diagrams is shown next, with a brief explanation of each to cover any new points.

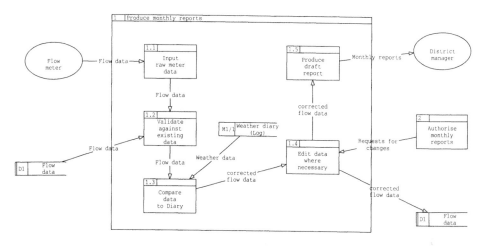

Figure 7.3 Explosion of required logical DFD Process 1

This is by far the most complex diagram as it covers the work of the DFO who performs most of the processing on the raw meter data to turn it into the processed data which acts as inputs to the other systems. Note that the diagram is consistent with the process box from which it is exploded, having two external entities, a data store and another process either providing or receiving data. The names and directions of the data flows into and out of the level 2 DFD should also be related to the flows on the original level 1 diagram. If, for any reason, it is found that the level 2 diagram requires any different data flows or sources in order to draw it correctly, then the level 1 DFD, and possibly the context diagram, must be also be changed to keep all the diagrams consistent.

Another item of note on this diagram is that the data store has been duplicated to avoid crossing the data flows, and the labels on the data flows have been made slightly different to add more detail to the process. The original label of 'River flow data', which refers to data measuring the river water not the generic name of the item on the DFD, was deliberately general to allow detail to be added to it at this level. Adding more detail is acceptable, changing the type or direction is not. The final new detail added to this diagram is to show the weather diary, or log, as a 'manual store'. This is similar to a data store but is given a different identifier to show that it is not a data store (i.e. it is not labelled D??) and is a way of holding or accessing non-computerised information internal to a low-level process. It would not have been wrong to show this as an external entity providing data, for example, but by making it internal to a low-level process its impact on the overall system has been minimised. This is especially so as it is effectively an exception (or error) procedure, and no part of the required system we intended to implement.

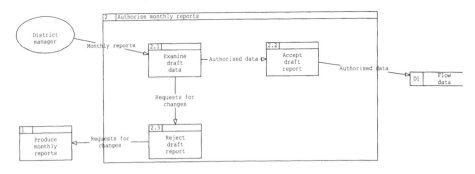

Figure 7.4 Explosion of required logical DFD Process 2

The method described above has been repeated for this process, and three level 2 processes has been suggested as being sufficient to deal with all of the work required. As this work is fairly straightforward, the diagram should be self-explanatory by now. The same is true for the remaining two diagrams. It could be argued that these did not even need exploding as they are so simple, but they are included below for completeness.

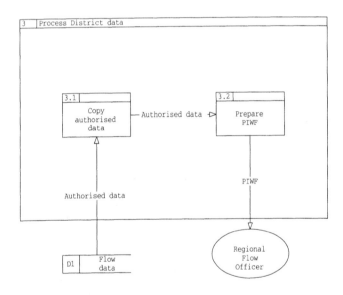

Figure 7.5 Explosion of required logical DFD Process 3

Finally, we can now replace the draft user/function relation matrix form used up to now with a correct version which list the actual functions shown in the set of DFDs generated. This work illustrates the method of generating a draft of the desired product, and then iteratively improving it until an acceptable version has been produced. It is rare in systems analysis and design that the first attempt at anything is good enough to be useful, so the experienced analyst accepts the need to check and re-check their work.

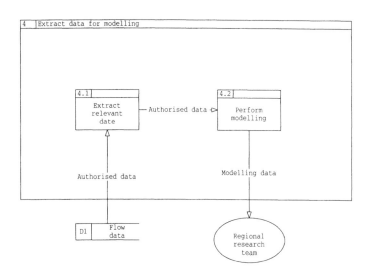

Figure 7.6 Explosion of required logical DFD Process 4

User/Function Relation Matrix Form											
Current System						Required System **YES**					
System **RIVER FLOW** Author **MJH** Date **2/3/98** Page **6** of **6**											
USER	A	B	C	D	E	F	G	H	I	J	K
A DISTRICT FLOW OFFICER											
B DISTRICT MANAGER											
C REGIONAL FLOW MANAGER											
D REGIONAL RESEARCH TEAM											
FUNCTION											
1 Produce monthly reports	C										
1.1 Input raw meter data	C										
1.2 Validate against existing data	C										
1.3 Compare data to Diary	C										
1.4 Edit data where necessary	C										
1.5 Produce draft report	C										
2 Authorise monthly reports		C									
2.1 Examine draft data		C									
2.2 Accept draft report		C									
2.3 Reject draft report		C									
3 Process District data			C								
3.1 Copy authorised data			C								
3.2 Prepare PIWF			C								
4 Extract data for modelling				C							
4.1 Extract relevant data				C							
4.2 Perform modelling				C							
Sample User/Function matrix Form. PISAD-UF1. Version 1.											

Several minor points are worth noting on the form above. Firstly, all of the process boxes have been shown to illustrate how the form is produced, but only the functions, the lowest level processes should really be there. Secondly, all of the activities are marked with a 'C' as being computerised, which is correct as the proposed system contains no manual processes.

7.3 Summary of the required data flow modelling activities

We have now defined what we require the implementation team to do logically to provide the required system. Before they, or we, can proceed into more detail there should be a definition of how we intend to accomplish the objectives in practical terms. It is very difficult to state at which point exactly in the life cycle this decision should be taken or documented. Different methodologies make different recommendations. In SSADM version 4 some tactical decisions will have been made when choosing the Technical Options and these will be made more explicit as the requirements specification progresses.

General guidelines can be given based on the evolution of system and software development techniques. It is generally a bad idea to start the project with a fixed idea of what type of equipment, for example, will be used. There may seem to be obvious exceptions to this, for example a systems programmer who is writing a specific driver file for a printer, modem or terminal. But even in this extreme case it has long been good practice to separate the logical functions from the physical solutions wherever possible: for instance by producing generic solutions based on tables keyed by type. This allows future expansion and modification to the functionality without re-writing the software. On the other hand a design which is not directed towards some physical functionality is not complete and becomes almost meaningless. All we can do is draw the best diagrams possible, with the information available to us at each stage. That is what we have done so far, by drawing the best DFDs possible based on the products of the analysis activities. However, it would be over-optimistic to believe that coding could now commence as no account has been taken of the data view of the system, which is all bundled into one data store marked 'D1 - Flow data'. In order to turn this initial attempt into something that could be implemented with confidence, we need several new tools and these will be described in the next few chapters.

7.4 Exercises

In order to gain more practice at **A first attempt at modelling the required system processes** you may now attempt the tutorial questions given below. Once you are confident of your skills in this topic you are in a position to complete the tasks within Section 13.7 if you wish to do so, before proceeding to the next chapter.

All of these questions assume that the User has decided that they want all of the functions to be centralised at the regional headquarters, as suggested in Exercise 6.2, but it is not necessary to complete that question before proceeding.

7.4.1   Imagine that the Regional Flow Manager decided that he wanted all of the procedures except visiting the river meters themselves to be completed at Regional Headquarters by a Regional Flow Officer. Modify the User/ Function Matrix Form shown below to reflect this decision.

User/Function Relation Matrix Form											
Current System	Required System **YES**										
System **RIVER FLOW** Author **MJH**	Date **2/3/93** Page of										
USER	A	B	C	D	E	F	G	H	I	J	K
A DISTRICT FLOW OFFICER B DISTRICT MANAGER C REGIONAL FLOW MANAGER D REGIONAL RESEARCH TEAM FUNCTION											
1 Collect river flow disk and pen chart	X										
2 Load fresh disk and pen chart paper	X										
3 Validate readings against previous reading	C										
4 Internally validate readings	C										
5 Validate readings between river flow meters	C										
6 Compare anomalous readings with weather diary	X										
7 Edit readings as necessary	C										
8 Enter new readings into system (database)	C										
9 Produce weekly reports (each month)	C										
10 Check diary and reports		X									
11 Request changes to unsatisfactory readings		X									
12 Authorise satisfactory data and reports		C									
13 Send data and reports to Regional HQ		X									
14 Read reports and store data from Districts into central database.			X C								
15 Use data for modelling				C							
16 Produce PIWFs			C								
17											
18											
Sample User/Function Matrix Form. PISAD-UF1. Version 1.											

7.4.2   If the system is changed in this way, will this affect the context diagram of the system?

7.4.3   Following on from the above changes, produce a new set of data flow diagrams to reflect this situation.

8 | The Business System Option

8.1 Introduction

The Business System Options is a report which lies close to the boundary between analysis and logical design, and serves as a document 'milestone' in that it is the last chance for the user to influence the outcome of the **way** in which the system is implemented with respect to their organisation.

There is rarely just one way in which a system can be implemented in terms of satisfying the user's requirements. Up until this point in the analysis process, the user requirements should be described using non-technical wording. For example, 'allow simultaneous access to customer records' as opposed to 'install a computer network using Microsoft Windows'. The latter may be one of the technical means of achieving the requirement, but it is not the requirement itself. By this stage the analyst should be trying to assess the impact on the organisation of allowing different groups of users different types of access to the customers' records. If only one group can update them, but many can read them, or vice versa then there will be consequences on the functional activities in the organisation.

Let us consider the case of a utility company (gas, electricity or water) which is spread over a large area and has a requirement 'to increase the productivity of clerks dealing with customer telephone enquiries'. The current system may be based on local area offices which only deal with their own area, but the company has a problem in that increasingly customers are telephoning to enquire about their accounts, rather than going into the offices. There are peak loads in some areas whilst others are underutilised, but it is impossible to predict where the load will occur. The options the analyst could recommend range from lots of relatively small groups of clerks dealing only with enquiries from their own area, right through to having one call centre which deals with telephone enquiries for the whole company. The implications for the company, and the telephone and computer networks, are enormously different, depending upon the option chosen. The analyst should not take it upon himself to choose the 'best' way, but to document a variety of options. They should use then use their skills to provide a sensible set of alternatives which involve different amounts of computerisation, as well as different approaches. Ideally the technical solutions should not be included, unless each different option enforces an obviously different method of use.

One acceptable instance of this is the non-computerisation or minimal computerisation option based on, say, a new approach to the manual procedures which has been identified from the analysis. Always try to start from this premise if possible. Often introducing a computer system forces new working practices on an organisation. It is possible that these practices alone would be enough to achieve some of the objectives, without putting a computer in at all.

The next level is often to make use of some parts of the manual procedures with a very simple computer system which just takes the drudgery out of the work, without requiring any massive changes to the current system. The options should be sorted into a sequence in which the clerical and administrative procedures, as well as the training needs for the computing aspects of the option are one level more demanding than the previous one. The final option can be the 'all-singing, all-dancing' fully automated system if that is appropriate.

8.1.1 The contents of the Business System Options

The analyst should include in the document an introduction and a list of the identified requirements, preferably in increasing order of user importance. An executive summary or contents list of the options is usually welcomed, followed by the details of each option in turn. For each option, the relevant information needed to allow the users to exercise their judgement, with a rich picture or any other means to make the Analyst's intentions absolutely clear, should be included.

Aim to present three or four viable alternatives which address the user's requirements in a progressive fashion. For each of them, the advantages, disadvantages and impact on the organisation should be clearly visible to the user. Obviously some options may not address all of the requirements, so the link between the requirements and the cost and complexity of each solution can be established. The implications of each choice are then obvious to the user, which puts them into the position of a consumer and aids them in the process of deciding upon one suitable option.

8.1.2 An overview of the river flow meter system business options

As described in Chapter 7, the business system options for the river flow meter system have already been decided for this case study. That is because they were set up this way, as in this book we are concentrating on the modelling techniques for the computerisation of user systems and have mentioned the business system aspect of development only for completeness. The proper treatment of proposing and adopting these options is the province of specialist Business Studies and Business Information Systems and lies outside the scope of this introductory text. However, in order to progress we will assume that there is no change to the current working practices in this case study. In practice the motivation for the systems analysis may be to introduce new practices which fundamentally change the operational aspects of the business.

After getting the user's agreement to the method in the initial required system design, the remaining tasks are concerned with checking that the design is as complete and correct as possible before coding commences.

8.2   Exercise

In order to gain more practice at **Suggesting various business options** you may now attempt the tutorial questions given below. Once complete you are in a position to complete the tasks within section 13.8, before proceeding to the next chapter.

These tasks specifically cover: 13.8.1 Producing the Business Systems Options.

8.2.1   Imagine that the idea of centralising the DFO functions described in the tutorial question 6.2 occurred to you rather than coming from the user. Produce a short report outlining the likely affect on the business of the users of the river flow system, of opting to implement the system in this way.

9 Relational data analysis

9.1 Introduction

Relational data analysis (RDA) is one name given to a set of techniques based on Codd's work on 'normalising' data. Relational data analysis is a 'bottom-up' technique. The procedure starts at the lowest level with the data items as they are appear in actual documents and reports. These data items are progressively refined into logical and efficient 'relations', using a multi-step process of normalisation. These relations may then be used to provide a second view of the data structure diagrams introduced in Chapter 5. For simplicity, we will refer to these diagrams as logical data structures, or LDSs, although there are other names used in different circumstances. This second copy of the logical data structure can be compared to the original copy to ensure that the two are in full agreement. The earlier techniques used to produce the logical data structure in the analysis phase, described in Chapter 5, are 'top-down' methods in which the analyst starts from a mental image of what is required, based on the fact-finding, and refines it by increasing the level of detail. The RDA method about to be described is much more rigorous and concentrates on the actual data items, and the two products may need to be resolved, giving a more complete picture that either method alone would produce.

The steps required to implement this method are described in the rest of this chapter which introduces the concepts, rules and terminology associated with relational data analysis, explaining normalisation up to third normal form. There are higher levels of normalisation but they are beyond the scope of an introductory text, and SSADM, and are only required for advanced database design. The normalisation process itself follows a set of fairly mechanical rules to process all the available data into a set of tables, also called relations, into 'third normal form' or 3NF. After completing the normalisation there is a set of related techniques to master before the tables can be turned into a useful LDS, and these will be covered in Chapter 10.

Relational data analysis tends to be one of the most difficult techniques for students to master, and whole books have been written about just this technique. Indeed you will find that, if you examine any of the current texts on proprietary database software, a large fraction of them will be devoted to explaining the methods described below. The good news for students is that, once they have mastered the concepts behind this topic, they should be able to use the latest database management tools with very little extra effort.

9.2   Basic terminology

Before considering the application of the process of normalisation, it is essential to first define the terminology and the context of what we are trying to achieve. RDA and normalisation share a common vocabulary which contains some terms not used elsewhere, so our first task is to become familiar with this.

9.2.1   Files, documents, relations and entities

A fundamental question is, 'what is it that we attempting to normalise?' The answer actually depends upon where we are in the life cycle. Generally we apply normalisation techniques to any examples of multiple data types that we have available to work on. These come mainly from two, mainly physical, sources.

The first source appears during the fact-finding phase when we normalise any existing input or output material that we discover. This material may be in the form of documents, files, records and screens as used on paper, magnetic media, visual display units, microfiche or any other form. What they should all have in common is that they contain items of data, often in a structure or layout. Note that, when modelling data we are as interested in the structure as we are in the data itself.

While RDA could have been used at the fact finding stage, it was not appropriate to introduce such an advanced technique at that point in an introductory text such as this, so a simpler method of producing the LDS was described. For details of this, see the sections on 'entity relationships' in Chapter 5. However, many of the structures and data items discovered during fact finding will have already been identified as entities in the system and will be of use during the later work on the required system.

The second source comes later in the life cycle, when we are getting close to the design stage. By then new or modified output screens, reports and file layouts will have been produced, each of which will also contain items of data in a defined structure. While these may be the result of processing normalised data from the fact finding during the progression through the analysis stages, this may not always be the case. Prototyping especially leads to the generation of input and output documents via discussions with the user which often by-pass the analysis process. In this case we have to 'discover' the source data from the result.

In both the above situations, the actual steps of normalisation are identical. In the first case, however, we are working 'forward' from physical files and documents to define an overall structure for the required application data, and in the second we are working back from design for such products, to impose an efficient structure on the result of the processing for the required system. The two results should be identical, but if they are not we have to decide on a consolidated data structure which we will actually implement.

In order to keep the discussions of the normalisation process logical, rather than physical, a whole new set of terminology was invented by Dr. Codd to apply to the items.

9.2.2   Records fields, tuples, attributes and keys

Anyone reading this book who is conversant with the standard terminology of computers will be familiar with the terms 'record' and 'field'. If you are not, the next few paragraphs is a brief synopsis for you.

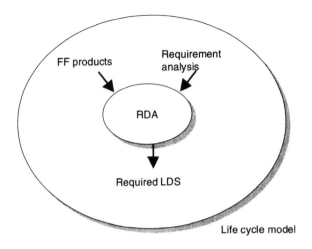

Figure 9.1 RDA in the Life-cycle model

Whenever we hold data it tends to be in groups of items. Let us say that we have a simple address book as in most personal organisers. These will typically provide a layout for each entry which consists of, say, name, address and telephone number. The computer term for each of these items is a 'field'. There are physical spaces on the page for the fields and each one holds a single item of data.

Field names   Data

Name	....
Address	....
	....
	....
Telephone	....

Figure 9.2 The physical data items and structure of an address book

We refer in computer terms to each full entry as a 'record', which is a set of the fields. Therefore the 'name' is one of the <u>fields</u> provided within each <u>record</u>. There may be literally dozens of ways of physically printing these items on paper, but when we wish to visualise them we typically draw out any groups of data which are held together as a list of rows and columns. Each of the rows represents one instance of a set of fields (i.e. a record) and each column shows the position of the corresponding field within it. The complete collection of records is called a 'file' and it is that which is named and accessed on all computer systems.

Name	Address	Telephone
Ahab, Captain	The Docks, Bristol	0231 321 7689
Hancock, Anthony A.	The Manor, 104 Railway Cuttings, East Cheam	0171 373 2121
Sykes, Bill	24, Abbey Croft Lane	
....	....	
....	....	
Zafarelli, Zaffaroni	Bella del Paise, Roma	0104 21 981 6781

Figure 9.3 A simple representation of the contents of an address book

Many practitioners refer to this representation as a 'flat file' layout. It is also called an un-normalised table, for reasons which will become clear later. There are many possible complexities in holding data in this way in practice, such as variable length fields and multiple occurrences of some groups, but for the moment let us ignore those and concentrate on our tidy simplification.

What we have done is to draw in Figure 9.3, a generic diagrammatic representation, in a simplified form, of the actual physical data items and structure as shown in Figure 9.2. This is the way we could imagine this simple data file if we were holding it in a computer instead of in a personal organiser. In fact the way the computer actually holds the data may look nothing like this, but it is the job of the systems software to present it to us in this way, so to imagine it like this is not a restriction.

However, we want to have an even more general view of the data than that, and in order that we do not constrain our thinking to that of computer files, we call the row and column entries not record and field, but tuple and attribute. Some people pronounce this as 'chew-pull' and others 'tup-ull'. My preference is the former, to rhyme with 'duple' and 'duplex'. The whole set of tuples, containing their attributes, is now called a table or relation, not a file.

File Notation	Field	A file or relation		Attribute	Relational Notation
Field Names (not part of the file)	Name	Address	Telephone		Attribute Names
A record >>	Ahab, Captain	The Docks, Bristol	0231 321 7689		<<< A Tuple
2nd record	Hancock, Anthony A.	The Manor, 104 Railway Cuttings, East Cheam	0171 373 2121		
	Sykes, Bill	24, Abbey Croft Lane			
	....	....			
	....	....			
Nth record	Zafarelli, Zaffaroni	Bella del Paise, Roma	0104 21 981 6781		

Figure 9.4 The notation for the contents of a table or relation

Note: Each of these relations may actually correspond to an entity, as in Chapter 5, in our logical data structure!

The reasons for these name changes may seem a little obscure, but they are required for the strict mathematical treatment which Codd wished to apply to the data. If it confuses you, just fix in your mind the terminology as shown in Figure 9.4, or if you are familiar with records and fields, the two translations of terminology between Figures 9.2 and 9.3. So long as you can remember those names and what they mean, you should be able to master the material in this unit.

The only thing we need to add now, before getting onto normalisation proper, is the concept of a key. It is used here to mean a pointer or clue, not something with which we open a door. In practice we use keys all the time in our brains. If someone says 'cat' we can easily picture what they are referring to, whereas a general description such as 'a small domestic quadruped' could mean a cat, dog, hamster and so on. Even more specifically 'your mother's cat, Moosey' would bring a specific animal into mind, if you knew it. In relations (cats we know) a key is something which when we insert its value (Moosey) into the correct attribute (cat's name) will only occur once. If that sounds over pedantic it is because it is really an easy concept which is quite hard to define precisely.

In our personal-organiser example, the key is implied to be the name of our acquaintance, and we have a problem on our hands unless each name occurs only once. If the address and telephone number is the same we are duplicating an entry and wasting space. On the other hand, if they are not we may remember for a while which is the correct one, but eventually we could get confused. (This is assuming, of course, that our friends do not really have multiple addresses.)

Let us say that we have accidentally put in an entry for the same person on two occasions and then we receive a change of address notification from them. We would probably just change the first entry found and hence would have another, incorrect entry to confuse us later. These may not be a problem in small examples where one has personal knowledge of the people involved, but imagine the chaos if there were millions of entries, as in the master copy of a telephone directory. It was computer problems just like these led to the invention of relational data analysis in the first place.

The other problem in choosing a key is in ensuring consistency. Names are what we use all the time to identify people, but they make poor computer keys because different people rarely write names the same way. Below is a small sample of the ways letters have been received, addressed to me over the last year.

Mr Martin John Hughes
M J Hughes
Martyn Hughes
M. J. Hughs
Dr. Martin John Hughes
Dr. Martyn J Hughes
Prof Martin J Hughes

Humans are very good at recognising these as variants of the same name, but to a computer they are completely different, unless you are using a special sound-related code. As we are trying to produce a simple example, however, let us assume that the form of the name in each address entry is consistent and unique. If so, we would have a 'candidate' key, meaning something that could be used as key.

There are a great many examples of how keys can be generated but typically we tend to use the shortest attribute and, if possible, one that is numeric. Numbers are simpler to encode, process and compress, and this is useful as keys often have to be held in several places or typed in many times.

If no suitable short, mainly numeric, key exists, then in most cases, even for manual and clerical applications, the user will create one. Once we have gone to the trouble of identifying someone and typing in their details, it is best if we can avoid having to do it all again! Examples of application-specific items created to be used as keys in real circumstances are national insurance numbers, student numbers, customer numbers, hospital numbers, bank account numbers and post-codes.

To use just one of these as an example, type in the post code and we will be defining a small section of a road or street which is uniquely defined in the post code list. Add the house number or name, and we uniquely identify the property. Now you know why most local authorities have a bye-law insisting that every property must have a number and it is used on the electoral register. They can cope with names but, even using a computer, they find it easier to type in numbers and prefer to enter: "1, The Mall" than "Buckingham Palace" quite apart from the possibility of mis-typing. Keys are so important that there are many versions and types, and these are summarised below.

9.2.3 Definition of key types

Having defined our key as a unique value which will identify the tuple in which it exists we can go on to look at the terminology to describe keys. In entity relationships we noted that important items tended to have more than one name, to describe various forms or states of the item. Some impression of the significance that keys have in computing can be gained from the following list of types of keys.

Key - an attribute or group of attributes which uniquely identify a tuple (or row) and has been chosen as the most suitable (see also candidate key). Also referred to as the primary key in some reference books.

- **Simple Key**. A key consisting of only one attribute.
- **Secondary Key**. An attribute or group of attributes which does not uniquely identify a tuple but can identify a cognate group of tuples.
- **Compound Key**. A key consisting of more than one attribute, each of which may be simple keys in other relations. Note that this latter statement may be enforced as a condition in some database applications.
- **Candidate Key**. An attribute or group of attributes which uniquely identify a tuple and which could be used as a key. This definition is only of use when there is more than one candidate key, otherwise the only candidate defaults to the (primary) key.
- **Alternate Key**. A candidate key which has **not** been chosen as the key.
- **Foreign Key**. An attribute or group of attributes which is used as the primary key in another relation or entity
- **Composite Key**. A compound key where one or more of the attributes are not simple keys in their own right.

- **Generated Keys**. A composite keys where one, usually the non-simple key, must be invented or generated to ensure uniqueness.
- **Primary Key**. The candidate key chosen as the key to be used to uniquely identify a tuple within a relation.

Whilst the above may seem very complicated, fortunately it is not as bad in practice as it may seem here. We only need the concept of a key for normalisation, and the most important of those listed above are the primary key and the foreign key. However, the other types may be important for later work, so it is as well to get used to them now and hopefully they will seem more familiar when they are found in case studies later. A simple example should help clarify any confusion. Let us extend our address book example to one used in most businesses, holding the personal details of our customers or clients.

9.3   Using a key to locate an individual, a hospital example

Because RDA is so important, it is worth introducing a few more examples to gain practice before we attempt the River flow Meter case study used so far. The extra example we will utilise here is the case of a hospital which holds medical records for their patients. This is a particularly interesting example as it is a case where the 'client' information must be identified no matter what length of time has elapsed since we last saw them. If we were selling say washing machines, we might keep our customer records for a few years or until the warranty expired. We do not expect to go back to a shop after ten years to have them produce every detail of our business with them. If there are unique circumstances, say having a large family which owns two washing machines at a time, the shop would happily keep the details twice, possibly with the full name on one record and just the name and initials on another. This may irritate the customer but it does no harm.

Hospitals are different. It is extremely important that they uniquely identify their patients whenever they turn up. If a person is registered under two slightly different names it is possibly for them to be treated by two physicians who have no knowledge of what medication the other is prescribing. This is the worst nightmare of most medical records officers and elaborate steps have to be taken to identify patients correctly. As no-one can be expected to remember the patient number they were allocated at, say, eighteen months old, the hospitals have to rely on the patients giving their personal details for identification. From that the hospital has to be able to locate their hospital number and hence their medical records.

Name, address and telephone number may be good enough for the local general practitioner who has fairly regular contact, but even they will want the name split up into first name, second name and last name, often called 'surname'. We have to be able to distinguish families, and even initials are not good enough. It is astonishing how many people in the same family share initials! There are cultural traps here as well and several systems have nearly foundered because the data entry clerks are not aware that some cultures put their title at the end, not the beginning. This is equivalent to putting 'Mr.' as the last name for the majority of males in this country. It wastes a field and complicates one possible key. But, as people care deeply about their titles it is essential to put that in as well.

So far we have identified essential attributes as:

- TITLE
- 1st-NAME
- 2nd-NAME
- SURNAME
- ADDRESS (which may have many logical lines)
- P-CODE
- TELEPHONE

Furthermore, the gender of the patient matters a great deal in this application. Wards, as well as clinic specialisms, can be gender specific so it is essential to make sure that there is a way of entering the sex. Specialisation raises another issue, age. There are specialisms for very young and very old patients, so the patient's age is needed. As people change age with time, the convention is that the date of birth is recorded, and the current age calculated from that. By the way, beware when implementing such a system: designers leaving only two characters on reports for age have caused people over one hundred years old to be allocated a place in a children's ward! (Note: This common error is often reported, incorrectly, as an instance of the 'millennium bug'!)

The figure below summarises the conversion of our personal address book to the information a hospital would need so far.

- TITLE
- 1st-NAME
- 2nd-NAME
- SURNAME
- ADDRESS
- P-CODE
- TELEPHONE
- DOB
- SEX

Figure 9.5 The minimum personal information that a hospital would need

The conversion is not complete for a real system, but let us summarise so far to see how this relates to our terminology for keys.

What values must we define to be sure that the person who fits them is unique? First name, second name and last, or surname, alone just will not do. There are thousands of Martins, even more Johns and heaven knows how many Hughes in any large geographical area such as that served by a hospital. It would be even worse if the surname was Smith or Jones. They are, however, secondary keys because they define a sub-group of all the possible nominees. The more items we add to the key, the smaller the group defined. Defining the surname to be 'Hughes' gives a large group, adding first name 'Martin' will give a small sub-group and a second name of 'John' an even smaller group. The first choice, last name, would be a simple key, but we know it will not be unique so we add first name and last name. Taken together, as a group of items, they make up a compound key. The distinction may have no meaning if there are no other data relations. The terminology used is slightly looser when we are discussing general principles, as we are here, than during formal relational analysis. So, if the combination is not guaranteed to be unique this is possibly a compound secondary key.

Summarising the position, and underlining the attributes chosen as keys which is the convention used to identify them, we have the following position.

- TITLE
- 1st-NAME
- 2nd-NAME
- <u>SURNAME</u>
- ADDRESS
- P-CODE
- TELEPHONE
- DOB
- SEX

This will give 1000's of people (a simple secondary key).

- TITLE
- <u>1st-NAME</u>
- 2nd-NAME
- <u>SURNAME</u>
- ADDRESS
- P-CODE
- TELEPHONE
- DOB
- SEX

This will give 100's of people, a compound or composite (we cannot tell which with the information available) secondary key.

- TITLE
- <u>1st-NAME</u>
- <u>2nd-NAME</u>
- <u>SURNAME</u>
- ADDRESS
- P-CODE
- TELEPHONE
- DOB
- SEX

This will give 10's of people (note that in some applications we could now treat the three components as one item as they are contiguous).

For a relatively small population that may be enough, but for large populations we may have to add another attribute. An obvious one is address, but that is not really so good because enough people give their children the same names as one of the parents to make this non-unique as they may all live at the same address for a long time. Date of birth would easily distinguish between individuals in these circumstances, the only exception being a parent who gave twins of the same sex identical names, a situation we can hopefully discount.

- TITLE
- 1st-NAME
- 2nd-NAME
- SURNAME
- DOB
- ADDRESS
- P-CODE
- TELEPHONE
- SEX

A unique compound primary key (we hope).

So, by adding date of birth to the items making up the key, we have produced from all the possible attributes a sub-set which we are reasonably confident will uniquely identify an individual: first name, second name, last name, and date of birth. This is a compound key made up of four attributes. There is no real significance in moving 'DOB' next to the other items, it just makes it easier to visualise them as one item, the key, although they retain their separate identities as attributes for all other purposes. We could add 'title' for completeness of the 'name' group, but this item does not normally give a more precise selection.

Following a similar rationale we may have chosen: first name, sex, date of birth, and address as providing a unique identification by reasoning that the chances of two people with the same first name, of the same sex, born on the same day and living at the same address is extremely small. If we had chosen that combination it also would be a compound key, and, as we have a choice of two keys, both would also be candidate keys. Once we have made a decision as to which one of the two candidate keys to choose as the primary key then the other would be relegated to the status of an alternate key. Where the candidate keys are unlikely combinations as in this second case, we rarely bother to identify them formally.

Even the example described is a simplification as we have not considered maiden names and so on, but we have now added enough detail to make the point about how difficult it can be to choose keys even in this simple example. All of the attributes are complex and messy, so most applications merely enter all the attribute details and then add one of their own which is unique to the system, in this example a patient number. As the Americans shorten 'number' to #, and a lot of the computer terminology is dominated by American practice, this is usually written as Patient#.

Now that we have a unique simple key available, Patient#, which can be used as a key most of the time, any other combination used, when the Patient# is not known, should be formally identified. This will probably be the name and date of birth combination discussed above which can now be relegated to the status of alternate key, but this is likely to be how it will be used in a hospital system.

To provide a practical application of normalisation, let us our imagine a local private hospital which has all the problems described above and which also has to bill the patients for any treatment they receive. This example has been chosen to be similar to the case study later in this book, but different enough to be make all the points we need to make to encompass all of the situations we are likely to meet in the case studies.

9.4   A first practical example of normalisation

In this part we will introduce the rules of normalisation and their practical application. The distinction is important. Firstly, although none of the actual steps are difficult in themselves, most students find normalisation the most difficult topic to grasp in systems analysis and design. There are two parts to ensuring a correct result. The first is to learn to follow the rules carefully and not worry about 'understanding' too much of what is going on. You will find that, if you trust the methods, the results produced will be correct. Secondly, the actual application of the rules relies in practice on a body of experience which you will need to acquire. In other words it is important to know that the items we are trying to normalise are in the correct state to have the rules applied to them.

This last statement may seem to contradict the first, but it is true of many subjects. In mathematics, for instance, we may know that we can calculate the area of a rectangle by multiplying the two sides together – that is a general rule. But we have also learnt to first put both measurements into the same units. Few people would expect a sensible result if they multiplied metric units by imperial. In fact many elementary mathematics problems are concerned with the practical application of basic arithmetic, and in the same way we have to learn general rules for analysis and design, and then the practical application of these rules.

In this text we will learn the basic procedures of normalisation up to third normal form. Then we can introduce some examples which will give experience of their practical application. Once we have seen one example of a certain type of problem, it is relatively easy to recognise it in other forms when we encounter them.

9.4.1   A private hospital as a simple normalisation example

The Private Community Hospital in East Morton provides a service to the local community. Below is an example of a typical invoice to a recent in-patient. Please note that this is only one instance of possibly thousands of similar documents. We work on this single layout but produce a model of the structure to apply to the multiplicity!

Do not be put off by the fact that some of the examples do not have all the items shown in the 'patient identification' example discussed above. It is quite common for forms or screens to contain only the information relevant to their particular use. The only items which must have everything are the complete data models, and the database which we finally implement.

```
┌─────────────────────────────────────────────────────────┐
│           Local Private Community Hospital                │
│            540 Monks Drive, East Morton                   │
│                  Patient Invoice                          │
│                                                           │
│  Statement for the account of:                           │
│                                                           │
│  PATIENT NAME :    Plod, Mike J.  PATIENT #:      3294    │
│  PATIENT ADDRESS:  24 Beech Lane, DATE ADMITTED:  23/02/93│
│                    Camtown       DATE DISCHARGED: 27/02/93│
│  POSTCODE :        CP8 9QT                                │
│                                                           │
│  PATIENT TEL NO.:  (01234) 76857                          │
│                                                           │
│  ITEM CODE   DESCRIPTION          CHARGE                  │
│  200         Room semi-pr         £150.00                 │
│  205         Television           £ 10.00                 │
│  307         X-ray                £ 25.00                 │
│  413         Lab test             £ 35.00                 │
│                                                           │
│              BALANCE DUE:         £220.00                 │
└─────────────────────────────────────────────────────────┘
```

Figure 9.6 A private hospital invoice as a normalisation example

9.4.2 The basic rules of normalisation

Now that we have introduced a suitable physical document we can proceed through the steps required to normalise it. These steps consist of removing repeating groups, removing partial key dependencies and removing non-key dependencies. If all that could have been written in Greek for all the understanding it gives you, do not worry as each step can be learnt separately. Not only that, but there is a simple form to depict precisely what we are doing.

We use the form for the first time by entering all of the data items into the first column. We ignore the values and just put the item names in. Some of the item names are a column header on the form, showing that there is more than one value. Where this occurs we put them together – this is how they usually occur – and put curly brackets to denote that there is repetition. The chosen key is underlined to identify it. The layout is precisely the same for a 'flat file' but with the items in a column rather than a row.

UN-NF	1NF	2NF	3NF	Relation
PATIENT #				
PATIENT NAME				
PATIENT ADDRESS				
POSTCODE				
PATIENT TEL NO				
DATE ADMITTED				
DATE DISCHARGED				
{ITEM CODE				
DESCRIPTION				
CHARGE}				
BALANCE DUE				

Figure 9.7 A Private Hospital invoice in un-normalised form

9.5   First normal form

The three items with the curly brackets around them, ITEM CODE, DESCRIPTION, and CHARGE are all there to represent a group of items which occur together more than once. Together they constitute what we call a 'repeating group', a group of items which are repeated, not alone but as a set. The first task is to remove repeating groups, if there are any. When we have done that our data will be in first normal form.

As always, it is not quite that simple. Whenever we go from one form of normalisation to a higher form, we must ensure that we able to re-construct the lower form for any possible sample. It is easy enough to just separate out these three items from the invoice and put them into another list, but how do we put them back together again to produce the original invoice?

This is in fact just one case of the general problem, called non-loss decomposition, which many beginners do not notice until they realise that they have not fully understood normalisation, so let us get it out of the way now.

When we put the data items in column one of the form in Figure 9.7 we were condensing down the information gained from the document in Figure 9.6. This is a conventional way of representing the data items as a simple structure but we must be aware that this is just one instance of many possible documents. As we discussed earlier the 'flat file' form consists of many attributes. (We do not call it a relation yet because it may not be one!) All we have done is to list in one column the items which head the columns in the 'flat file' representation.

PATIENT # I PATIENT NAME I PATIENT ADDRESS I POSTCODE I PATIENT TEL NO I DATE ADMITTED I DATE DISCHARGED { ITEM CODE I DESCRIPTION I CHARGE } BALANCE DUE

Figure 9.8 Simple normalisation example, a Private Hospital, normal 'flat file' representation

Even this is a simplification as the group {ITEM CODE, DESCRIPTION, CHARGE}, should really be repeated over and over, enough times to fill the maximum space on the form. Even when we do this some patients will have too many items and will require continuation forms. This class of problem is the bane of the report designer's life, but one other reason for normalisation is to predict these situations whilst allowing us to concentrate on the data structure.

The way that we remove the repeating group is to treat it like a completely different table in its own right. Of course we then have to go through the process of deciding what we should use as a key for this new group. By now it should be fairly obvious that we would choose the ITEM CODE, although DESCRIPTION is also a candidate key. We show this by underlining ITEM CODE in its new 'flat file'. Unfortunately this is not enough. If we were just to remove the repeating group and create a new relation (we can start to use this word now) then all of the repeated columns on all the invoices would be jumbled up together. We must be able to get back to the original form and for this we need to identify the source in the first relation of each tuple in the new relation. Fortunately we already have a defined way of uniquely identifying each tuple, the key. This is the PATIENT # and by adding it, as an attribute in the new relation we ensure that each and every tuple can be related back to its original position.

PATIENT # I PATIENT NAME I PATIENT ADDRESS I POSTCODE I PATIENT TEL NO I DATE ADMITTED I DATE DISCHARGED I BALANCE DUE

PATIENT # I ITEM CODE I DESCRIPTION I CHARGE

Figure 9.9 Normalisation example

The lists in the last two figures are merely over-explanations to relate the work to the earlier table form of the process in case some extra explanation is required. Once we are used to the process of duplicating the key of the original relation in order to be able to undo the split, we can normally go straight to splitting the attributes and in putting them in the correct column on the form.

UN-NF	1NF	2NF	3NF	Relation
PATIENT #	PATIENT #			
PATIENT NAME	PATIENT NAME			
PATIENT ADDRESS	PATIENT ADDRESS			
POSTCODE	POSTCODE			
PATIENT TEL NO	PATIENT TEL NO			
DATE ADMITTED	DATE ADMITTED			
DATE DISCHARGED	DATE DISCHARGED			
{ITEM CODE	BALANCE DUE			
DESCRIPTION				
CHARGE}	PATIENT #			
BALANCE DUE	ITEM CODE			
	DESCRIPTION			
	CHARGE			

Figure 9.10 A Private Hospital invoice, 1NF

9.6   Second normal form

Fortunately once we have introduced the first step in normalisation the rest follows relatively easily. That is because we have had to introduce several basic concepts while discussing going from an un-normalised form to first normal form. The rest of the process is just a repeat of those procedures, but each time looking for slightly different configurations in the data. When we find them we deal with them in the same way, by splitting the group into two sub-groups, both with unique keys.

In second normal form we are looking for 'partial key dependencies'. In other words we want to see if any of the non-key items are only dependent on part of the key. Say, a group has six data items, A, B, C, D, E, and F. The key is A and B, that is why they are underlined. The non-key items are C, D, E, and F, and they can be dependant on either A, B, or A and B together. The concept of dependency is similar to the discussion earlier on identifying keys. There we were interested in finding a combination of attributes which would give us a unique value to identify the whole group of attributes. Here we are only interested in inter-attribute relationships. If C and D are only dependant on A, while E and F are only dependant on B then we have two groups of attributes ([C, D] and [E, F]) which are dependant on part of the key. We can hence split them into two new groups of three items each ([A,C, D] and [B,E, F]) with A as the key for the first and B as the key for the second. Watch out though, as we still need to keep the A and B together so that we can re-assemble the original structure as we must need it for the application.

Some papers and texts treat the topic of dependency very formally, which can be useful if you do start to get confused. If we say that C and D are dependant on A what we really mean is that if we know the value of A, then we know the corresponding values of B and C, but not necessarily vice versa. There are several standard texts on RDA which cover this topic in considerable detail under the headings of 'functional dependancy' or 'determinancy'. For the moment we have sufficient knowledge to solve most of the problems in simple systems.

UN-NF	1NF	2NF	3NF	Relation
PATIENT #	PATIENT #	)		
PATIENT NAME	PATIENT NAME	)		
PATIENT ADDRESS	PATIENT ADDRESS	) ⟶		
POSTCODE	POSTCODE	)		
PATIENT TEL NO	PATIENT TEL NO	)		
DATE ADMITTED	DATE ADMITTED	)		
DATE DISCHARGED	DATE DISCHARGED	)		
{ITEM CODE	BALANCE DUE	)		
DESCRIPTION				
CHARGE}	PATIENT #	PATIENT #		
BALANCE DUE	ITEM CODE	ITEM CODE		
	DESCRIPTION			
	CHARGE	ITEM CODE		
		DESCRIPTION		
		CHARGE		

Figure 9.11 A Private Hospital invoice, 2NF

We have applied this process above by splitting off item code, description and charge into a separate relation as description and charge are dependant on item code only, which becomes the key of the new relation. Patient no. and item code have been retained as a key-only relation so that we can always go back to 1NF if we wanted to do so. Note also that we just draw an arrow through this column to show that the top relation is already in 2NF. It must be because it only has one key!

9.7 Third normal form

In order to convert the second normal form relations to third normal form we go though a similar procedure to previously but aim to remove any 'non-key dependencies'. This is very comparable to the procedure outlined above, but so far we have always looked for relationships between the keys and the non-keys.

Now we are looking, firstly, to see if any of the non-key items can be associated with other non-key items. If we find such instances we remove the dependant item from the original relation and also make the pair of items to another relation, with the first item as the key.

Secondly, we look for any attributes which do not depend upon non-key items but are still not dependant on the key. In a way it is the second case which is the most troublesome, because they seem to depend upon circumstances rather than data. If that is the case then we can simply remove these 'transitory' items from the relation. We must note in the data structure from which they came how they are to be re-created. Often they are calculated from the other attributes or depend upon the time or date of reporting.

Also in the example, the attribute BALANCE DUE can be removed as, in this instance, it is calculated at the time of printing the invoice by summing all of the charges due to that patient by going round the set of ITEMS linked to that patient and accumulating the CHARGE values. This is not to say that there may not be another structure in the system which holds the BALANCE DUE in some other way, say, outstanding invoices. To deal with that situation we have to normalise all of the inputs and outputs and then consolidate them. This complication is covered in detail in the next chapter.

Once we have checked for these circumstances, we can copy forward the modified relations to the 3NF column, or simply draw arrows for those relations which are already in third normal form. There is then only one simple task left to do before we have finished the process of normalising this particular structure, and that is to give the third normal form groups relation or 'table' names. In the example below we end up with four relations or tables: PATIENT, SESSION, TREATMENT, and ITEM.

In the SESSION relation, one of the dates must be added to the key to conform to the rule that no two relations may have identical keys, and PATIENT# is already used alone as the primary key of the relation PATIENT.

UN-NF	1NF	2NF	3NF	Relation
PATIENT #	PATIENT #		PATIENT #	PATIENT
PATIENT NAME	PATIENT NAME		PATIENT NAME	
PATIENT ADDRESS	PATIENT ADDRESS		PATIENT ADDRESS	
POSTCODE	POSTCODE		POSTCODE	
PATIENT TEL NO	PATIENT TEL NO		PATIENT TEL NO	
DATE ADMITTED	DATE ADMITTED			
DATE DISCHARGED	DATE DISCHARGED		PATIENT #	SESSION
{ITEM CODE	BALANCE DUE		DATE ADMITTED	
DESCRIPTION			DATE DISCHARGED	
CHARGE}	PATIENT #	PATIENT #		
BALANCE DUE	ITEM CODE	ITEM CODE	PATIENT #	TREATMENT
	DESCRIPTION	DESCRIPTION	ITEM CODE	
	CHARGE	ITEM CODE		
		DESCRIPTION	ITEM CODE	ITEM
		CHARGE	DESCRIPTION	
			CHARGE	

Figure 9.12 A Private Hospital invoice, 3NF

9.8 Getting more RDA practice using the River flow meter system

We can now use the documents we discovered during the fact finding and soft system work in earnest. These are shown in Figures 3.8, 2.9 and later in Figure 6.4

What we have to do is to normalise each of these documents in turn up to third normal form (3NF) as described in the previous paragraphs. It is well worth going over these river flow meter reports in detail as the practical application of normalisation has several common pitfalls which are rarely seen in simple exercises such as the ones used up to this point in order to introduce the topic.

9.8.1 Normalising the raw river flow meter data

We may as well start with the data as it enters the system, the raw river flow meter data. Figure 3.8 showed the raw river flow meter data used to record the river flow data every 15 minutes at the point of collection as it appears when listed from the disk. This figure is reproduced below to save referring back.

12.67	12.84	13.23	12.95	13.14	13.70	13.50	13.19	13.27	13.44	13.20	13.53
13.77	14.07	13.43	13.27	13.46	13.20	13.61	14.24	13.83	13.32	13.97	14.26
14.35	14.57	14.77	15.43	15.17	15.76	15.91	16.27	15.70	15.75	15.57	15.39
15.35	15.77	15.71	15.34	14.74	14.79	14.76	14.69	14.02	14.16	14.69	14.22
13.74	13.74	14.40	13.72	14.21	14.73	14.75	14.58	15.18	15.51	14.87	14.89
14.75	15.44	16.08	16.28	15.89	16.67	16.82	17.09	16.82	17.36	17.77	17.36
17.31	16.60	17.23	17.24	17.44	17.61	17.25	17.77	18.34	19.12	19.04	19.77

Figure 9.13 Raw river flow meter 15-minute data (repeated)

As stated previously, it can be difficult to get users to incorporate the things that they know into the documents and reports. However, the DFO knows that each table also has associated with it the meter identity and the start date because he writes them onto the disk when he collects them so he can identify each one correctly later. As well as this he knows that each reading represents a quarter of an hourly recorded river flow, and that the system holds these values in memory and writes them to disk at midnight every night. This information needs be added to the physical data structure, as shown in the figure below. This means that the parts in italics have been added to show the structure. These items are not really on the disk, but as it is impossible to normalise the data as it physically appears, it is essential that the whole structure is available. This is one instance of a case which is quite common, where the physical data appears on one media and is inserted into a context which gives the complete picture. In this case the data on the disk, which is really the raw data, is logically inserted into a system to allow the DFO to calculate the daily average river flow for each meter for each day (Figure 9.14).

We can now start normalising this data by putting the data items into the first column of the normalisation form, and applying the rules as defined previously. Meter and date are both keys, as we need them to distinguish this set of data from all the others on different disks. The rest of the data consists of a set of times and readings, in other words a repeating group. Do not be confused by the table layout of the times which allows the re-use of information: this is just a shorthand way of showing the time of each reading. Therefore, within the repeating group is a set of times and readings. as shown in the table in Figure 9.15.

Meter: x   Start date 13/2/95

Time	*+15*	*+30*	*+45*	*+1hr*				*+2hr*				
00:00	12.67	12.84	13.23	12.95	13.14	13.70	13.50	13.19	13.27	13.44	13.20	13.53
03:00	13.77	14.07	13.43	13.27	13.46	13.20	13.61	14.24	13.83	13.32	13.97	14.26
06:00	14.35	14.57	14.77	15.43	15.17	15.76	15.91	16.27	15.70	15.75	15.57	15.39
09:00	15.35	15.77	15.71	15.34	14.74	14.79	14.76	14.69	14.02	14.16	14.69	14.22
12:00	13.74	13.74	14.40	13.72	14.21	14.73	14.75	14.58	15.18	15.51	14.87	14.89
15:00	14.75	15.44	16.08	16.28	15.89	16.67	16.82	17.09	16.82	17.36	17.77	17.36
18:00	17.31	16.60	17.23	17.24	17.44	17.61	17.25	17.77	18.34	19.12	19.04	19.77
21:00	18.99	19.05	19.78	20.32	21.28	22.22	23.18	22.90	22.56	22.41	21.98	22.30
+1day	21.47	22.13	22.09	22.18	21.46	20.75	20.48	20.45	20.70	21.37	21.74	20.85
Etc.	21.24	20.34	20.98	21.92	21.62	20.88	20.79	19.79	19.13	19.55	20.02	20.38
	20.87	21.79	22.85	22.59	23.08	22.13	21.22	21.42	22.32	23.38	24.31	23.77
	....	....	....	....	....	....	....	....	....	....	....	....

Figure 9.14 Raw river flow meter data with the known structure added

Figure 9.15 The normalised raw river flow meter data

The repeating group is turned into first normal form by copying forward the key of the owning group, meter and date, and making one of the items a key, in this case the time, as it is this which identifies the reading, rather vice versa. As there are no other data items outside the repeating group, the first normal form looks almost identical to the un-normalised form. However, the removal of the repeating group brackets and the insertion of the extra key makes it a genuine normalised table, or relation, which could legitimately be included in a relational database. The rest of the work in this case is trivial: there is only one data item outside of the key. That means that, unless there is some redundancy in the key items so that they depend upon one another, the table is already in second and third normal form. All that remains is to give a name to the table, such as '15MIN-READING'.

9.8.2 Normalising the District River flow Authorisation Report

The next report is the District River flow Authorisation Report as shown in Figure 2.9. Again this is reproduced below to avoid having to refer back.

```
Flow Meter report for
District                    Bourn Brook
Week Beginning              22/06/98
Daily Aves
Meter      1      2      3      4       5      Temp C   Rainfall
Mon      12.67   13.01  14.20  15.06   15.55  26.00    0.57
Tue      12.48   13.25  13.36  14.01   14.87  26.80    0.55
Weds     12.41   12.52  13.64  14.26   15.52  27.63    0.55
Thu      11.68   12.69  13.66  14.31   15.41  28.03    0.54
Fri      11.33   11.80  12.07  12.23   12.61  26.98    0.51
Sat      11.28   11.70  12.38  13.20   13.63  25.12    0.12
Sun      10.70   11.47  11.79  12.49   12.86  25.90    0.35


Weekly
AveFlow 11.79   12.35  13.02  13.65   14.35

Prepared by: Jim Ladd
Authorised By: Alan Cambridge
On Date: 1/7/98
```

Figure 9.16 A sample District River flow Authorisation Report (repeated)

This may seem very similar to the previous example and it appears obvious that there is a repeating group in the form of a table in the centre of the form. There is a trap for the unwary here which requires a little more thought before we proceed. It may appear that the un-normalised row on the RDA form should be entered by copying from the form, as in the list of attributes given next:

District, Week-begin, {Meter, Mon, Tue, Weds, Thu, Fri, Sat, Sun, WeeklyAveFlow, Flow, Temp, Rainfall}, Prepared By, Authorised By, Authorised On

This is not correct. Firstly, the set of days Mon, Tue etc. is actually a repeating group of days, secondly, this implies there is an average daily river flow reading just for one meter, and thirdly there is no real justification for writing the attributes down in the order shown, as there are several ways the headings could be read. We can put another set of repeating group brackets in to try to show that there are more river flow readings by writing it as shown next:

District, Week-begin, {Meter, {Day, Flow, Temp, Rainfall}, WeeklyAveFlow} Prepared By, Authorised By, Authorised On

This is a lot better because it gives the set of meters, each with a set of days, each day having a flow, temperature and rainfall. The problem with this layout is that it implies that there is temperature and rainfall reading for each day **and** meter, just like the river flow reading. If we try to turn it around and have a set of days with a set of meters, then it looks like the notation given next:

District , Week-begin, {Day, {Meter, Flow, Temp, Rainfall}, WeeklyAveFlow} Prepared By, Authorised By, Authorised On

This is wrong too, as it implies that there is a weekly average for every day rather than every meter. In fact none of the ways of using nested brackets works properly. The difficulty we are having in trying to use nested repeating group brackets to denote two sets is that no two of these sets are distinct, but overlap.

This happens quite often with layouts of this kind and results from the fact that we really have more tables in the central part of this report than appears at first glance. There is a table of daily average flows for a week with a flow for each day and each meter, a table of days with temperature and rainfall for each day, and a table of weekly average flows with a flow for each meter. These three separate tables are as shown below.

Meter	1	2	3	4	5
Mon	12.67	13.01	14.20	15.06	15.55
Tue	12.48	13.25	13.36	14.01	14.87
Weds	12.41	12.52	13.64	14.26	15.52
Thu	11.68	12.69	13.66	14.31	15.41
Fri	11.33	11.80	12.07	12.23	12.61
Sat	11.28	11.70	12.38	13.20	13.63
Sun	10.70	11.47	11.79	12.49	12.86

	Temp C	Rainfall
Mon	26.00	0.57
Tue	26.80	0.55
Weds	27.63	0.55
Thu	28.03	0.54
Fri	26.98	0.51
Sat	25.12	0.12
Sun	25.90	0.35

Meter	1	2	3	4	5
WeeklyAveFlow	11.79	12.35	13.02	13.65	14.35

Figure 9.17 The centre of the authorisation report expanded

What the user has done in the original report, quite reasonably, is to re-use the row and column heading to condense the report down to a manageable size. Human beings are quite good at reading such layouts, and will usually read out the correct values once they have been shown what they mean. What creates the difficulty, when trying to represent these repeating groups in order to normalise them, is that some of the items are missing.

Notice that in the three expanded tables the first row and column are not values at all but headers. Note also that in the remaining entries there is a value for each of these headings. The first box (row one, column one) can be left blank or used to label either the heading row or column, but other than that a simple table would have no gaps at all. It is the gaps in the original body of the report that should alert us to this problem.

Using this information, we can suggest a layout for the un-normalised form as follows:

District, Week-begin, {Meter, {Day, Flow}},{Day, Temp, Rainfall}, {Meter, Week-lyAveFlow}, Prepared By, Authorised By, Authorised On

In fact we could get away with combining any two of the above groups, and keeping one separate, but having gone to the trouble of separating the three sets it makes sense to keep them that way.

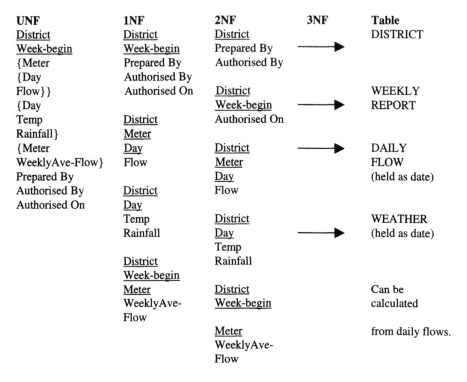

UNF	1NF	2NF	3NF	Table
District	District	District	→	DISTRICT
Week-begin	Week-begin	Prepared By		
{Meter	Prepared By	Authorised By		
{Day	Authorised By			
Flow}}	Authorised On	District	→	WEEKLY
{Day		Week-begin		REPORT
Temp	District	Authorised On		
Rainfall}	Meter			
{Meter	Day	District	→	DAILY
WeeklyAve-Flow}	Flow	Meter		FLOW
Prepared By		Day		(held as date)
Authorised By	District	Flow		
Authorised On	Day			
	Temp	District	→	WEATHER
	Rainfall	Day		(held as date)
		Temp		
	District	Rainfall		
	Week-begin			
	Meter	District		Can be
	WeeklyAve-Flow	Week-begin		calculated
		Meter		from daily flows.
		WeeklyAve-Flow		

Figure 9.18 The normalised authorisation report

The weekly river flow data disappears between second and third normal form as the only data item can easily be calculated from the average of the corresponding seven daily averages. The only other parts of the above which may need explanation is the choice of keys.

In the first instance it would seem that either 'District', or the date 'week be-gin(ning)' are candidate keys. However, it is the date of the week which uniquely iden-tifies each table from all of the other identical reports produced within that District. Looking ahead to the required system, when all of the data is held at the Regional Headquarters as well as at the District, it should be clear that including the District as well will enable the consolidated records to be identified. If the data was only going to be held at the District then this would not be required. The choice of 'day' as a key item within the removed repeating groups may seem odd as it raises the question as to how all of the 'Mon' etc. entries can be linked back to their original weeks. However, if we decide at this point that 'day' can be held as a date, then this problem disappears. It is one of the advantages of using computers that a date can be displayed as the day of the week, but the real data that is being held is a code for that unique day, i.e. a sequential date field, which is much more useful.

9.8.3 Normalising the PIWF report

Performing the normalisation on the final report is quite simple after all the previous hard work. The layout is repeated from Figure 6.4 to save you looking back.

DRAFT PIWF
ROOM 460 'J BLOCK', REGIONAL HQ, WASH ROAD,
WATERBOROUGH

Average flow readings for all meters in Bourn Brook District (in litres per second). 1998

WK	Week-begin	Meter 1	Meter 2	Meter 3	Meter 4	Meter 5
1	05/01/98	12.67	14.63	20.11	25.08	28.98
2	12/01/98	12.94	14.12	20.36	25.91	28.51
3	19/01/98	12.99	13.92	20.37	26.47	27.09
4	26/01/98	13.33	14.54	21.20	27.52	28.25
5	02/02/98	13.32	14.21	20.24	26.97	28.22
6	09/02/98	10.42	12.49	16.26	29.33	32.50
7	16/02/98	9.96	12.40	16.98	28.72	31.93
8	23/02/98	9.81	12.61	16.15	28.03	31.62
	etc.	10.26	12.98	15.60	28.62	30.54
	up to date	...	....	....	.....	....

Figure 9.19 Draft layout for the PIWF report (repeated)

There are none of the missing items which made the authorisation report so problematical here. This seems to be a simple table of dates and values. Each date is given as a 'week beginning' and as a week within the year, as the latter occurs many times over time, there is a week 1 every year, the actual date is the only unique value and hence becomes the key. The repeating group of meters and flows can be resolved, as described previously, by making the meter a key item. To put the table in 3NF, it can be noted that 'WK' can be calculated and hence can be removed.

UNF	1NF	2NF	3NF	Table
WK	WK		Week-begin	PIWF ENTRY
Week-begin	Week-begin		Meter	
{Meter	Meter	⟶	WeeklyAve-Flow	
WeeklyAve-Flow}	WeeklyAve-Flow			

Figure 9.20 The normalised PIWF report, version 1

In fact there is a serious error in this which is easily overlooked. As previously noted, when all of the data is held at the Regional Headquarters as well as at the District, the District will be required to uniquely identify the source of the data. If the data was only going to be held at the District then this would not be required.

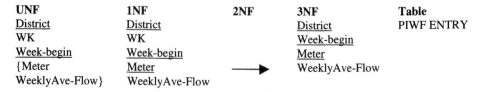

UNF	1NF	2NF	3NF	Table
District	District		District	PIWF ENTRY
WK	WK		Week-begin	
Week-begin	Week-begin		Meter	
{Meter	Meter	⟶	WeeklyAve-Flow	
WeeklyAve-Flow}	WeeklyAve-Flow			

Figure 9.21 The normalised PIWF report, version 2

The interesting thing about this is that it is identical to the result of the weekly report table that was removed in the last stage of normalisation in Figure 9.18, a piece of information that will be useful later.

9.8.4 Normalising the meter record card

There is one other item left to deal with, and this is even more simple than the previous report. The layout is repeated from Figure 3.7 to save you looking back.

Meter:	x
Location:	Bourn brook, upstream of Biba Gaga
Grid Ref:	TN1234
Type:	W-clump weir
Last serviced:	1/3/94

Figure 9.22 A sample meter record card

This data is obviously already in second normal form as there are no repeating groups, and a single key of 'meter'. None of the items are dependant upon, or can be calculated from, the other data items, so the table is also in third normal form. There is just one thing wrong with the result. The meter actually resides within a District and we take that for granted at the moment, but when all of the Districts are put together into a Regional system then the District will need to be added, and will become part of the key.

District view	Regional view
Meter	Meter
Location	District
Grid Ref	Location
Type	Grid Ref
Last serviced	Type
	Last serviced

Figure 9.23 The meter record card normalised

This table can be named METER, for example and with it the task of normalising the river flow meter data has been completed. These tables can now be used as input to the next design task. This concludes the normalisation part of the relational data analysis for the required River flow meter system, but there is more work to be done before we have a complete data model. The additional steps are covered in the next chapter.

9.9 Exercises

In order to gain more practice at **Modelling the required system relations** you may now attempt the tutorial questions given below. Once you are confident of your skills in this topic you are in a position to complete the tasks within section 13.9 if you wish to do so, before proceeding to the next chapter.

These tasks specifically cover:

13.9.1 Normalising the Data into Tables

9.9.1   The form in Figure 9.24 is used as customer bills by a local dairy for its roundsmen to issue to customers. Turn this into a 'flat file' format suitable for normalisation.

9.9.2   Turn the result of Exercise 9.9.1 into first normal form.

9.9.3   Turn the result of Exercise 9.9.2 into second normal form.

9.9.4   Turn the result of Exercise 9.9.3 into third normal form.

HAPPY COW DIARIES
Vat No. H7 710 3874 41

Customer No. CH1234
Name   Mrs A. Christie...............   Week Ending 2 July 1999.
Address The Spinney.............   Round No.   CH1..........
          1144 Old Kent Road.....
          London SW14..........
Item   S   M   T   W   T   F   S   £-P
G7 Milk.   ..   .4 ..   .4 ..   .3 .. .2-20
White bread .1 ..   ..   ..   .1 .. .1-20
....-..
....-..
....-..
                   Total for week   .3-40
                   Balance B/fwd   .9-90
                   Total   13-30
                   Cash Rec'd   10-00
                   Balance Due   .3-30

Figure 9.24

Relational data analysis   131

10 Producing the Required LDS from Normalised Tables

10.1 Introduction

This chapter explains how to consolidate the tables produced from the normalisation process into a 'realistic' set, so called because we rarely encounter the circumstance when learning normalisation on single worked examples. It then goes on to deal with the production of a logical data structure from the normalised relations produced from consolidated tables. If the data items used in the normalisation process come from products designed for the required system, as in Chapter 9, then the LDS produced is the required logical data structure, and the tables used to produce it provide a good starting point for the design of the physical database schema.

Whilst this technique is quite distinct from the normalisation process described in the previous chapter, understanding the process depends upon a good knowledge of the terminology used in both normalisation and in producing a logical data structure described in Chapter 5. The advantage of having this separate approach is that it provides an independent check on the correctness of this crucial product, the LDS. Because of the rigorous principles built into RDA, all of the available data are guaranteed to be incorporated into the final model, making this process an ideal complement to the more conceptual method described in the previous chapters. To remain consistent with the increasingly practical nature of the subject by this stage, the method followed below will be to describe in detail what you actually have to do to the products available so far to produce the required result.

10.2 Organising the normalised tables into a consolidated set

To get started we should gather together the results from the previous chapter and lay out the RDA forms so that the tables can all be seen at once if possible. Take the form with the largest number of tables and copy the 'Table Name' from the biggest table, and all of the data items that go with it, onto a large sheet of paper. Start in the top left hand corner and make sure that you copy the items accurately. The table name should be in block capitals and the key items should be underlined. Draw a light pencil line through the table and items which you have copied on the original form.

Next go through all of the other forms looking for tables which have an identical key to the one you have copied onto the new sheet. Ignore the number or size of the data items other than those in the key. Whenever you find such a table, whether it has the same name or not, carefully merge the data items together into the table you copied over in the previous task. Typically, most of the items will be identical. What you are looking for are items in the table you have just identified, with the same keys, but which are not in the first table. If you find any items you should add them to the list of data items on the new sheet of paper. They will, of course, be non-key items because you would not be performing the process if the keys were not identical.

Draw a line through the second table you found and note the table name if it is different from the first table. Continue this process with every one of the RDA forms, looking for any other tables with exactly the same key as the first table you copied. If, whilst doing this, you find two tables with identical keys on the same RDA form, then you are in trouble because that means you did not do your normalisation correctly.

When you have looked at every table, and merged any relevant ones with the first table, consider any multiple table names you have noted. Now is your opportunity to give the consolidated table the most appropriate name from those available to you. If you did a good job originally just stick with that name.

10.2.1 Normalising the different results

Now for the bad news! It is just possible that you broke some of the rules of normalisation in consolidating your table. Quickly check over the new consolidated table. If it is still in third normal form everything is fine. Otherwise you must find out why it is not, normalise the new table and break it into two or more tables which are in third normal form. Strictly speaking this should never happen, but if you made any errors previously this is when they will show up and you must correct them now.

As a final check, make sure that all of the names and key items on the tables are different. Watch out particularly for very similar table and data item names: they will cause confusion all the way through implementation so correct them now, if necessary, by giving them obviously different names.

10.2.2 Transitory relationships

When you have formed your consolidated set of tables there are still some attributes (or data items) which may be lurking within them which do not need to be held explicitly. These are the items which depend upon the attribute values, or time, when the structure which was originally normalised was produced. Typical of these items are totals, aggregates, and statistical indicators such as count and mean. These can be removed so long as they remain as a requirement elsewhere in the system documentation. Date and time can be particularly troublesome and the trick here is to remove any of these items which only refer to, for example, the date of producing a report, as soon as possible. This always assumes that the above condition holds, and that the requirement has been documented elsewhere. Always check this condition is true before removing transitory attributes or relations.

10.3 Turning the normalised tables into entities

The rationalisation of the normalised data, like the process of normalisation itself, can be broken into a series of clear procedures or rules. These are summarised below using single character data items to illustrate the principles involved. These can then be worked through using the examples of normalised data available to us from the previous section.

10.3.1 Converting tables to working entities

The result of the normalisation process is a set of relations, also known as tables, each of which lists the attributes or data items belonging to it. The convention is that the key of each relation is listed at the beginning of the list of data items in a group, and are underlined to make them easily identifiable. The first step in the rationalisation process is to convert the relations into entities, i.e. boxes with names, so that they appear as they would in a Logical Data Structure diagram. All of the attributes are not required, so we remove those not needed for the remainder of the process.

10.3.2 Removing common data errors in normalised tables

There are two types of elementary error which can stop the rationalisation process in its tracks. The accuracy of the process is only affected if these errors occur in a key item, but it is good practice, and possibly your last chance, to correct this type of error before it is passed forward into the design phase. The first error is having the same data item, or attribute, with two names, and the second is having the same name for two different data items.

The problem of different names is quite tricky. Firstly we may not have noticed that we are calling essentially the same item by two different names. That is a fault in analysis technique, and your job is to spot these duplications and resolve them. The second difficulty is that these situations are often user generated. It frequently occurs that there are two 'popular' names for an item used in two different parts of an organisation. Even worse it may be a fundamental item and the variations in naming have evolved because it is used, or misused, so often. In the Hospital Out-patient system, the item which came to be accepted as PATIENT-NUMBER was known in various Hospital Departments as PATIENT-ID, PAT-ID, PATIENT-NO, PATIENT-CODE as well as simply NUMBER, ID and CODE! Users can be as attached to their group's usage of names as they are to their own. One individual, in another project, insisted on referring to a process which everyone else called 'transmitting' as 'dumping' for several years, despite the fact that he had to explain what he meant every time he said it.

The second mistake is unusual and should be easy to rectify. It often arises from simple carelessness on the part of the analyst, or two analysts using the same name, say DATE without consultation or qualification. Adding additional information, 'ORDER-DATE', 'DELETION-DATE' is often enough to correct the problem. Always try to avoid 'meaningless' qualifications – for example 'DATE-1' – you will regret it later when you and the implementation team have to keep looking up what it actually means in the Data Dictionary.

The solution is to come to some consensus regarding naming wherever possible. Failing that, adopt the most popular form as the main name and use the other forms as an ALIAS of the standard name. Many Data Dictionary standards, CASE tools and Computer Languages allow an aliasing feature because this situation is so prevalent. It may not remove the problem entirely but at least the design and implementation can proceed smoothly.

TWO RELATIONS	PATIENT		APPT	
And their attributes	Patient-id	<<--?-->>	Patient-no	*<< Should be Patient-id??*
	Name		Clinic	
	Addr		Time	
	Tel		Date	*<< Duplicate Name*
Date-of-birth?	Date	*<<Duplicate Name*		

Figure 10.1 Two common naming errors

10.3.3 Identifying foreign keys

Having resolved, or at least identified any naming problems, the next step is to identify any foreign keys among the attributes in your entities. Foreign keys are attributes of one entity which are used as the key in another entity. We need to keep the actual keys of the entity plus any foreign keys. The other attributes can be removed from the copy of the entities and attributes which we are working on at this point to allow us to concentrate on the next process. Remember that some of the attributes which are foreign keys may be part of the key of the table we are working on.

TWO RELATIONS		PATIENT		APPT	
And their attributes	*Key >>*	Patient-id	*Gives a 1:N Relationship*	Patient-id*	*Foreign key*
		Name		Clinic	}
		Addr		Time	}*Composite Key*
		Tel		Date	}
		Date-of-birth?			

Figure 10.2 Showing that any patient may have many appointments, for example

10.3.4 Creating working entities

At this point it is worth actually creating a working sketch or diagram with an entity box for each relation, clearly named, and with the entity key plus any foreign keys written within each entity. Leave yourself as much room as possible to add the relationship lines between the entities. It may seem like 'cheating' a little, but a quick glance at your Logical data structure at this point to place your working entity boxes in roughly the same position relative to each other will make cross-checking the two diagrams much easier at the final stage. It is also useful to make sure that the relations, or tables, have ended up being called the same as the corresponding entities on this new diagram.

As always do not spend too much time on the artwork! A rough sketch is good enough for your purposes and the hour or so you might spend drawing a marvellously neat laser-printed diagram will not add anything to the correctness of the result. It may even be counter-productive if you use up your available time and enthusiasm on the diagram rather than the thinking.

10.4 Turning the keys into relationships

We have now reached the stage where we can start adding the relationships to the working entities we just created. This is an iterative process in which we identify different types of relationships, depending upon the location of the foreign keys. Basically, if an entity has a data item, or several data items, within it which is a foreign key to another entity then there is a one-to-many relationship between the two entities, with the entity holding the foreign key at the 'many' end. The rest of the paragraphs of this section are concerned with identifying instances of foreign keys, the existence of some of which can only be deduced, and then drawing in the required relationships.

This means that we must examine the items within the entity boxes and prepare them, if necessary, for use in identifying the order of relationship required between the entities. We can draw in the obvious relationships first from the existence of the foreign keys in non-key items. As we have already done the bulk of the work for this it should be straightforward. The next section depends upon familiarity with the types of keys. These were introduced and discussed under 'Normalisation' but it is essential that you understand clearly what is meant, so a brief revision might be in order before we proceed.

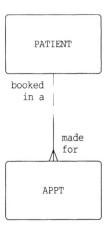

Figure 10.3 The foreign key information from 10.2 shown as an LDS fragment

About now is the point where anyone who is confused about the terminology starts to get really lost, so it is worthwhile having a brief re-cap. The main point of misunderstanding is often the terminology involving the term 'relation'. The solution to understanding this topic is to keep very clear in your mind the distinction between the TABLES which are the result of the third normal form process which Dr. Codd called, for very good reasons at the time, RELATIONS, and the lines between the ENTITIES which give the order and type of the RELATIONSHIP. The problem is that the latter are often referred to as a RELATION as well, so that we can easily muddle up what we mean. This is a classic example of the problems which arise from unclear naming customs as we discussed earlier in this section.

If the entity with a compound key has a three, or more, element key, then try to identify an entity which has all the elements but one as its primary key and join them by a one-to-many relationship. Find an entity with the remaining element as its simple primary and join them by a one-to-many relationship. Otherwise you will have to join it to all of the relations with the relevant simple primary keys.

10.4.1 Tidying up the new LDS

You probably have a rather complex LDS in front of you by this time because you have been creating entities and joining them by relationships following a set of rules to make certain that every possible combination has been represented. In your original LDS you only used the minimum number of relationships to join the structure together. Before you compare the two diagrams you need to generally tidy up the latest. This mainly consists of removing any redundant relationships.

Examine all of the entities in which all of the attributes are used as keys. We may be able to remove them, and join the ends of the relationships left behind, without changing the overall structure of the diagram. Look also at any relationships which bridge intermediate entities which are already joined – they are probably redundant and can be removed.

Any many-to-many relationships are immediately suspect. If they occur between entities which are already linked by a pair of one-to-many relationships look to see if they are key-only entities, and if so they can probably be removed.

10.5 LDM for the River flow Meter system

The procedures described above can now be applied to the case study used to illustrate the techniques. Applying the instructions in Section 10.2 above, the result of gathering all of the tables together is as shown in the figure below. For ease of reference the sources of the tables have been put in the top row, although is not strictly necessary in practice.

Whilst examining these data items in their entirety, several aspects should become clear for this particular example. Firstly, all of the key fields are closely related but distinct, so no actual consolidation of tables is required in this instance. Secondly, as already suggested the dates fields may become problematical. The 'day' in the weather table, the 'week-begin' in the weekly report table, and the 'date' in the meter reading table are all linked together. In fact they are all dates referring to different types of reading as they are recorded or calculated.

This leads to the third issue which is more problematical. When gathered together it is obvious that the daily average could be calculated from the quarter-hourly readings for that day, and also that the weekly average flow could be calculated from the daily average flows (referred to as 'flow' in the daily flow table). These items are apparently transitory items and could theoretically be removed. As they are both the only non-key data items in their respective tables, just like the example in Figure 9.18, then the whole tables would be removed, as the keys are really only there to provide access to the data.

Meter card   **PIWF**   **Authorisation**   **Raw data**

METER	PIWF ENTRY	DISTRICT	METER READING
Meter	District	District	Meter
District	Week-begin	Prepared By	Date
Location	Meter	Authorised By	15min time
Grid Ref	WeeklyAve-Flow		Reading
Type			

WEEKLY REPORT

District
Week-begin
Authorised On

DAILY FLOW
District
Meter
Day
Flow

WEATHER
District
Day
Temp
Rainfall

Last serviced

Figure 10.4 The normalised river flow meter tables gathered together

There are two conditions which may persuade the analyst not to follow the normalisation rules and remove the tables at this point. The first condition is where either or both of the values exist as entities in their own right, and are not really transitory. This may sound odd, but the solution lies in the authorisation process. If the District Manager and the Flow Officer agree that the raw data is incorrect, say because of faulty or jammed equipment, then the reading recorded may be an estimate based on the weather conditions and the adjacent averages. In this case the 'authorised readings' may be entities, or tables, in their own right and therefore must be held separately. This condition only has to apply very occasionally, say once a month, for the database to have to hold all of such readings. It is only when this is completely impossible that the table can be removed.

The second condition is really beyond the scope of this book, but is worth mentioning briefly, and that is when the system is to be implemented as a distributed system. This means that the disk holding the raw data is produced at one location, the daily averages are calculated and authorised and are held in one data store (D1) at another, and the weekly average values are similarly held at another location, the Regional HQ. For example, let us say that the raw data is held on the DFO's personal computer while he performs the calculations, that the daily averages are then held on a District computer and cannot be changed once authorised, and the weekly averages are similarly held on a Regional computer. In this case the values could be kept at each location for reasons of efficiency and ease of enquiry, even though they are not strictly required and the whole system database is not in third normal form. What we are discussing in this paragraph is the physical data structure, and in fact the design at this point is still only producing a logical structure which may become more complex when implemented.

In practice, the safest course at this point is to note the possible redundancy of these items, but keep using them in the design process until it became absolutely clear whether they were needed or not. Sooner or later a firm decision needs to be made, but removing an item which is needed is less safe than keeping redundant data until the decision to remove it is a firm one.

10.5.1 Turning the tables into entities

The next step is to apply the procedures described in Section 10.3 above by concentrating only on the primary and foreign keys. Copying the tables forward, and leaving the two 'doubtful' ones present for the moment, would give the result shown in the figure below.

METER	PIWF ENTRY	METER READING
Meter	District	Meter
District	Week-begin	Date
	Meter	15min time
DISTRICT		
District	WEATHER	WEEKLY REPORT
	District	District
DAILY FLOW	Day	Week-begin
District		
Meter		
Day		

Figure 10.5 The reduced tables with keys shown

Applying the rules described in Section 10.3, for example to the two tables DISTRICT and METER, the attribute District is common to both tables. However, District is the primary key of DISTRICT, but is one attribute of the compound key of METER, and hence is a foreign key in this table. It is therefore marked with an '*' in the table, which can be interpreted as 'there may be many METERS per DISTRICT' as shown in Figure 10.6.

Marking all of the foreign keys in the tables shown in Figure 11.8 gives the results shown in the Figure 10.7.

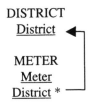

DISTRICT
District

METER
Meter
District *

Figure 10.6 Tables with relation from primary key to foreign key shown.

METER	PIWF ENTRY	METER READING
<u>Meter</u>	<u>District</u> } *	<u>Meter</u> }
District*	<u>Meter</u> }	<u>Date</u> }*
	}	
	<u>Week-begin</u> }*	<u>15min time</u>
DISTRICT		
<u>District</u>	WEATHER	WEEKLY REPORT
	District*	District*
DAILY FLOW	<u>Day</u>	<u>Week-begin</u>
<u>District</u> }*		
<u>Meter</u> }		
<u>Day</u>		

Figure 10.7 The reduced tables with keys shown

Relating the foreign keys to the respective relations can be difficult to see at first, but by comparing the rules given above with Figures 10.4 and 10.5 the application of the methods should soon become apparent. If you still have difficulty visualising what is going on, try looking at the example reports used to generate the normalised tables. Some people find real data values helpful, whilst others find them a distraction.

The labelling on the LDS should also help as it allows the relationships to be read as sentences, again helping clarify the situation. The table below expands the relationships shown in the LDS into sentences.

Entity	**Relationship(s)**
15-min Reading	may be used in one Daily Average Reading
Daily Average Reading	must be owned by one Meter
	must be printed on one Weekly Report
	must be made up of many 15-min Reading(s)
	must be related to one Weather
	must be used in one PIWF Entry
District	may be using many Meter(s)
	may record many Weather(s)
	may be in many Weekly Report(s)
Meter	must be installed in one District
	may own many Daily Average Reading(s)
PIWF Entry	must be printed in one Weekly Report
	may be calculated from many Daily Average Reading(s)
Weather	may be used by many Daily Average Reading(s)
	must be recorded in one District
Weekly Report	may be a listing with many Daily Average Reading(s)
	may contain many PIWF Entry(s)
	must be reporting on one District

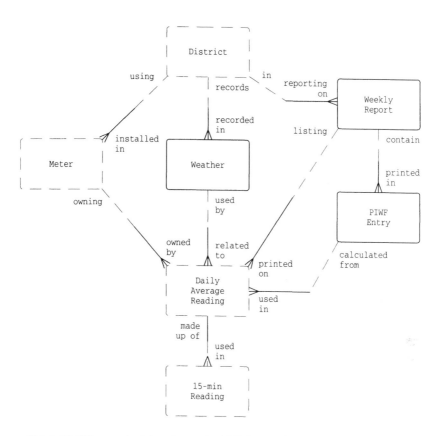

Figure 10.8 The required river flow meter LDS diagram based on the RDA process.

Comparing this version, generated from the RDA process, to Figure 5.26 there appear to be many differences, but in fact the diagrams are logically very similar, especially if an entity 'Region' with many Districts is added. In fact, given the information available at the time, the original LDS is a reasonable guess at the required data model, and was good enough to allow us to progress. If all the physical entities are removed on the grounds that they are either not relevant to the database, or can be used as attributes in 1:1 relationships with required entities, then the diagrams become very similar. The ones shown as 'dotted boxes' perform the same role in both versions, and the only remaining differences are in the names of the entities which are more precisely defined in Figure 10.8 above. The next step is to check this refined view of the required data against the latest view of the processes, as defined in Chapter 11, and then we will be ready to produce a definitive document of the required system for the implementation phase.

10.6 Exercises

In order to gain more practice at **Producing a LDM of the required system** you may now attempt the tutorial questions given below. Once you are confident of your skills in this topic you are in a position to complete the tasks within Section 13.10 if you wish to do so, before proceeding to the next chapter.

These tasks specifically cover:

13.10.1   Rationalising the Normalised Tables
13.10.8   Producing a LDM from the required RDA

10.6.1   Using the result of the normalisation process in the tutorial questions at the end of the previous chapter, rationalise the normalised tables, marking the foreign keys with an '*'.

10.6.2   Using the result of the above tutorial question, produce a logical data model in the form of a logical data structure diagram.

10.6.3   Imagine that you discovered an additional form that when normalised gave you an attribute pair {item, unit-cost). Modify the logical data structure diagram you produced as the answer to the previous question to incorporate this additional information.

10.6.4   Using the result of the above tutorial question, produce a text description of the logical data structure diagram.

11 Analysing the Entity Life History Events

11.1 Jackson Structured Programming (JSP) notation

As we get further into the process of designing the required system there are an increasing number of items which have to be represented in far more detail than is possible with the diagrams introduced so far. By far the most important of these items are the entity life histories or ELHs. The level to which these need to be specified conforms very much to the detail required when defining the code of a program or module. Every process that it is possible to write as a computer program can be expressed in terms of three basic constructs: sequence, selection and iteration, and a diagrammatic representation of these constructs is fundamental to logical design.

In 1975 the computer consultant Prof. Michael A. Jackson introduced a notation for programming design applicable to all programming languages in *Principles of Program Design* published by the Academic Press, London. This book introduced Jackson Structured Programming based on a simple but powerful way of representing structures, known as using JSP diagrams. This notation has not only been used extensively as one of the standard methods for communicating program designs ever since, but is now the basis for the notation of a variety of diagrams used within several modern methodologies, such as SSADM.

11.2 JSP diagram notation

Once you have grasped the basic use of the notation, then all of the other applications follow on naturally. For this reason a simple introduction to the notation is presented below, so that any of the tools and techniques which rely on JSP can be used later if required.

11.2.1 Sequence

The simplest structure that we may wish to represent is 'sequence', meaning a simple list of tasks or events. For example, to instruct a robot to enter a house we may tell it to: go up to the front door, open the door, and then go through the door. This is an almost trivial set of instructions to give a human, but the order is important in the robot if it has no other information. Such sequences can be drawn as a diagram as shown in Figure 11.1.

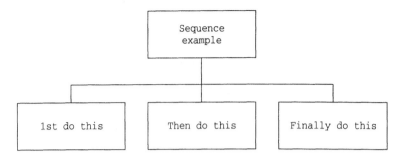

Figure 11.1 A simple JSP sequence example

Obviously we can have more than three boxes at the bottom if there are more than three items in the sequence being depicted. However, too many can be confusing to read so we may bundle them into groups of activities which will need exploding into lower levels to give even more detail. This is analogous to the way that we hid the complexity of the system processes within 'high-level' DFDs based on the fundamental system skill of 'structuring'. More than four or five items on a line can get confusing, but the notation allows a process of nesting. Let us say that if the middle activity above had three sub-activities, then it could be drawn as shown in Figure 11.2.

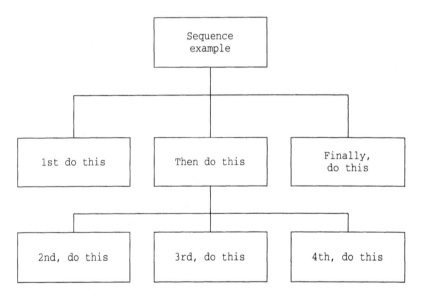

Figure 11.2 A more complex JSP sequence example

This diagram shows a sequence within a sequence, and is an example of how the JSP diagrams can be structured. Any, or all, of the boxes on the bottom line could have sub-structures connected below them in exactly the same way as the middle box on the line above.

All JSP diagrams can be structured in this way, with the higher-level boxes called structure boxes or branches, and any which do not have anything connected below

144   *Mastering systems analysis and design*

them is called a 'leaf'. In the example above, all the boxes are leaf boxes, except the two labelled 'Sequence example' and 'Then do this' which are structure boxes. There must be at least one structure box on a line by itself at the top of the diagram to label the structure being represented.

All the different types of JSP diagrams call the higher level boxes 'structures', but each leaf may have a specific name when a diagram is used for a particular purpose. For example, on a JSP representing the life history of an entity, each leaf would be an event, but in a program design diagram a leaf would represent a module, i.e. a block of code performing that function.

11.2.2 Selection

Now that we have introduced the basic rules for drawing JSP diagrams, we can add another type of construct. We do this by adding a character into the top right-hand corner of a box. If an 'o' is shown then we are indicating that the boxes in that branch are alternatives to one another, and hence that only one of them should be selected, often depending on some criteria or condition which may be shown on the diagram or added within the boxes.

There is an additional JSP convention that we do not mix different types of construct at the same level within a single branch. This implies that, if one of the boxes linked below a structure box is shown as a selection, then all of the other boxes are also selections. It is not enough to imply this: an 'o' must be put in each box to clearly show that that is what is intended. A simple example of a selection is shown in Figure 11.3.

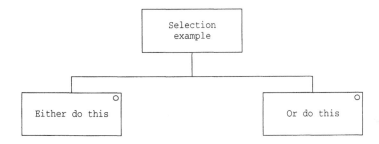

Figure 11.3 A simple example of JSP selection

11.2.3 Iteration

There is only one other type of structure that we need to use the JSP notation within this text, and that is the iteration box. We do this by adding an '*' character into the top right-hand corner of a box. By doing this we are indicating that the actions shown by the boxes in that branch are to be repeated two or more times.

11.2.4 Putting all the JSP types together

So far we have shown all of the three basic constructs in isolation, but the real value lies in putting them together to give a diagrammatic view of a complex scenario. If the use of the diagram was to show how we wanted something doing, then we could use a JSP diagram using all of the constructs arranged to indicate the order of the actions.

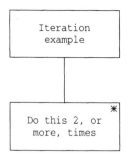

Figure 11.4 A simple example of JSP iteration

Figure 11.5 shows a rather contrived example which uses all of the constructs intro-duced so far. The top two lines are structure boxes, but each box on the bottom line is a leaf showing the different type of events. The 'full example' consists of a sequence of three structures to be performed in the order shown. Each structure branches into one of the three types of construct. The first offers a choice of two actions, the second section has one action that should be done many times, and the third is a sequence of two actions. Even though all of the leaves are on the same line, the convention is cor-rectly followed as each type belongs to a different structure or 'branch'.

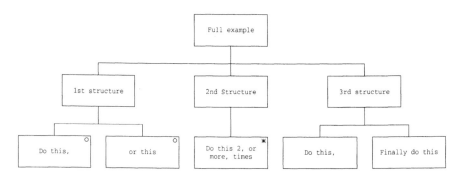

Figure 11.5 A single JSP diagram showing the three type of construct

What we mean by this diagram is that to perform the *full example* we need three steps: firstly, *do this, - or this*; secondly, *do this two or more times*; and thirdly, *do this* and *finally do this*. Now we have the basic notation it can be applied to a variety of dia-gram types. However as this is an introductory text we will deal with the most impor-tant example, and one which allows us to complete the design process to the level needed for this book, the entity life histories.

11.3 Producing the Entity Life Histories

One aspect of the required system modelling neglected so far is the time element. This aspect was excluded from both the data flow processing and the logical data structures, but it must be included to give a complete view of a logical system model. The processes are considered to be instantaneous events, so we only need to model the time element of the data, or at this stage of the life cycle, the entities identified in the LDS or LDM. We can perform this type of analysis by using a variant of the Jackson Structure Charts just introduced, the Entity Life History (ELH) diagrams. Entity life histories, together with DFDs and LDSs are one of the fundamental tools used to document a system and are a very important product of the analysis and design activities. They can also be used to check that the logical data structure or model is consistent and compatible with the data flow model, which greatly extends their usefulness. With three basic views, data structure, process and time, it is possible to be provide a cross-checked model, because we can use two of any of these products to check or correct the remaining one. We can use this in practice by following a series of simple steps, to produce a set of ELHs.

11.3.1 The Event–Entity Relation Matrix

Firstly we need to make a list of all of the Entities which occur in the system. This can be the current or required system, depending on where you are using this technique in the life cycle. The process works the same way in both circumstances. The list can be obtained by examining the logical data model produced as part of the previous analysis, as each box on the diagram represents an Entity. We also need to identify the 'life events' of each entity. These usually consist of the creation, deletion or modification of the entities and we should have noted these events during the fact finding process. It becomes second nature to note the entities after a while, and if a user refers to changing one, we should automatically ask how it is created as our next question. If we cannot find the life events it is sometimes possible to 'reverse engineering' them at this point by asking for each entity: 'What event causes it to be created?', 'What event causes it to be modified?', and 'What event causes it to be deleted?'. In fact, the generic ELH diagram for any entity can be drawn as shown in the Figure 11.6. This illustrates that an entity tends to be created, modified many times and finally deleted. Each of these events will have to be implemented in some way, which in practice means that a function must operate on the entity. By checking that these processes exist to perform these operations on all of the entities, we can relate the three diagram types to one another.

However there is an even more simple way to produce this list, and that is to copy it from the functions on the final version User/Function Matrix Form produced when we were modelling the system processes, at the end in Section 7.2.5. After all, everything we do in the system should be identified as a function within the system. Whichever method we use, it should enable us to fill in the first column of an entity/event matrix, such as the one on the sample form given below. The same is true of the entity names which were identified in the final section of Chapter 10. These names are used to label in the small columns, labelled A B, etc., or produce a separate key, whichever is most convenient. The partially filled matrix shown below is for the River flow Meter case study. Please note that we have removed the top-level processes from the form, leaving only the genuine functions, in this system all of the level 2 DFD processes.

Event-Entity Matrix Form											
Current System						Required System Yes					
System **Meter v.1**	Author MJH				Date **2/12/98**			Page of			
Entity	A	B	C	D	E	F	G	H	I	J	K
A 15-min Reading											
B Daily Ave Reading											
C District											
D Meter											
E PIWF Entry											
F Weather											
G Weekly Report											
Functions											
1.1 Input raw meter data											
1.2 Validate against existing data											
1.3 Compare data to Diary											
1.4 Edit data where necessary											
1.5 Produce draft report											
2.1 Examine draft data											
2.2 Accept draft report											
2.3 Reject draft report											
3.1 Copy authorised data											
3.2 Prepare PIWF											
4.1 Extract relevant data											
4.2 Perform modelling											

We consider each event in the first column and record the effect that that event has on each entity by putting a 'C' for creation, a 'D' for deletion, or an 'M' for modification on the same row in the column below the required Entity name.

Some events may have two effects on an entity. This is almost invariably to create a default entity, and then modify the entity based on current conditions. In this case we enter a 'C/M'. No other combinations should occur. It just does not make sense to create an entity, or modify it, and then immediately delete it. Similarly, it is impossible to delete it and then do anything else to it. You could delete an entity and then create it, but this is logically the same as modifying but is very inefficient. As explained previously, the best explanation of the use of a form is to present an example of its use. Following the procedure used so far, the form below has been completed for the River flow Meter System using the information carried forward from the earlier fact finding and other analysis.

	Event-Entity Matrix Form										
Current System					Required System Yes						
System **Meter v.2**		Author MJH			Date **3/12/98**			Page of			
Entity	A	B	C	D	E	F	G	H	I	J	K
A 15-min Reading											
B Daily Ave Reading											
C District											
D Meter											
E PIWF Entry											
F Weather											
G Weekly Report											
Functions											
1.1 Input raw meter data	C	C									
1.2 Validate against existing data	M	M									
1.3 Compare data to Diary						C					
1.4 Edit data where necessary	M	M									
1.5 Produce draft report		C				C	C				
2.1 Examine draft data											
2.2 Accept draft report							M				
2.3 Reject draft report		M				M	M				
3.1 Copy authorised data					C						
3.2 Prepare PIWF					M						
4.1 Extract relevant data											
4.2 Perform modelling											

11.3.2 Drawing each ELH as a JSP diagram

Having created a table as shown in the previous section, it is relatively easy to produce an Entity Life History diagram using the JSP notation introduced at the beginning of this chapter. Each diagram should consist of a single box labelled with the Entity name at the top, and with the various life events shown as boxes underneath. If we have identified, say, five entities along the top of the form, then we should have five different ELH diagrams, each with the name of one entity in the top box. Below the entity-name box we draw the second level boxes, progressing from left to right. The creation events come first, being shown as options if there is more than one of them. Next we have the modification events, and the deletion events come last. We can use the normal Jackson notation to show optionality and iteration, and we keep expanding the diagram to as many levels as is necessary to show all the events on the matrix above.

As this is an introductory text dealing with relatively simple case studies, we will not go into the detail of the ELH for each entity. It is sufficient that we are familiar enough with the notation to recognise and read any such diagrams, and have the information required to complete a final check on the DFDs, as described below. That means ensuring that every entity is created, modified and deleted, or if not, there is a good reason for any anomalies in this system.

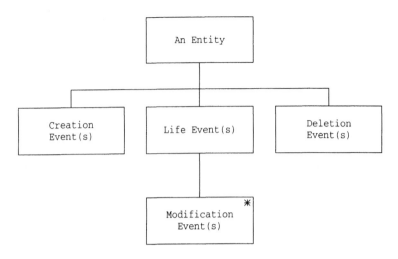

Figure 11.6 A generic ELH diagram for any entity

11.4 Producing the corrected DFDs using the ELH

Once a complete set of ELH events is available we can use them as a final check on the correctness of our analysis of the system by comparing them against the data flow diagrams. What we are trying to ensure is that all of the data flow processes are compatible with the logical data structures by using the entity life history events as a cross-check between them. Firstly, we should have a list of ELH events for each of the entities on the LDS diagrams. That is the work described on the event-entity matrix form above, and is easily completed. On this form we also used the data flow diagrams and their documentation, to ensure that there is a process for every event. What we check next is if there is an event for every process. Whilst this is not absolutely necessary, it raises the question as to whether the function is required if it does not affect any entity in any way. It is not essential that every function is associated with a life event, but it a good way of identifying potentially redundant functions before the implementation starts.

We cross-check the DFDs by assembling all the sets of documentation. It is advisable to make a copy of the documents to work on, as it is much easier to keep a check on our progress if we mark the diagrams as we go along. The Event/Entity Matrix Form we produced earlier is a good working document to check for consistency. However, as we produced the ELHs from this form the DFDs should be available to consult and check any discrepancies. In this way we avoid propagating any errors that may have been made when completing the event/entity matrix form.

We take each event in turn and find the process or processes that deal with that event for each entity it affects. Remember that, in this context, an event is something that causes an entity to change state. Well-structured DFDs are a great aid to efficiency in this process, as we want to trace the explosion paths down to the lowest level function that causes an entity to be created, modified or deleted. We should be able to identify an event which is linked to each function. If we cannot identify any event for a given function, it begs the question 'why is that function in the system, and is it still required?' When we have done this we can draw a light pencil tick through the process on the DFD and also on the row of the form, to show that you have dealt with both of them.

If we are fully documenting the system, we need to enter the reference number of the process into the 'DFD Processes' box on the corresponding Function Definition Form, as shown in Section 4.7.3. We can also record the reference(s) of the event in the 'Events' box on the same form, which we left out when completing the documentation for the current process model. The events themselves do not have specific references, but we can use the matrix entry from the event/entity matrix form. For example, if you are dealing with the third entity and the first function on your form, the box on the matrix will be 'C1' (column C, row 1).

When we have gone through every one of the low-level processes, or functions, on the whole of the event/entity matrix form we can then turn the technique around and look at each of the entity columns to make sure that one of each type of event has occurred for each entity. Once that has been done we can be fairly well satisfied that our process modelling, and that the three documents are correct.

If there is an entity which has one of the three life events missing, we have to decide how our proposed system will deal with this event. For example, looking at the form above, none of the entities are ever deleted! This should send you back to the user to check if this is correct. You may receive information of the form, 'environmental data must be kept in perpetuity', or you may find that different types of data have to deleted after a certain length of time. Either situation is going to cause problems eventually as the database will get enormous after a certain length of time and special backup procedures will have to be implemented to keep the current databases clear and un-fragmented. This is a problem for the physical database design, which is outside the scope of this book.

11.4.1 Entity life histories (ELH) in the river flow case study

Going through each of the entities in turn, the 15-min Reading, Daily Average Reading, PIWF Entry, Weather, and Weekly Report are all created and modified, which is reassuring. However, the District and Meter entities are not operated on at all. This makes some sense in the current system as they are physical objects, and the information on them will be held on paper documents, such as the DFO's meter cards. In the proposed system we need some information on the computer database, so these entities must be present and capable of modification, say in the case of a new meter being installed or an existing one moved. Again we have to go back to the user to check how they want to handle the situation. Let us say that, after a meeting with the RFO, the DFO and the DM they decide that this is a management issue and, as the DM is now using the computer to authorise the reports, it would be proper for that person to create and modify these entities. By the way, you can never allow them to delete these entities if the meter data has to be kept in perpetuity, as that would remove an 'owning' record in the database and break an RDA rule to do with referential integrity, so that function need not be implemented. It is also clear from the form that 'examine draft data' is not a computer function and so can be removed. We can now modify the form to reflect these changes.

Event-Entity Matrix Form											
Current System						Required System Yes					
System **Meter v.3**		Author MJH			Date **4/12/98**			Page of			
Entity	A	B	C	D	E	F	G	H	I	J	K
A 15-min Reading											
B Daily Ave Reading											
C District											
D Meter											
E PIWF Entry											
F Weather											
G Weekly Report											
Functions											
1.1 Input raw meter data	C	C									
1.2 Validate against existing data	M	M									
1.3 Compare data to Diary					C						
1.4 Edit data where necessary	M	M									
1.5 Produce draft report		C				C	C				
2.1 Accept draft report							M				
2.2 Reject draft report		M				M	M				
2.3 Create/edit District			C/M								
2.4 Create/edit Meter				C/M							
3.1 Copy authorised data					C						
3.2 Prepare PIWF					M						
4.1 Extract relevant data											
4.2 Perform modelling											

Having done that, the DFDs have to be changed to reflect the modifications, starting with level 2 processes and progressively correcting any 'parent' diagrams affected.

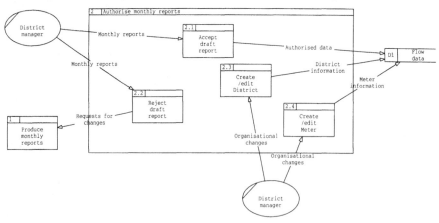

Figure 11.7 The corrected case study level 2 DFD

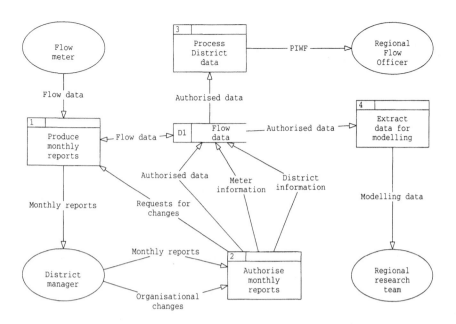

Figure 11.8 The corrected case study level 1 DFD

Having performed all of the checks described, and found the model to be satisfactory, we can be reasonably sure that our logical design for the system is correct and complete. We can never be completely certain of this, as the absence of identified errors is not a proof of the total correctness of the design. All we can do as analysts is to perform as many paper checks as possible so that we minimise the possibility that things can go wrong. Checking we have a full tank of fuel before we start a journey does not guarantee we will not have a breakdown, but at least we should not run out of petrol. It is a matter of minimising the risks and trying not to make careless errors. In our simplified life cycle model, we are now ready to document our logical solution, ready for the implementation team to start the physical design and coding.

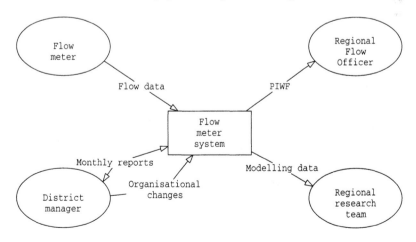

Figure 11.9 The corrected case study context diagram

11.5 Exercises

In order to gain more practice at **Using the Entity Life History events to check the DFM** you may now attempt the tutorial questions given below. Once you are confident of your skills in this topic you are in a position to complete the tasks within section 13.11 if you wish to do so, before proceeding to the next chapter.

These tasks specifically cover:

13.11.4   Checking the DFM using the Entity Life Histories
13.11.6   Producing the definitive Required Logical DFDs

Draw a JSP structure to represent the following situations.

11.5.1   A train has either one or two engines. These are followed by a number of carriages: the first is a 1st class passenger carriages, and the rest are 2nd class passenger carriages. The train has a goods wagon at the end, followed by either a guard or brake van.

11.5.2   If you telephone me at home my number is engaged or not. If it is engaged then 'call waiting' will beep me, and I can put the other caller on hold or ignore you. If I ignore you, you can wait, hang up or press a key to leave a message on the call monitoring service. This also an option to leave a message if there is no reply after 5 rings.

System Specification

12.1 Introduction

As with the previous documents, there is no single specific definition of what should or should not be included in a systems specification. The analyst(s) should look to the purpose of the document, and decide if the contents are necessary and sufficient to fulfil that purpose. The purpose of a system specification is to define the requirements of the system to sufficient detail that an implementation team can carry on with the coding and testing without further information from the analyst. This is, of course an ideal, but if it is kept in mind the resulting documentation should be of a higher standard than otherwise. In other words the specification should convey to the reader, in a clear and structured fashion:

- All the objective(s) of the proposed system.
- The functions of each of the parts of the proposed system.
- A complete definition of all the inputs to each part of the proposed system.
- A complete definition of all the outputs from each part of the proposed system.
- An acceptance test plan for the complete system.
- A schedule of timescales, resources and costs.

The systems specification should contain enough material for the reader to completely understand what is required of the system and should leave no logical design decisions to be made by the implementation team. The specification should also be written and structured well enough to communicate that understanding easily and efficiently.

The following contents list is offered as a pro-forma. It can be used as a basis for your specification, but feel free to add or subtract sections if you think your system has different needs. However, do be sure of your ground if you decide to deviate. Remember that the order is not definitive! The clarity of layout of *your* system documentation is paramount.

12.2 Suggested contents for a systems specification

a) Contents list and summary of the proposed system.
   A Description of the major parts of the system with a diagram of how these parts interact. E.g. rich picture or context diagram.
   Identify any manual procedures needed to support the computerised functions.

155

b) Detail of the System Processes.
   Process Descriptions and Diagrams (level 1, 2 etc DFD's).
c) Detail of the System Data.
   Definition and description of Entities and their attributes.
   Logical Data Model.
   Entity life history information.
d) Identification and detail of all reports and outputs.
e) Identification and detail of all screens and inputs.
f) Project Control and System Management.
   Timescales and deadlines.
   Test procedures required.
   Manual and clerical procedures required to run the system.

The analyst will have produced all the specialist products referred to by working through the material in the preceding chapters. The purely descriptive material can be produced using normal report writing skills.

12.2.1 An overview of producing the required system specification

The preceding chapters show how the specialist diagrams are used in practice to develop a model of the system from several different views. They have also described the analyst's thinking at each point in the process. The diagrams and forms have been kept in step as the work progressed, and used to update one another as more was discovered about what was required and how to go about achieving it.

The work covered in this chapter actually spans a large part of the analysis and design activities and would, in practice, be punctuated by many other activities. Most modern methodologies use many more diagram types that we have shown, but they all tend to be used in the same way, to generate one view and then to crosscheck that result with a previous product.

Exactly what techniques are used, and where and how the related diagrams are produced is the major difference between the structured methodologies. Real-time systems have different requirements from business and scientific systems. An inspection of the overviews of the methodology in any textbook on SSADM, for example, will clearly show the stages and steps where a data flow diagram should be produced or used. For the moment you have completed your first pass through the work that an analyst completes in implementing a small-scale real-life project.

12.3 Exercise

Due to the nature of the topic, in order to gain more practice at producing **the requirements specification** you need to have worked through all of the analysis and design for a complete case study. Therefore you are now in a position to attempt the tasks within section 13.12 only if you have completed all of the previous sections in chapter 13 as you progressed through this book.. If you did not, you may now proceed to the next chapter, 13 and work your way through sections 13.1 to 13.11, and then attempt section 13.12.

13 | A Task-Driven Example

13.1 Introduction

Chapters one to twelve of this book introduced the basic tools and concepts required to perform the techniques of system analysis and design, using a simple case study to explain each technique and its use in the phase in which it is first encountered. This chapter takes a different approach and works through another complete case study, assuming that the reader is already familiar with the technical material, and adding additional advice on how to deal with some of the problems which can occur in practical situations. This method of working is suitable for:

- Revising and consolidating the previous work for beginning students.
- A guide to practical work for solo or group assessment in this topic.
- Updating existing skills by experienced students and practitioners.
- Allowing 'task-driven' learning for those who prefer a more active approach.

This type of approach is valuable because it separates out the skills relevant to a particular case study from the generic techniques which are used in every situation. Ideally the tools and techniques should be able to be applied in a mechanical way to each example encountered. In practice, each application will tend to throw up 'special' cases and problems which require experience and judgement to be applied by the analyst. As described in the Preface, the analyst is assumed throughout to be the reader.

The River Flow Meter case study used to introduce the material was deliberately simplified to allow each technique to be covered with the minimum of distraction by the example. By covering another case study, giving only minimal explanation, we can start to extend our skills to the practical application of theoretical techniques. This is a process that will probably continue throughout your working life as you gain more experience and insight into the use of systems analysis and design techniques in practice. The good news is that, as you gain this experience, your skills will become more valuable to potential employers.

In order to be able to cross-reference between the techniques more easily, the section numbering (13.n.) of this chapter matches the previous chapter headings. For example, all of the tasks to do with finding out about the current system are numbered as 13.2... in this chapter, and are covered in Chapter 2 of the main text. Soft System tasks have numbers beginning with 13.3, matching the descriptions covered in Chapter 3, and so on. This first part corresponds to Chapter 1, which describes the fundamental concepts and has no related tasks, so the real work starts in the next section.

13.2 Finding out about the current system

This unit covers the essential steps leading up to the fact-finding interviews with the user. The initial interview is usually with the most senior person in the company and covers strategic issues. The next interviews tend to involve people further down the organisational structure until the current users explain the present operational details.

13.2.1 Preparing for an interview

The first thing to be done when starting a new systems analysis project is to learn as much as possible about the system. There is frequently a great deal of information available to you before you even meet a user. Often the first contact will be through a letter, a tender request or an advertisement; because you quickly accumulate a variety of notes and material you should always start the analysis by getting organised.

13.2.2 Task

To get yourself into good personal organisation habits, why not work through this case study as if it were a professional project? This involves using a suitable ring binder or document wallet, and labelling it "Wooden Windows Project". You will need about 50 sheets of A4 paper and a similar amount of scrap paper to complete the project.
You can carry on by:

- Creating a project folder in to which you can put all the information collected.
- Carefully studying whatever information you have available.
- Attempting to find any other details about the company or individual.
- Preparing an interview plan prior to meeting the user(s).

13.2.3 Task

Study the memo in Figure 13.1 and make notes to guide you on the key points about the company. HINT Remember that you eventually want to produce an interview plan so divide your notes into two general sections. One section that will help you under-stand the character of the company, and another for specific needs covering the likely requirements of the application.

13.2.4 Suggested result of previous task

- User company 'Wooden Windows', makes windows.
- Owner Mr. Macdonnel, friend of my boss's boss!
- Wants 'simple' system to 'streamline' existing paperwork.
- Expects robust reliable system, but prepared to pay for it.
- Current functions identified: ordering and production.

From: Mr. Bigg, The Chief Executive
To: The Senior Analyst
(Note For the purposes of this chapter, that is your boss!)

At the local Business Club last night I met Mr Macdonnel, the owner of the Wooden Windows Company. He wants a good simple computer system to streamline the paperwork in his existing ordering and production system. Your job is to produce the documentation for such a system and, if we win the next tender, to implement it.

As the Wooden Windows Company is in a production industry, they understand about planning, scheduling and quality control and do not mind paying for it. They do, however, expect the computer system to work at least as well as their own products!

I know that this is likely to be a small project by our standards so you can put someone new on it. But remember that, as always, our company's reputation is on the line so I expect the normal standards to be maintained. I want to be able to the face the Business Club after this job is finished!

Figure 13.1 Internal Memo re: The Wooden Windows Company

13.2.5 Task

Using Figure 13.2, assume that you have discovered the following article in the local press. Study it carefully and use the information to add to your notes.

13.2.6 Suggested result of previous task

- User company 'Wooden Windows'.
- Makes all-wood domestic windows from own supplies.
- Owner Mr. Macdonnel, friend of my boss's boss!
- Wants 'simple' system to 'streamline' existing paperwork.
- Expect robust reliable system, but prepared to pay for it.
- Current functions identified: sales?, ordering, sawmills and production.
- Sell through small retail and mail order. No 'Wooden Windows' shops?
- 50 Employees. How distributed?
- Sales increasing by 25% pa. Policy on staff growth?
- Small number of standard parts and embellishments.

13.2.7 Task

You should now be in a position to produce a draft interview plan. Assume at first that you have a one-hour meeting with the owner of Wooden Windows in his office at 3pm on the 14th of October. HINT Study the section on interview plans in Chapter 2. From now on, if you are in doubt what to do, refer back to the chapter with the same number as the section, and locate the topic in the text where it is first described.

Newspaper Cutting on the Wooden Windows Company

One of our most colourful residents and employers is Mr. Macdonnel. An expatriate American of Scottish descent, he is the owner of Wooden Windows Company, a small company which specialises in the manufacturing of all-wood windows. Their distinctive log-cabin style offices are situated just outside town on Urnold Street. The company has a number of product lines including dining room, library, living room and bedroom window frames. They market their goods through a wide variety of retail outlets, and by direct mail order to the DIY market, especially to people renovating period homes.

At the present time the company has about 50 employees and sales are increasing by 25% per year. Their marketing policy is simple but effective: 'If you want cheap windows which are just like your neighbour's, and you want them fast, go somewhere else.' Whilst this may sound like a recipe for disaster several factors have contributed to the firm's success.

Firstly, in the 1970's Mr Macdonnel bought several thousand acres of disused training grounds from the Ministry of Defence for a song. The land consisted mainly of pine forests together with a few sawmills. It was a condition of the purchase that the buyer promised to keep the mills in business and to use the wood productively. When asked by a previous reporter, some years ago, why his windows were twice as heavy as anybody else's he replied 'Because, Sonny, I have loggers to feed and pine trees growing like weeds.'

Another factor is that Mr Macdonnel's uncle lost his livelihood in the American Mid-West due to soil erosion. Determined that this would not happen to him he has carefully re-planted all the trees as they were cut down, long before renewable resources became an issue. This policy has led to our retaining the beautiful wooded aspect of the region, although Mr Macdonnel admits that he felt at the time that this would slow down the loggers a bit; as he puts it, 'while they are planting they aren't cutting'. But it also means that Mr Macdonnel is now the darling of the conservationists. If you are a public figure being photographed at home it is essential to have some 'Wooden Windows' in the background!

The windows are very easy to recognise; they are twice as thick as they need to be, and are not made with wood from a threatened rain-forest. The designs are also based on unpretentious traditional designs which Mr Macdonnel shamelessly appropriated as it simplified manufacture enormously. Most of the windows are assembled from a small number of standard parts, with an even smaller number of decorative embellishments to add 'a touch of class'. 'Neat but not gaudy', as Mr Macdonnel constantly says.

Figure 13.2 Newspaper article about the Wooden Windows Company

13.2.8 Suggested result of previous task

1st INTERVIEW   Wooden Windows Company System
3pm, Thurs 14th October 1997
Wooden Windows Company Offices, Urnold Street
MEETING WITH: Mr. Macdonnel, Owner

Suggested Basic Questions

- What are your reasons for considering computerisation?
- How much impact do you expect the new system to have on the present structure and working practices of the company?
- What do you wish to retain about the current system?
- What would you like to gain by changing from the current system to the new system?
- Do you have computers in your company at the moment?
- Do you have a guideline budget for implementing the new system?

Suggested Specific Questions

- Would you describe how the sales and accounts departments work at present?
- Are the sales and accounts departments essentially integrated?
- How much of the work is mail order?
- How much of the work is with already existing customers?
- I notice that your windows are all wood and you provide that yourself. Do you deal with any suppliers?
- If so, would the supplier accounts be part of the system?
- Would you identify the 'functional areas' within your organisation?
- What is their structure and who manages them?
- Can I arrange to meet them to pursue the analysis?

Suggested Timings

		Be early.
Start time:	3.00pm	Introductions (and Coffee?)
	3.05pm	Basic Questions
	3.30pm	More detailed questions
>>>>	3.50pm	Sum up and arrange next meeting
Be ready to		Same time and place in 1 week?
leave by	4.00pm	Do not let it over run.

Remember to take diary, project folder and spare paper

13.2.9 The Formal User Interviews

Below is a transcript of several interviews with staff of Wooden Windows Company which is essential to provide material for the initial analysis. (Remember that these are taken from actual transcripts. They have been edited to remove the worst errors, but still expect less than perfect grammar, repetition, and occasional contradictory descriptions. The skill is to work out what is meant, not what is said!).

13.2.10   Task

Study the interview transcript below annotating it to mark key points.

Wooden Windows Company System
                 3pm, Thursday 14ᵗʰ October 1993
                 Wooden Windows Company Offices in Urnold Street

Analyst   "Good afternoon Mr Macdonnel. Thank you for letting me come to see you at such short notice. I am a trainee analyst with Mr Bigg's company, and he said that you were both talking about the computerisation of your company. I am here to get the basic facts in order to see how we can help you."

Mr Macdonnel "Good of you to come. Let's sit over there. I usually have coffee around this time. Would you like some?"

Analyst   "Yes please. I was just admiring your offices. Log cabins are unusual buildings for this purpose but it gives a very friendly atmosphere."

Mr Macdonnel "Well spotted. I like my staff to be happy and comfortable. It makes it nice for me and they work better."

Analyst   "I noticed as I came in that there seemed to be no computers around. Are your staff happy at the idea of computers being introduced? A lot of people aren't."

Mr Macdonnel "You are right, we are probably the last firm in town not using computers. Oddly enough it is the staff who have pushed me into it. Most of them have families who use computers at home. They tell me that they are finding it difficult to cope with the increased workload and that computers would help them. We don't want to bring lots of new people in. Just let the existing ones get through the paperwork more easily."

Analyst   "That is actually very helpful. So you do not want to lose staff or make immediate savings, just increase productivity so that your existing people can cope with your 25% per annum sales growth?"

Mr Macdonnel "Very impressive, I can see that you have done your homework. Yes, no changes in working practice. Just streamline what we have got."

Analyst   "Isn't that only the sales and accounting side? What about production? Do you expect that to be affected?"

Mr Macdonnel "I don't see how computers can help there. The saw mills are pretty independent, turning trees into standard parts and stocking them in advance. The production people only get one report which is a 'work order' telling them what to assemble every week from the orders which have come in."

Analyst   "I would like to go into more detail on that in a little while. For the moment I am just trying to get to grips with the big picture. What about suppliers? I know you produce all the raw wood materials but what about glue and nails. Do you have an ordering system and if so does it need to be included in the computer system?"

Mr Macdonnel	"We don't use nails! Good Heavens, haven't you seen our windows? It's all joints and dowels. Still I suppose you wouldn't know about that, you are an expert on computers. No, you needn't worry about external supplies. I have a barter deal with a chipboard firm. They take away all our sawdust and scrap and supply us with glue in return. It works very well."
Analyst	"Please excuse my ignorance. When I said nails, I really meant anything else you may use. So, to summarise, it is just your customer ordering side we are talking about, and you want the same basic procedures to be maintained as in the present system, with the same people using the computers to do the paperwork as at present?"
Mr Macdonnel	"That is nearly right. At the moment the office staff divide the work fairly rigidly between processing orders and dealing with accounts. We haven't actually discussed how the staff deal with the paperwork, and I think you had better talk to Mrs. Jones, the office manager about that."
Analyst	"That's fine. I have several questions on the detailed handling of the paperwork but I will leave them until I see Mrs Jones. I see we have about 15 minutes left of our hour. Could I talk about a few more general issues before we finish?"
Mr Macdonnel	"Of course. I suppose you are going to ask about money?"
Analyst	"Actually that was one of the questions, so could we deal with it now? Do you have a guide-line budget for implementing the new system?"
Mr Macdonnel	"No! I don't have clue what it will cost. I trust Mr Bigg to do an honest deal. That's not very business-like of me is it? OK, how about this. We have ten staff in the office of whom eight work on the orders and accounts. If we keep growing at the present rate we will need at least two extra staff a year for the next three years. That is six staff costing me about £20,000 a year each in salary and overheads. If you can put in a complete system with minimum disruption for half that, say £60,000, you will have a happy customer."
Analyst	"Thank you, that is very frank. It is never quite that simple, though. Do you have any computers at all in your company at the moment?"
Mr Macdonnel	"No, why?"
Analyst	"Well, putting the system in is one thing, but running it is another. You really need someone who is trained up in these things actually on the premises or you will have to bring people in every time there is a minor hiccup in the system. It is a bit like having someone handy around rather having to call a builder or plumber for every little job."
Mr Macdonnel	"Don't tell me, maintenance on my buildings and machines cost a fortune until I sorted it out. But that's another story. Is this likely to be a big problem? I thought you just put computers in and for-

Analyst	got about them?"
	"In situations like this we try to arrange that that is how it works, but it really depends on how complex your systems are and what we can do to simplify them. Theoretically it shouldn't be a big problem. One well-trained member of staff should be able to do almost everything, barring absolute disasters, when you would need specialist help anyway. Why don't we go as far as we can and I will advise you on the likely support needs when I have more idea."
Mr Macdonnel	"OK, is that it?"
Analyst	"Almost. Can I just go briefly over what we have discussed so far. You want a simple, robust, computer system to make your existing ordering and accounts staff more productive so that they can cope with expanded sales without extra staff. You envisage some greater flexibility in the way they perform their work, but no major re-structuring or procedural changes. You want to spend about £60,000 for all the equipment, software development, training and support and you want the system to cope for about three years without modification."
Mr Macdonnel	"Correct!"
Analyst	"The way our company usually works is that someone like myself will do the necessary interviews and initial analysis and then produce a feasibility report. If that is satisfactory, then we go on to more detailed analysis with a complete requirements specification and then a system specification. Up to that point you are really only paying for my time and getting a paper plan of your system. When we have a specification we can actually get the system coded and start buying and installing hardware, which costs a lot more."
Mr Macdonnel	"So what do I pay, and when?"
Analyst	"My time is charged to you at £500 a day. However, if I only need one more interview, with Mrs Jones, I estimate that it is will only take two or three days' work to do the feasibility report. That will mean a maximum cost of £1500 for that, and then we will be in a position to roughly cost out the rest of the system. The estimates will become more accurate as we do more analysis. If at any time it looks as though we cannot complete the work within your budget I will tell you immediately. Is that all right?"
Mr Macdonnel	"All right. Would you like me to check Mrs Jones' diary and arrange a meeting between you while you are here?"
Analyst	"Yes please. I take it that you do not want to be involved in that, but would it be all right for me to arrange another meeting with you if I need one?"
Mr Macdonnel	"Of course. Mrs Jones is away on holiday now but could see you on Monday morning."
Analyst	"That's fine. Monday the 18th, shall we make it 10am? Well, goodbye Mr Macdonnel, and thank you for all the information

Mr Macdonnel	and, of course, the coffee."
	"No problem. Goodbye."
	End of interview

13.2.11   Task

You should now produce an interview plan for the second interview, with Mrs Jones. Carry forward any unanswered questions and add any points raised from the first interview. Are there any details which you got from Mr Macdonnel which you should avoid mentioning?

13.2.12   Suggested result of previous task

2nd INTERVIEW   Wooden Windows Company System
10am, Monday 18th October 1993
Wooden Windows Company Offices, Urnold Street
MEETING WITH: Mrs Jones, Sales and Accounts Office Manager.

Ask about holidays!

GENERAL QUESTIONS
- Mainly asked at 1st interview.
- Summarise what Mr Macdonnel wants to get positive feedback.
- But leave out reference to budget unless she is obviously in his confidence!

SPECIFIC QUESTIONS
- Would you describe how the sales and accounts departments work at present?
- Are the sales and accounts departments essentially integrated?
- How much of the work is mail order?
- How much of the work is with already existing customers?
- Would you identify the other 'functional areas' within your organisation?
- What is their structure and who supervises them?
- Can I arrange to meet them to pursue the analysis if necessary?
- Is there anyone who is a computer enthusiast who could do local support?

TIMINGS
Be early.
Start time :	10.00am	Introductions and Coffee?
	10.05am	Summary of 1st Interview.
	10.20am	More detailed questions
>>>>	10.50am	Sum up and arrange next meeting if necessary.
Be ready to		Same time and place in 1 week?
leave by	11.00am	

Do not let it overrun.
Remember to take diary, project folder, notes from 1st interview and spare paper.

Study the interview transcript below annotating it to mark key points.

2nd INTERVIEW   Wooden Windows Company System
                               10am, Monday 18th October 1993
                               Wooden Windows Company Offices in Urnold Street

Analyst	"Good morning Mrs Jones. I am a trainee analyst with Mr Bigg's company, and I met Mr Macdonnel last week to talk about the computerisation of your company."
Mrs Jones	"Yes, he told me about it. I was away on holiday at the time."
Analyst	"Oh really, did you go anywhere pleasant?"
Mrs Jones	"I went with my family to a big theme park. We didn't expect to enjoy it, it was just for the children really. As it happened we were very impressed, especially with some of the machines. Do they have computers in them?"
Analyst	"I read somewhere that they have lots of computerised machines, although I am not an expert on robotics. A friend told me that they had some very impressive systems. I cannot promise anything like that I am afraid."
Mrs Jones	"I don't expect it. Simple desk-top computers will do for us."
Analyst	"Are you familiar with office computers then? Mr Macdonnel said that some of the staff were the instigators of this feasibility study."
Mrs Jones	"Yes I am one of the new technology fanatics. Myself and several of the other women in the office have husbands who are self-employed and we do their paperwork and accounts on our own computers at home. It is quite frustrating to come into work and use typewriters and card files when you know how much easier it could be. However, here there are lots of us using essentially the same information so I suppose that means it will be more complicated?"
Analyst	"Almost certainly, but perhaps not too much. If we go over the details I can get a better idea. Would you describe how the sales and accounts departments work at present?"
Mrs Jones	"Departments is rather a grand title for them. As you can see we have several offices each spread over a couple of the log cabins. Why don't we walk around them and I will describe what is going on as we go?"
Analyst	"Fine so long as you do not mind me having to stop to make notes occasionally."
Mrs Jones	"OK. Well here in the main sales office the staff open the post which has already been identified as orders by the post room. They do this as a background job and stop if they get a telephone order to deal with that."
Analyst	"Is there any difference between the two types of order?"
Mrs Jones	"No. The telephone orders tend to be from private customers, and

the written ones from retail stores, but it can be the other way around. They are quite similar really. Because, our products aren't cheap most of the stores hold very small amounts of stock and they re-order when they sell an item. In the same way a lot of our private customers have been dealing us for years and slowly filling their homes with matching windows as they can afford it"

Analyst "So you tend to do small amounts of steady business with a lot of customers over many years? How is it that your sales are increasing so much then?"

Mrs Jones "That's correct. We keep both types of customer for life it seems. That is why the sales are increasing. We constantly get new customers and do not lose the old ones. At least not yet; I suppose we must start to, after thirty or forty years."

Analyst "So you have a steady stream of orders coming in. What happens to them?"

Mrs Jones "We check the customer identity and order details to make sure that they are correct. Then we type out a combined invoice, payment document, packing slip and record of order which we use to process the order. We pass the bottom copy to the accounting staff for our files and send the top three copies to the warehouse. The copy we keep is used for two purposes. Initially we add the items to a cumulative work order report which we send at the end of every week to the assembly shop. They use that to assemble the orders from the previous week from the standard components and send the finished goods to the warehouse who use the top three copies to assemble and despatch the customers orders. When .."

Analyst "Excuse me interrupting but you are losing me a little. Can we go over some of that? Why do you keep the bottom copy of that combined order?"

Mrs Jones "To make up the weekly work order report in the first instance."
Analyst "What do you do with it when you have made up those reports?"
Mrs Jones "The accounts staff hold it until the payment comes in, or fails to arrive. This copy is the only record we have if we have any queries. All the other copies go to the warehouse."

Analyst "I see. Why do the warehouse get three copies and what do they do with them all?"

Mrs Jones "They don't need three copies, one will do for them, the packing slip, but they send them all to the customer with the goods. The order is made up from the packing slip, the customer signs that when they take delivery and the driver gives it back to the warehouse staff who keep it for a few weeks in case of any queries. The customer is then left with the goods and the other two copies. One is the invoice, which tells them how much to pay, and which they keep for their own records, and the other is the payment slip which they send back to us with a cheque, so we know who is paying and what they are paying for."

Analyst	"Heavens, it sounds complicated. In what way are these four copies different?"
Mrs Jones	"Only in colour, so we can distinguish them. They are multi-part stationary. We type all the order details onto the top copy and it goes through all the others using pressure sensitive paper. The lower copies, like the packing slip, may have blanked out parts so that you cannot read the money columns, but that is all. That is because the drivers do not need to know the value of the load, just the items and who they are going to."
Analyst	"I think I have got it now. Do you have a copy of one I can take away."
Mrs Jones	"Not really. You see they are all consecutively numbered and we would wonder what had happened if an order number was missing. I can photocopy one of the old ones so long as you treat it in confidence, as it has customer information on it."
Analyst	"We assume everything you give us is confidential unless you tell us otherwise. Isn't it difficult to produce the work order report?"
Mrs Jones	"Yes, it is sheer drudgery. We have to keep track of all the items separately and then count them up. If we get behind it is easy to forget and then the assembly shop do not make up enough items for the warehouse to despatch and they have to carry them over to the next week. It doesn't happen often but we would like it not to happen at all."
Analyst	"What other problems do you have with this system?"
Mrs Jones	"Lots. The customer index is on cards which means that we are always getting in one another's way trying to get at them. The cards are filed by customer name which references the full record number and there are two copies, but it is just not enough so there is a bottle-neck there sometimes. We keep the customer records separately, which is where we file the order copy when we have used it. As you can see we have the office set up so the clerks can reach everything fairly easily but it is still quite hectic at times and no more than two people can be answering the phone at once or it gets impossible. The mail orders can be dealt with a little more leisurely, so anyone doing those keeps out of the way of someone dealing with a telephone order. It worked very well when the turnover was small, but gets fraught at times now, as you can see. As well as all that we have to keep typing in the product description on the orders, which is time consuming and tedious. We are hoping that a computer system would help us with those things."
Analyst	"So when an order comes in, the clerk looks up the customer name in the index and then gets the customer number to access the customer file in the central index. What are they looking for specifically?"
Mrs Jones	"Just the name and address, and customer discount status which depends on whether they have paid their last bill. The discount is

Analyst	based on a scale of the value of the order, before you ask. We give 2.5% discount for every full £500 of the order value, up to a limit of 40% discount. It is easy to work out. An order of £900 would get a 2.5% discount, one of £1100 would get 5%, and so on."
Analyst	"So why do you need the customer record to work out the discount?"
Mrs Jones	"They only get the discount if they have paid for all their previous orders. I know it sounds strange but it works for our customers. When they pay, by sending their payment and the payment slip back to the accounts department over in another cabin, one of the other clerks comes over with a list of payments received so that the clerks here can update the customer records. They try to do it just after lunch when there is a slack period for the telephone orders and when they have processed most of the post for that day."
Analyst	"What about non-payment?"
Mrs Jones	"Fortunately we have very little of that but it does happen. The accounts department know about bad payers because they have the order copy waiting. After four months they start chasing the customer up and we cannot give a discount to those customers. After eight months we do not accept any more orders from them at all until they have settled up. Accounts put a yellow or red coloured slip on the customer file for those conditions so that we know what to do."
Analyst	"How do you know that there is an outstanding order if the order copy goes to accounts?"
Mrs Jones	"Didn't I say? We write the order number inside the customer file and accounts cross it out when the payment comes with the invoice copy to show that it has been paid."
Analyst	"Thank you. I think I have seen everything. Normally I would attempt to sum up at this point but I see we have used up all the available time, and I know that you are busy. What I would like to do is go away now and study what we have discussed. Then I would like to come back in a few days with my assessment of what you do now and what you want from the computer system and go over it with you. Is Thursday at the same time all right?"
Mrs Jones	"Thursday is fine but the afternoon would be more convenient, say 3pm."
Analyst	"Thursday the 21st at 3pm then. Thank you very much for all your help, Mrs Jones. Goodbye for now."
Mrs Jones	"Goodbye."
End of 2nd interview

13.2.14   Task

Identify the information the analyst has gathered so far. What, if anything, is still needed? Suggest what else the analyst should have done. What additional documents should be available after the completion of the interviews?

13.2.15   Suggested result of previous task

OVERVIEW OF THE INFORMATION GATHERED SO FAR.
- Identified owner, current and proposed users.
- Overview of the owner's strategy for the company.
- Terms of reference from the owner.
- Draft budget from the owner.
- User's description of the current system procedures.
- List of problems and requirements from the user.

MISSED OUT.
- Summary of Mr. Macdonnel interview to get feedback. (Too busy chatting about holidays and then computers!)
- Examples of documents.
- Exactly who was going to use the new system.
- Whether the informal debtor reporting should be formalised.
- Numbers of: active customers, orders per day, items per order.

SHOULD HAVE.
- Got the documents during the interview so they could look at them as they were described.

13.2.16   Producing an initial problem requirements list

This unit provides practice in summarising the initial analysis to produce a catalogue of basic requirements, together with a list of problems in the current system to be resolved in the required system.

Lets assume that Mrs Jones remembered your request for copies of the current working documents and has sent you examples of the Customer Order and the Work Order Report, copies of which are given in Figure 13.3.

```
WOODEN WINDOWS COMPANY - WORK ORDER REPORT
Week ending: 28th August 1993
Product No.  Description                Quantity to make
B381         SASH                            32
B382         SASH (with panels)              21
B383         SASH (double width)              2
M121         SLIDING (study)                201
M123         SLIDING (small)                 52
M126         SLIDING (wide)                  31
M128         SLIDING                         12
R210         CASEMENT                       107
R211         CASEMENT (double)               11
R212         CASEMENT (half)                 71
R213         CASEMENT (triple)               23
R215         CASEMENT (1/2 height)           19
...   ......   ...
...   ......   ...
...   ......   ...
...   ......   ...
...   ......   ...
```

Figure 13.3 The Work Order Report

There are four identical copies on multi-part stationary as listed in Figure 13.4.

13.2.17   Task

Use the documents in Figure 13.4 to check that you fully understood the current system requirements as detailed in Chapter 2.

13.2.18   Task

Study your results from the tasks so far and use them to produce an initial list of user requirements. Separate out the items in your draft list into two types: new user requirements and problems in the current system which need to be avoided or improved. You may find it difficult to distinguish between these, but if you can it helps to clarify the situation. HINT Do not worry about order or type of item. You will almost certainly have to re-write the list so treat the first attempt as a draft and then refine it.

Additional Volume And Frequencies Information

Assume that you have contacted Mrs Jones and got the following additional information from her.

Wooden Windows Company currently:

- Has 5000 active customers.
- Gets 50 orders per day on average, by post and telephone.
- Orders have between 1 and 12 items each.
- An average of 3 items per order.

BOTTOM COPY WOODEN WINDOWS - OFFICE INVOICE COPY

3rd COPY WOODEN WINDOWS COMPANY - PACKING SLIP

2nd COPY WOODEN WINDOWS COMPANY - PAYMENT SLIP

TOP COPY WOODEN WINDOWS COMPANY - CUSTOMER ORDER
WOODEN WINDOWS COMPANY - CUSTOMER ORDER

CUSTOMER NUMBER: 1273   INVOICE NUMBER: 06391
                              DATE: February 10, 1991
CUSTOMER NAME: Robert Lilleys RE. ORDER NUMBER: 61384
CUSTOMER ADDRESS: 123 High Street,
                      Saffron Walden,
                      Suffolk, SA3 3TI
                      United Kingdom

Product No.	Description Ord.	Qty.	Unit Price	Total Price
B381	SASH	2	150.00	300.00
M128	SLIDING	2	200.00	400.00
R210	CASEMENT	1	500.00	500.00
			TOTAL AMOUNT	1200.00
			5.0% DISCOUNT	60.00
			TOTAL AMOUNT DUE	1140.00

Please retain one copy for your records and return the other copy along with your payment.

Wooden Windows Company, 'Quality without compromise'.

Figure 13.4 The four Wooden Windows customer order copies

13.2.19   *Suggested result of previous tasks*

Draft problem/requirements Catalogue

LIST OF REQUIREMENTS
1 Simplify paperwork in the sales system
2 Increase productivity of existing staff
3 Improve communication between sales and accounts
4 Ease the production of weekly Work Order Report
5 Simple system with minimum maintenance and support
6 Total cost less than £60,000.

PROBLEMS IN THE CURRENT SYSTEM

A Identifying customers (sales)
B Multiple access to records (sales)
C Keeping customer payment records up to date for discounts
   (sales and accounts)
D Keeping work order report up to date (sales)
E Typing in product descriptions (sales)
F Dealing with bad debts (accounts)
G Dealing with bad debts (sales)

13.3 Producing a 'soft' system overview of the current system

This unit provides practice in summarising the initial analysis to produce a 'soft system' overview of the current system to allow discussion with the user and clear up any issues before the formal, or 'hard methodology' tasks are started.

13.3.1 Task

Study your notes from the Unit above and produce a 'soft system' sketch, or 'Rich' picture of the current system. Try not to look at the figure below until you have totally completed your own efforts. HINT Do not worry about making it neat or professional at first. The main purpose is to fix the system procedures in your mind.

13.3.2 Task

You have to imagine that this task is a replacement for the next visit to the Wooden Windows Company to see Mrs Jones. You should go over the processing of the customer orders on your sketch as though you were explaining them, and check the details against Figure 13.5 .
   HINT If possible actually do this by persuading a friend to be 'Mrs Jones' and look at the figure below, without letting you see it, while you explain the procedures to them using your own diagram.

13.3.3 Task

Go over the people identified so far and try to associate them with the roles identified for a general system as described in Section 3.3 of Chapter 3.

Suggested answer to the above task:

- Owner   Mr. Macdonnel
- Current user(s) Mrs Jones & the sales clerks
- Proposed user(s) Mrs Jones, the sales & accounts clerks
- Other Players   Possibly the spouses of the above

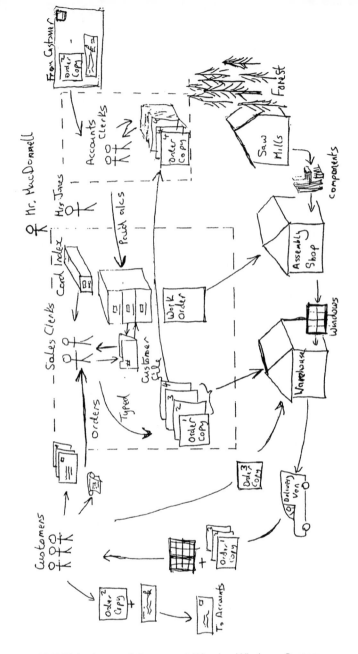

Figure 13.5 Rich picture of the current Wooden Windows System

13.4 Modelling the current system processes

13.4.1 Producing the Current Context Diagram

The relation of the system to the external entities is explored, and an initial view of the functionality of the current system produced in terms of the system inputs and outputs. A Context Diagram is produced and checked to ensure that the analysis of the system can proceed in a systematic and structured manner.

13.4.2 Task

Make a list of the information you expect this to contain. You must now translate the Rich picture into a context diagram of the current system. This is a formal diagram which clearly defines: who contributes data to the system, who receives data from the system and where the boundaries of the current system lie.

This is a little like trying to do a jigsaw puzzle without seeing the box lid. In the same way that with a jigsaw we can start by finding all the edge pieces and then trying to assemble them, in systems analysis we must first find the boundaries of the system. This is, of course, logically impossible because we cannot define the boundaries to something when we do not know what that object is. The first step is to define all the objects which we do know are **not** part of the system, but which are related to it, the external entities.

List all the objects identified at this point which are possible External Entities to the system. HINT Use the section on the Systems Approach and the section 'Data flows and external entities' in Chapter 4. The reference material suggests that the next task is to cut down all our possible External Entities to those which are actually relevant from a systems analysis viewpoint. Using the systems approach, these are the entities which either **contribute** data or **receive** data in the context of the system we are defining. You must then draw this information in the form of a diagram which can be understood by another analyst.

13.4.3 Task

Modify the list of possible External Entities you made in the above task by crossing out those which do not contribute or receive data. Which are you now left with?

The reference material states that there are two types of input and output at this point. The first type is the logical component. This consists of the raw data, which are the system inputs, and the processed data as these are our system outputs, which appear mainly in the form of print-outs or reports. There is also the physical aspect of the system, which is shown by any is real objects which transfer between the system and the external entities. If you are puzzled about the products themselves, and are wondering how to represent them in the diagram, the reference material explains that you ignore physical transfer in a logical data flow diagram. The delivery of the windows is implied by transfer of the packing slip, to show the movement of the data.

13.4.4 Task

Using the list you produced in the above task, suggest what is transferred into and out of the current system. If you are puzzled by the relationship between what you are doing in the analysis and the required physical system, the reference material explained in

Chapters 1 to 3. If you started actually coding without them, you will soon be utterly lost in the detail of the implementation. For instance, these data flows you are currently trying to identify will eventually become the data items and structures for your system inputs and outputs. If any of them are missed or wrongly defined at this point then the system will be fundamentally flawed. It is therefore vitally important that this initial stage is complete and correct before real progress can be made. The pains taken now will save considerable time, money and effort later in the Life Cycle.

13.4.5 Task

Can you explain why the staff who actually enter the data are not classed as External Entities? Many beginners think that they are a direct link between the customer and the system. Sherlock Holmes is going to be one of your role models during this initial process. Practical systems analysis seems to consist of frantic information-gathering exercises followed by intense periods of intellectual activity, much of it solitary. The analyst is expected to master the details of the system and then assemble them in their brain, just like a detective solving a mystery. When conclusions, even partial ones, have been formed, they must be written down or they will be forgotten. This is why the documentation is so essential. The thought processes should not be impaired by having to remember the detail. In this way the analyst can formulate and define for them-selves, and other people, a picture of the system.

The very act of trying to draw the diagrams will force you, the analyst, into per-forming the analysis in a correct and rigorous fashion. In addition you can show your diagrams to other analysts or to other students and lecturers to get feedback. The main problem is that this intellectual activity is lonely and difficult, similar to mathematics and hence unpopular with many students.

13.4.6 Task

You should now be able to draw a draft context diagram for the Wooden Windows Company's current system. You may be astonished that such a simple diagram should have taken so much time and effort to produce! There are two reasons for this. Firstly it is vitally important to get this diagram right. Just like the foundations of a building, the context diagram is the foundation upon which your system will be built. The over-all size and weight of a house is set by the foundations, and any mistakes only show later and are costly to correct. In exactly the same way the context diagram is used to define the boundaries of your system, and nothing may be output from it or used within it which has not been defined. Each data flow will eventually be expanded to show the exact data items which are available to the System, but for the moment we are satisfied to bundle these under a vague name.

Secondly, it is necessary to explain and discuss every step in the reasoning which got us to this point. It is like solving an algebraic equation by explaining every addi-tion, subtraction and so on. In a similar way the processes described above will soon become second nature and you will be able to produce solutions as quickly as you can do simple multiplication, without having to look up 'times tables'.

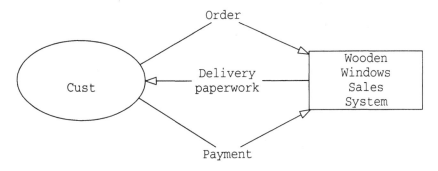

Figure 13.6 Context diagram of the current Wooden Windows System

13.4.7 Answer to the above tasks

- The customer is the only obvious External Entity. Note the use of the singular, Customer not Customers. The rationale behind this is discussed in the section on Entity Analysis in Chapter 5.
- The production department appears to be a process at the moment, but may be an external entity, depending on how we treat it in the system model.
- The Customer orders goods, takes delivery of them, and (hopefully) pays for them.
- The Staff are not included because they are only processing the data, they are not the originators of it.

To expand on the last item, the staff are considered to be a part of the system itself. There will be, for example, a manual data entry process defined at the design stage and probably performed by them. If we could get the customer to enter the data directly into the computer we would, and the staff are only there when we cannot do this. If we went over to some form of automatic telephone entry, then the staff would vanish from the diagram *without changing the concept of the system* and they are therefore only performing a function within the system. This is tricky point which catches many people out. It does not do any real harm to make this type of error but it will complicate the later analysis and design until it is noticed and corrected.

13.4.8 Producing the Level 1 Data Flow Diagram

This section describes the techniques required to fill in the details on the current system context diagram to produce the Current System Level 1 Data Flow Diagram.

By now you should have formed an impression of the relationship of the actual area you are defining to be the current system to those entities which provide data to it and receive information from it. The next step involves acquiring and documenting a clear view of the internal workings of the system in a more formal representation than was provided by the rich picture.

There are several ways of viewing a system: one concentrates on the processes and the other is based on the data items and their relations to one another. Both approaches give related and complementary views of a model of the system. You can consider these two approaches like a pair of two-dimensions which define a three-dimensional object; by concentrating on one to the exclusion of the other only a partial picture is ever built up.

In this unit we will concentrate on building the process-driven view of the system. Replacing any activity by a process box, and inventing data and resource stores to show how items are held does this. All of these are linked by data flows which follow strict rules, almost like the syntax of a programming language.

13.4.9 Task

Take a blank sheet of A4 paper and copy the context diagram onto it. Make sure you spread the external entities apart near to the edges of the paper, leaving as much room as possible for the central system processes, and leave this blank. Draw the data flows from, and to, each of the external entities only a short distance, and label them. Turn the paper sideways if you wish – many people are more comfortable with this orientation.

Using the information in the interviews in Section 13.2, and the rich picture from Section 13.3, extend the end of one of the flows into the central box and draw a process box for the first action that is performed on it. Continue tracing the flow, inventing processes and data stores as necessary, until you reach another external entity or you run out of inspiration. HINT: You are probably best starting with the 'order' flow from the customer.

Continue this procedure until each of the flows on the context diagram is connected to a process on your level 1 diagram. Carefully check that each of the objects and flows which appear on your context diagram is also on the level 1 diagram and that they are identical. Make sure that you have not broken any of the rules for drawing and exploding data flow diagrams.

Are there more than eight processes and data stores in your system diagram? If so, your diagram may be too complex, so try to combine groups of processes related to a single function into one process to simplify your diagram. A suggested 'model answer' is given in Figure 13.7. By the way, 'cust' is repeated three times and is an external entity so we are allowed to do that. We have shown production as a process for the moment but it looks suspiciously like an external entity. Do you know why?

13.4.10 Producing the Current Logical Data Flow documents

Completes the preparation of a logical model of the current system by removing any physical elements from the current data flow diagrams and by producing the supporting documentation.

As a trainee analyst you are now starting the loneliest and most academic phase of your work. After the excitement of starting the new system and meeting the users you are left alone with your notes and the results of the fact finding exercise. In this phase the analyst(s) are expected to work mainly by themselves until they have produced enough of the proposed system documentation to present to their superiors, the users or the implementation team. Whilst the users know a great deal about the current system, you as analyst have a unique overview of it based on a professional evaluation of the problems and procedures. In practice there is often also only a vague notion of how the ideal proposed system might develop from this, but this is all right as it prevents the analysis being biased by previous systems.

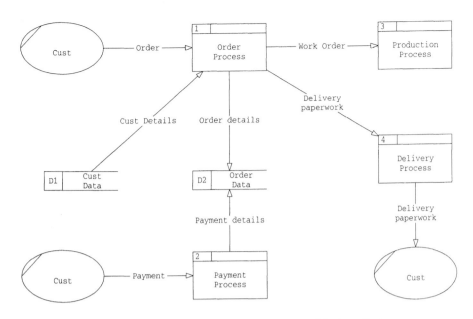

Figure 13.7 Level 1 DFD of the current Wooden Windows System.

The commonest response to this situation is for the analyst to attempt to start to design those parts of the new system for which they feel they have identified good solutions. This is an inefficient response because there are almost certainly other parts of the system requirements which are likely to very complicated, which is why a complete solution cannot be seen with the present knowledge. The analyst may irretrievably flaw the final system if they produce a partial solution based on their current understanding.

The solution to this problem is to accept that the understanding of the system is far from complete and that you, the analyst, must work through the logical modelling process until you have a thorough understanding of all the system requirements. The distinction between open-mindedness and ignorance can be a fine one at this stage!

13.4.11   Task

Assemble the set of current data flow diagrams, and if possible take photocopies of them to work on. Make sure that you keep copies of the masters to refer to as reference.

Using the level 1 current logical data flow diagram as your reference, take each of processes in turn and add them to the blank 'Function Summary Form' provided below after filling in the header section details. In the main body of the form, enter one line for each of the process boxes on the data flow diagram. For each line you should give the reference number, the function name, the type of process and any comments or notes you have. Add any tasks which this process consists of under the process name. This is the opportunity to add information which cannot fit in the box on the level 1 diagram. HINT You may want to use a pencil for your initial attempts so that you can make corrections as you go along.

Function Summary Form				
Current System		Required System		
System	Author		Date	Page of
Description				
Ref	**Function Name**		**Comments**	
Sample Function Summary Form. PISAD-FS1. Version 1				

Figure 13.8 A blank 'Function Summary Form' for the current system.

For a fully documented system there should be a Function Definition Form for each of the level one functions. The main fields on these forms are the Function Description and the Error Handling entries. You can gain experience by deciding what information you would put in each of these fields if you were completing the forms in a real system. Remember, there should be one form per level 1 process at this stage. It may help you to try this before attempting the next task.

13.4.12   Task

Use the blank 'user/function relation matrix' form provided below to relate each of the processes in your 'Function Summary Form' to the actual person or department who currently performs the task. (NOTE - This is how we resolve the 'clerks and external entities' problem referred to above).

User/Function Matrix Form												
Current System			Required System									
System	Author		Date			Page of						
User	A	B	C	D	E	F	G	H	I	J	K	
FUNCTION												
Sample User/Function Matrix Form. PISAD-UF1. Version 1.												

Figure 13.9 A blank 'User/Function Relation Matrix Form' for the current system

Function Summary Form				
Current System **yes**		Required System		
System **Wooden Windows**	Author **MJH**		Date **2/3/98**	Page **1** of **6**
Description Summary of the high-level functions performed in the current logical system				
Ref	Function Name		Comments	
1	Process order a) Identify Customer b) Create new order c) Accept order details d) Produce weekly work order		Check Customer Status Use customer discount status Use o/s orders	
2	Accounts processing a) File o/s Orders b) Process payments c) Process 4-month bad debts d) Process 8-month bad debts		Use o/s orders Use o/s orders	
3	Production			
4	Delivery a) Assemble goods & deliver b) File delivery notes			
Sample Function Summary Form. PISAD-FS1. Version 1				

Figure 13.10 The completed 'Function Summary Form' for the current system

Function Definition Form				
Current System **Yes**			Required System	
System **Wooden Windows**	Author **MJH**	Date **3/3/98**	Page **2** of **6**	
Function Name - **Process orders**		Function Ref. **1**		
Type Manual/Clerical **Manual**		Initiated By - **Customer**		

User Roles - **Sales Clerks**

Function Description

Process order

a) **Identify Customer**

b) **Create new order**

c) **Accept order details**

d) **Produce weekly work order**

Error Handling

New customer, create customer record

Check Customer Status to allocate discount status

Use o/s orders :-

None - Discount 2.5% per 500 pounds

4 month non-payment - no discount

8 month non-payment - no new orders

DFD Processes **1**

Events

I/O Descriptions

I/O Structures

Requirements Catalogue Reference - **No change to these procedures.**

Volumes **50 per day**

Related Functions

Enquiries - **Customer name search for cust-no.**

Common Processing - **N/A**

Dialogue Name - **N/A**

Service Level Requirements Service Level - **N/A**

Description	Target Value	Range	Comments

Sample Function Definition Form. PISAD-ED1. Version 1.

Figure 13.11 A completed 'Function Definition Form' for the current system

Form	Function Description	Error Handling
Page 3 of 6	Accounts processing a) File o/s Orders b) Process payments c) Process 4-month bad debts d) Process 8-month bad debts	
Page 4 of 6	Production	
Page 5 of 6	Delivery a) Assemble goods & deliver b) File delivery notes	

Figure 13.12 Contents of the remaining 3 function definition forms for the current system

User/Function Matrix Form											
Current System **YES**							Required System				
System **wooden windows** Author **MJH** Date **2/3/98**							Page **6** of **6**				
User	A	B	C	D	E	F	G	H	I	J	K
A Sales B Accounts C Production D Delivery FUNCTION											
1 Identify Customer	×										
2 Create new order	×										
3 Accept order details	×										
4 Process order	×										
5 Produce weekly work order	×										
6 File o/s Orders		×									
7 Process payments		×									
8 Process 4-month bad debts		×									
9 Process 8-month bad debts		×									
10 Production			×								
11 Assemble goods & deliver				×							
12 File delivery notes				×							
Sample User/Function Matrix Form. PISAD-UF1. Version 1.											

Figure 13.13 The completed 'User/Function Relation Matrix Form' for the current system

13.5 Analysing the current system data

13.5.1 Producing the Current Logical Data Structure

This section introduces the concept of relationships between the entities and of drawing the data items of the current system in the form of a logical data structure diagram. In this unit we will concentrate on building a data-driven view of the current system. This is best done independently of Section 13.4 so that the logical data structure diagram can be used as an independent check on the data flow diagrams, and vice versa. We will be ignoring processes completely here and concentrating on the objects defined as entities and their relationship to one another.

13.5.2 Task

Make a list of all the objects in the system which may be an entity. HINT See the corresponding section in Chapter 5.

Choose the first entity on your list and associate it to each of the other entities in turn. Is there a relationship between any two of the entities? If so what is the degree of that relationship? Draw out each of the binary relationships as you discover them. Take care to get the direction and style of the arrows correct. Do not overlook the possibility of an entity having a relationship with itself.

Continue the above procedure considering each of the entities on your list, and relating it to those below it, until you have compared each entity with every other entity. You should now have a set of binary relationships.

Are any of your relationships many-to-many? If so take each of the pairs in turn and try to find a 'revealed' relationship which converts each of them to two one-to-many relationships.

Consolidate the set of relationships you have drawn from the above tasks into one composite diagram. It may take you several attempts to produce a neat final version so only sketch each attempt. Try to make the one-to-many relationships point down on the paper if you can.

Remove from your diagram any redundant relationships. Let us say we have three entities A, B and C. If there is a relationship between A and B, B and C, and A and C then the latter is redundant. You cannot remove the first two relationships but the last one, A to C, is implied by the other two.

Add the optionality and contingency to each of your relationships on the draft diagram. You can now compare your results with the following suggested 'model answer'.

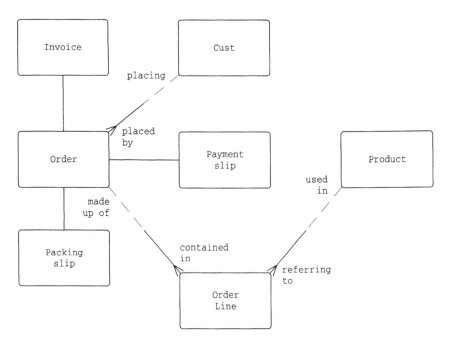

Figure 13.14 A completed Logical Data Structure diagram for the current system

13.6 Assembling a document proposing how to proceed

Simulates the production of the first piece of formal system documentation, the initial proposal, or feasibility, report. By this point in the analysis you should have completely examined the current system in outline, and formed an assessment of the basic user requirements.

13.6.1 Producing the Initial Proposal (Feasibility) Report

Before proceeding you should consolidate the work that you have done so far and present it formally to your superiors and the user to seek approval to proceed with the project. How much work you have to present will depend very much upon the size of the project and the formality of the structure or methodology within which you are working.

As a minimum, where it is a small system probably involving only yourself and the owner of the current system, you can deliver a simple system proposal. For a large or complicated system you will have essentially the same products but, as they will be correspondingly more complex, you will have probably had to do considerably more work to reach the same point. The amount and complexity of the documentation, together with the supporting analysis will reflect this. In these cases the work you present is usually referred to as a feasibility report, as it is no simple matter to decide if the requirements are indeed achievable within the terms of reference and budget. In addition this report may have to go before committees and consultants who want to review the fact-finding and analysis, and there must be enough detail to allow them to do so.

The content is roughly the same in both cases, but the quantity can vary enormously. For a simple proposal you may have only ten or twelve pages, but a feasibility report can run to many hundreds of pages. Needless to say the amount of care taken should be the same. However, the effort goes up more than linearly with the complexity.

13.6.2 Task

Write a clear and concise definition of what you believe the user wishes to achieve in developing the proposed system. This should be as short as possible, no more than three sentences at most. It must be written in clear non-technical terms which can be understood by the user. At the same time it should be precise and unambiguous enough to be used, if necessary, to settle legal disputes as to the fitness of purpose of the delivered system by comparison of actual performance and facilities against the statement.

Assemble a definitive description of the current system consisting of the analysis products of the previous units. Produce them in a report format with a contents list and suitable sub-headings.

Specifically these should include:

- A Diagram of the current system, either the level 1 Data Flow Diagram, the Rich picture or both if they complement one another.
- An explanation of the processes shown in the diagram with a short statement of who performs which task and what it involves.
- Identification of the reports (outputs from the system) with a brief informal description of their purpose and destination.

13.6.3 Task

Provide a section in report format describing your understanding of the user requirements of the proposed system without going into technical detail.

This should include:

- A description of the changes, or lack of them, to the present organisational structure.
- The identification of any new reports.
- The identification of new tasks.
- A statement of the likely range of costs of equipment required to implement the system.
- Possible software costs required to implement the system.
- An operational overview of the proposed system if this can be made at this time.
- An estimate of the total timescales and costs.

Note that most of these will be at best educated guesses or estimates at this stage, but you should have a feeling for the overall scale of the project and attempt to pass it on to the user. Some analysts use a rule of 'form your best estimate and double it' to ensure that their projects come in under budget.

13.6.4 Task

Collect all the products of task in this section into a folder labelled 'System Proposal'. No 'model answer' is given for this Section as the detail is not required to complete the work covered by this book, and the mass of documentation would detract us from learning the generic skills. However, most of the specialist documents are the products shown in the preceding figures.

13.7 A first attempt at modelling the required system processes

This section follows the procedures to make a first attempt at the detailed analysis of the processing for the required system. As previously described, current structured methodology practice is to draw the whole data flow view from a set of diagrams which form the basis of a data flow model, rather than one cluttered diagram. When completing Section 13.4 above, you were advised to consolidate groups of processes into one high-level process to simplify the level 1 diagram. The procedure here is to put that detail back, but this time including the user requirements to produce a first pass at the required system.

13.7.1 Task

Go back to the User/Function Relation Matrix Form completed in Section 13.4 and edit it by entering the identifier of each of the process boxes on the lowest level data flow diagrams in one of the lines (1-12) on the form. These are a first guess at the functions to be performed by the proposed system. You need not enter any of the processes on the higher level diagrams unless they have no 'explosions' as these are only present to give the structure of the system. When you have entered all of the process identifiers, you should complete the form by also entering the identity of the users of the system along the top of the form. You can now mark the boxes where the two coincide with an 'x' if it is a manual process in the required system, and a 'C' if it is to be computerised. For example, if there is a process 'validate cust id' (Process Id 1.1) in line 1 and you know it is performed on the proposed computer system by a 'sales clerk', as identified in column A, then an 'C' should be entered in the top left hand box. Note that this time, we are familiar with the technique, we have added suggested process identifiers 1.1, 1.2, etc. in step to help us draw the DFDs. These are bundled together related to the person who performs the task, i.e. all the processes by the sales clerks are numbered '1.?'. Compare your results with the suggested answer given below.

User/Function Matrix Form											
Current System	Required System **YES**										
System **wooden windows** Author **MJH**	Date **2/3/98** Page **6** of **6**										
User	A	B	C	D	E	F	G	H	I	J	K
A Sales B Accounts C Production D Delivery FUNCTION											
1.1 Identify Customer	C										
1.2 Create new order	C										
1.3 Accept order details	C										
1.4 Process order	C										
1.5 Produce weekly work order	C										
2.1 File o/s Orders		×									
2.2 Process payments		C									
2.3 Process 4-month bad debts		C									
2.4 Process 8-month bad debts		C									
3 Production			×								
4.1 Assemble goods & deliver				C							
4.2 File delivery notes				C							
Sample User/Function Matrix Form. PISAD-UF1. Version 1.											

Figure 13.15 The initial 'User/Function Relation Matrix Form' for the required system

We can now be fairly certain that the production process should be treated as an external entity, as it clearly is a physical activity and does not seem to process any data in the required system. Using this information we can re-draw the context diagram as a first attempt at the required system.

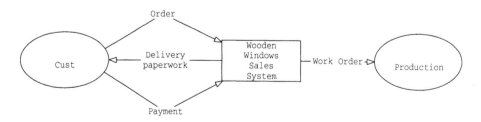

Figure 13.16 The first attempt at the required system context diagram

13.7.2 Task

Using the context diagram shown above as a reference, re-draw the external entities near to the edge of a new blank page. Using the information in the interviews in Section 13.2, and the rich picture from Section 13.3, extend the end of one of the flows and draw a process box for the first procedure that is performed on it. Continue tracing the flow, inventing processes and data stores as necessary, until reaches another object external to the exploded process or you run out of inspiration. In this way you should be able to make a first attempt at the required system Level 1 DFD. HINT, start with the 'order' flow from the customer. Compare your result to the suggested model answer shown in Figure 13.17.

We can now make an attempt at updating the Function Summary Form from the Section 13.4 reflecting this new information. All that seems required at the moment is to remove the production process, Function 3, and hence re-number the old Function 4 as Function 3 to avoid having any gaps in the numbering of the required system .

For a fully documented system, the analyst should now complete a Function Definition form for each of the functions in the User/Function Relation Matrix Form. This can be a tedious process but it is essential in practice to explain the analyst's understanding of the proposed system to other professionals. However boring it may be to write the details down, it is much worse to keep explaining them to the programming team and then to find that they misheard or misunderstood. For completeness a description of this process is given below, together with sample products to indicate how these would appear, but whether you attempt it yourself will depend upon how much practice you want to get at completing the full documentation.

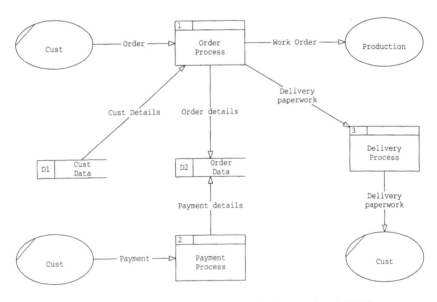

Figure 13.17 The first attempt at the required system Level 1 DFD

Function Summary Form				
Current System		Required System **yes**		
System **Wooden Windows**	Author **MJH**		Date **2/3/98**	Page **1** of **6**

Description Summary of the high-level functions performed in the current logical system

Ref	Function Name	Comments
1	Process order a) Identify Customer b) Create new order c) Accept order details d) Process order d) Produce weekly work order	Check Customer Status Use customer discount status Use o/s orders
2	Accounts processing a) File o/s Orders b) Process payments c) Process 4-month bad debts d) Process 8-month bad debts	 Use o/s orders Use o/s orders
3	Delivery a) Assemble goods & deliver b) File delivery notes	

Sample Function Summary Form. PISAD-FS1. Version 1

Figure 13.18 The completed 'Function Summary Form' for the required system

To complete these forms, first enter all the header information and put the name of the corresponding process in the Function Name box, and the line number from the matrix form in the Function ID box. The letter identifying the users of the function can be read from the previous form and entered as A, B etc. as required.

You will now have to provide a short but accurate description of the function in the Function Description box. Try to be concise whilst including all the relevant detail. There is quite an art to this so do not be discouraged if you find it difficult at first. Any conditions which cause the function to be abandoned or re-started can be entered in the Error Handling box.

The Data Flow Diagram identifier (e.g., 1, 2, 3) and the label, usually a shortened form of the Process Name, should now be entered into the DFD Processes box. The next three boxes can be skipped for the moment as the information required to complete them is not available at this point. The references to the Requirements Catalogue which this function satisfies is entered next if they are available. The remaining entries are concerned with more advanced aspects of design which are outside the scope of this book, but which appear on the sample form so that you will recognise them when you encounter them in practice.

Function Definition Form			
Current System	Required System **Yes**		
System **Wooden Windows**	Author **MJH**	Date **3/3/98**	Page **2** of **5**
Function Name - **Process orders**	Function Ref. **1**		
Type **Computerised**	Initiated By - **Customer**		
User Roles - **Sales Clerks**			
Function Description **Process order** **a) Identify Customer** **b) Create new order** **c) Accept order details** **d) Process order** **e) Produce weekly work order**			
Error Handling **New customer, create customer record** **Check Customer Status to allocate discount status** **Use o/s orders :-** **None - Discount 2.5% per 500 pounds** **4 month non-payment - no discount** **8 month non-payment - no new orders**			
DFD Processes **1**			
Events			
I/O Descriptions			
I/O Structures			
Requirements Catalogue Reference - **No change to these procedures.**			
Volumes **50 per day**			
Related Functions			
Enquiries - **Customer name search for cust-no.**			
Common Processing - **N/A**			
Dialogue Name - **N/A**			
Service Level Requirements Service Level - **N/A**			
Description	Target Value	Range	Comments
Sample Function Definition Form. PISAD-ED1. Version 1.			

Figure 13.19 A completed 'Function Definition Form' for the current system

The main fields for the remaining two forms are shown below for completeness.

Form	Function Description	Error Handling
Page 3 of 5	Accounts processing a) File o/s Orders b) Process payments c) Process 4-month bad debts d) Process 8-month bad debts	
Page 4 of 5	Delivery a) Assemble goods & deliver b) File delivery notes	

Figure 13.20 Contents of the remaining 2 function definition forms for the required system

13.7.3 Task

We now have to make an attempt at exploding the level 1 process boxes into level 2 DFDs. Take a blank sheet of A4 paper and copy onto it the first process from the level 1 data flow diagram, produced in the previous unit as a large central box. Spread the objects directly connected to the process apart near to the edges of the paper, leaving as much room as possible for the central system box, and leave this blank for the moment. Draw the data flows from and to each of the other objects only as far as the edges of the box and label them. Turn the paper sideways if you wish, many people are more comfortable with this orientation.

Using the information in the interviews in Unit 13.2, and the Rich picture from Unit 13.3, extend the end of one of the flows into the central box and draw a process box for the first function that is performed on it. Continue tracing the flow, inventing processes and data stores as necessary, until the flow leaves the process and reaches another object external to the exploded process or you run out of inspiration. HINT - Start with the 'order' flow from the customer.

Continue this procedure for each until each of the flows going into or out of the process are correct. Carefully check that each of the objects and flows which appear on your level 1 diagram is also on the exploded (level 2) diagram and that they are identical. Make sure that you have not broken any of the rules for drawing and exploding data flow diagrams.

Are there more than eight objects in your system box? If so your diagram is too complex. Combine groups of objects into processes to simplify your diagram. Label the completed box in exactly the same way as the process you derived it from. Label the new lower level processes uniquely starting each label with the reference number of the original parent. For example if you are filling in the detail on process 3 then each new process should be: 3.1, 3.2 and so on. Also label the data stores that you are using but make them unique or lower level decomposition of existing data stores.

Repeat the above tasks for each process box on the level 1 data flow diagram. You should now have a complete set of level 2 data flow diagrams which you can compare with the suggested model answers given in Figure 13.21.

Finally we can edit the first attempt at the user/function relation matrix form to reflect these changes. It is attention to these kind of small details that ensures that the final system specification is unambiguous and hence serves it purpose for the implementation team.

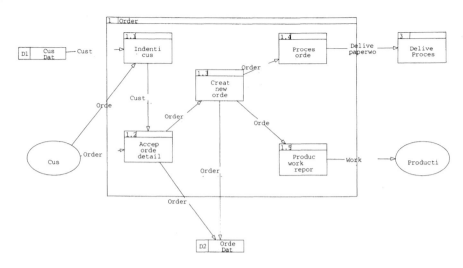

Figure 13.21 The first attempt at the required exploded process 1 from the Level 1 DFD

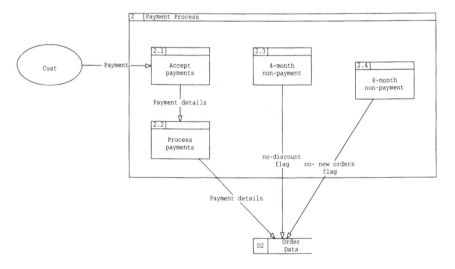

Figure 13.22 The first attempt at the required exploded process 2 from the Level 1 DFD

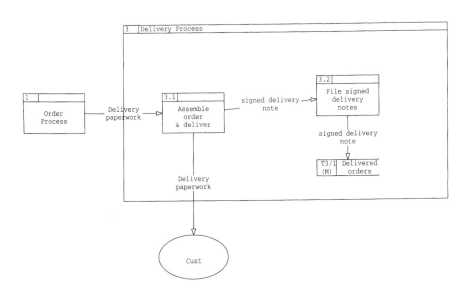

Figure 13.23 The first attempt at the required exploded process 3 from the Level 1 DFD

User/Function Matrix Form											
Current System				Required System **YES**							
System **wooden windows** Author **MJH**				Date **2/3/98** Page **5** of **5**							
User A Sales B Accounts C Production D Delivery	A	B	C	D	E	F	G	H	I	J	K
FUNCTION											
1.1 Identify Customer	C										
1.2 Create new order	C										
1.3 Accept order details	C										
1.4 Process order	C										
1.5 Produce weekly work order	C										
2.1 Accept Payments		X									
2.2 Process payments		C									
2.3 Process 4-month non-payment		C									
2.4 Process 8-month non-payment		C									
3.1 Assemble orders & deliver				C							
3.2 File signed delivery notes				C							
Sample User/Function Matrix Form. PISAD-UF1. Version 1.											

Figure 13.24 'User/Function Relation Matrix Form' edited for the required system

13.8 Suggesting various business options

13.8.1 Producing the Business Systems Options

In this unit you assemble a complete copy of the relevant documentation produced to date in a form suitable for presentation to the user(s), in order to lay out the various strategic options which you have identified from your analysis.

Your object in doing this is to involve the user in the process of making a decision as to how to proceed, and to get their agreement to the consequences of that decision. It is important that you present all of the available options in such a way that the user is fully aware of the choices they are faced with, the pros and cons of each option and the fact that, whilst you may advise them on these topics, the ultimate decision must be come from them. You may find this difficult in practice as this will involve management and people skills, rather than technical ability. However, the people side of this process can be eased by following an efficient administrative procedure as outlined below.

13.8.2 Task

Using the rich picture, the logical data structure and the data flow diagrams for the required system, draw a variety of system boundaries which could encompass a new system. You may find it helpful to take a photocopy of one diagram to work on, and then depict the different proposed system boundaries by drawing 'lasso-lines' on it in different colours.

13.8.3 Task

For <u>each</u> of the above try to imagine the effect on the operational running of the business. You are specifically interested in:

- Whether automating or changing this area or areas will address any of the problems raised in the user needs/requirements list.
- What the cost in terms of extra staff, equipment and software will be.
- What the savings in terms of the above will be.

Remember that you are generating business options, so avoid the temptation to start providing details of what specific equipment you may need. This is a fine line to follow, as you must have 'ball park' figures in mind for the total cost. If you find yourself getting bogged down remember that this level of option is concerned with WHAT not HOW.

13.8.4 Task

Cut down your options to three or four sensible business-like ones. If you only started out with that many, make sure that you considered all the possibilities. You either have a very simple organisational situation, or you are not being as open minded as this situation demands.

The trick here is to include every possible approach and then discard the illogical or intermediate ones. You should now be left with two or three options which involve modifications to various functions, or combinations of functions, within the organisation. Each of these options should then be expanded to describe the **tactical** changes required to each existing business function. This must include clerical and administrative procedures, as well as the training needs for the computing aspects of the option.

You should go over the advantages and disadvantages very carefully trying to give as full a picture as possible of how much the user must pay and what they will gain by each of the options. It is quite reasonable to include a non-computerisation or minimal computerisation option based on, say, a new approach to the manual procedures which you have identified from your analysis.

13.8.5 Task

Order the chosen options from the previous section in order of increasing effect on the organisation. In practical terms this usually also means increasing cost and benefit. If any option is more costly or complex than a prior one, without additional benefits you should not include it. Consider the latter situation carefully. Is it just that you have not spelt out the benefits properly?

Finally you should prepare, for each of the options, a professional-standard business report. This report should also include a contents list and an executive summary. You should now be in a position to visit the Wooden Windows offices and present your options to the staff of the company. Who would you expect to attend and why? Would you take anyone from your own company with you?

13.8.6 Task

If at all possible you should actually present the options to a panel of 'users' who have been carefully chosen to role play a sympathetic but critical audience. Try to assemble a group of people to role play the users that you have identified in Section 13.2 above. If you are following a course, the lecturers will probably make this presentation a major assessment element and will play the parts themselves. If you are studying alone, try to persuade other students or friends to play the part of a user panel. Either way you will probably find the experience of presenting your options the most painful ordeal in your studies to date. Console yourself with the knowledge that it will be a very valuable experience and that your future performance will be improved because of it. It is much better to gain presentation skills now, rather than when your real job is on the line.

13.8.7 Task

If you performed the previous task correctly you should have identified a single acceptable approach from your suggested options. You should now add as much detail as possible, including clean copies of your analysis products and assemble this option as a formal proposal to the user or client. As in Section 13.6, we will assume that there is only one option available to us in order to avoid deflecting this text from the main purpose of covering the specialist analysis and design skills.

13.9.1 Normalising the data into tables

Once a Business Option is agreed, the input and output documents can be identified from the context diagram, and they can be 'normalised' into a set of tables which have the property of being in third normal form. This is an efficient way of holding data and removes redundant or duplicated items.

13.9.2 Task

Identify the Input/Output documents defined in the previous sections which have more than one data item. Take the first of these, and copy all the data items to the first column, labelled 'UN-NF', onto a blank Relational Data Analysis Form (now you are familiar with the layout, normal lined paper can be used). Underline the items which make up the key to this single group of data items, and make sure that any repeating groups are clearly shown by enclosing them in curly brackets.

13.9.3 Task

Turn the first, unnormalised, column into 'first normal form' by copying forward all of the data items except those in repeating groups to the next column along, labelled '1NF'. At the same time you should put any repeating groups into another, separate, group of data items in that same column. If there are no repeating groups, your first column is already in 'first normal form' so draw an arrow through the 1NF column to the 2NF column to indicate that you have considered the situation and are carrying these groups forward.

When you have completed this process, you should have in the second column a set of data items corresponding to the original column one, minus any repeating items, together in one group. In addition there should be a set of data items for each of the repeating groups you removed. For example if you start with **one** repeating group, the most common situation, you should have **two** groups of items separated by a few blank lines in column two.

Underline the key data items in each of the first normal form groups. The original main items should have the same key. However, the set made out of the repeating data items may need additional items to be classified as keys.

13.9.4 Task

Look at each of the groups of data items in turn which are in first normal form, either from the UN-NF column or the 1NF column, and look to see if they have more than one data item in the key. If they do not, that group of data items is already in second normal form, so draw an arrow through the 2NF column alongside that group of data items to the 3NF column, and proceed to the next group.

If there is more than one data item in the key, look at each of the non-key data items in turn. These will depend upon the whole of the key or part of the key. For example, if there are two data items in the key, any non-key data item could depend upon either of the two key items or both. (If it depends upon neither ignore it as it will be dealt with in the next task.)

For any set of data items that only depend upon part of the key, create a new group of data items in the 2NF column containing that partial key and the data items which depend upon it. Do this by removing these data item from the original group into the new group of data items. You must leave the partial key in the original group, and duplicate it in the new set of items. Continue this process for each non-key data item in the group, and perform the same process on each group of data items. Remember that the new group is shown as a separate list within the 2NF column. When you have considered all of the data items and processed them, then copy forward the remaining portion of the original group which was in first normal form to the 2NF column. All the new groups are now in second normal form and you can proceed to the next task.

13.9.5 Task

You must now examine all of the groups of data items which are in second normal form and remove any item or items which are not dependant on the key to a new group. This involves considering each of the non-key items in each list in turn and asking yourself if it depends upon the 'whole key and nothing but the key'. There are two circumstances where you need to take action.

The first case is where an item depends upon another non-key item. In this case you write them as another list of data items in the 3NF column, exactly as in the previous tasks. Usually the second data item will become the key of the new group, but by this stage the groups are often very small and the choice of key can vary depending on uniqueness. Any new or modified groups should be entered in column four of the normalisation form under the heading '3NF'. Any groups you do not modify must be in third normal form and can be indicated as such by drawing an arrow through the 3NF column.

The second case is where an item is calculated from the values of another group of data items, or only exists because of its context, such as the time of printing. You need not hold such 'transitive' values and they can simply be removed from your lists. Do not worry that they have disappeared from the system, as the original data structure you were working on still exists and will show them. What we are concerned with at the moment is to try to form an efficient model holding all of the data for the new system.

Finally you must give each of the groups of data items which are in third normal form a unique table name. This should be entered in the last column on the form in block capitals. If you have difficulty in naming the tables look at the key items and use these as a basis for the name.

13.9.6 Task

You must repeat the above process for each of the documents identified in the fact-finding exercise. Use a separate form to normalise each flow. Carefully follow through each of the above tasks trying to be as accurate as possible. Use pencil rather than ink to allow yourself to correct errors without spoiling the rest of the work. This is one of the most difficult intellectual jobs in analysis, but it is crucial for the successful outcome of the new system.

Do not worry if you seem to be creating the same list as you did in a previous RDA exercise. Just note the point and try to give it the same name, when you come to it, as you did in the previous task.

When you have completed all your tasks in this unit, compare your results with the model answers given below. If you find a discrepancy, go back immediately to that stage in your own work and repeat the process you did, correcting the mistake and re-working the rest of the normalisation process through to the end. Do not just copy the answers, as in the long run you will learn nothing by doing that.

Sample Relational Data Analysis - Customer Order (copied from Figure 13.4)

UN-NF	1NF	2NF	3NF	TABLE NAME
Customer Number	Customer Number	)	Order Number	ORDER
Customer Name	Customer Name	)	Customer Number	
Customer Address	Customer Address	)--------->	Date	
Order Number	Order Number	)	Invoice No.	
Date	Date	)		
Invoice No.	Invoice No.		Customer Number	CUSTOMER
{Product No	Total Amount		Customer Name	
Description	Discount		Customer Address	
Quantity Ordered	Total Amount Due			
Unit Price			Order Number	ORDER LINE
Total Price}			Product No	
Total Amount	Order Number	Order Number	Quantity Ordered	
Discount	Product No	Product No		
Total Amount Due	Description	Quantity Ordered	Product No	PRODUCT
	Quantity Ordered	Total Price	Description	
	Unit Price		Unit Price	
	Total Price	Product No		
		Description		
		Unit Price		

Figure 13.25 The RDA form normalising the Customer Order

There is no need to normalise the other documents as they are exact copies of the order. Note that 'order no.' was chosen as the key as the document is an order!

UN-NF	1NF	2NF	3NF	TABLE	NAME
Week Ending	Week Ending		Week Ending		(1)
{Product No.}					
{Description}	Week Ending				
{Quantity Ordered}	Product No.	Product No.	Product No.	Product No.	PRODUCT
	Description	Description	Description	Description	
	Quantity Ordered				
		Week Ending	Week Ending	Week Ending	W/O LINE
		Product No.	Product No.	Product No.	
		Quantity Ordered	Quantity Ordered	Quantity Ordered	

Figure 13.26 The RDA form showing the normalisation of the Work Order (from Figure 13.3)

(1)   WEEK ENDING is a key only entity, and is a transient value so it should be removed, even though it is also part of the key of the following relation.

13.10 Producing a LDM of the required system

13.10.1   Rationalising the normalised tables

Having normalised the Input/Output documents into separate sets of third normal form tables you must now consolidate them into one 'super-group' of tables which together defines all of the data items in the required system.

13.10.2   Task

Gather together the results of the previous unit and lay out the forms so that you can see all of them at once if possible. Take the form with the largest number of tables and copy the Table Name from the biggest table, and all of the data items that go with it, onto a large sheet of paper. Start in the top left hand corner and make sure that you copy the items accurately. The table name should be in block capitals and the key items should be underlined. Draw a light pencil line through the table and items which you have copied on the original form.

13.10.3   Task

Next go through all of the other forms looking for tables which have an identical key to the one you have copied onto the new sheet. Ignore the number or size of the data items other than those in the key. Whenever you find such a table, whether it has the same name or not, carefully merge the data items together into the table you copied over in the previous task. Typically, most of the items will be identical. What you are looking for are items in the table you have just identified, with the same keys, but which are not in the first table. If you find any items you should add them to the list of data items on the new sheet of paper. They will, of course, be non-key items **because you would not be performing the process if the keys were not identical**.

13.10.4 Task

Draw a line through the second table you found and note the table name if it is different from the first table. Continue this process with every one of the RDA forms looking for any other tables with exactly the same key as the first table you copied. If, whilst doing this, you find two tables with identical keys on the same RDA form, then you are in trouble because that means you did not do your normalisation correctly in Unit 13.9.

When you have looked at every table, and merged any relevant ones with the first table, consider any multiple table names you have noted. Now is your opportunity to give the consolidated table the most appropriate name from those available to you. If you did a good job originally just stick with that name.

13.10.5 Task

Now for the bad news! It is just possible that you broke some of the rules of normalisation in consolidating your table. Quickly check over the tasks in previous unit again on the new consolidated table. If it is still in third normal form everything is fine. Otherwise you must find out why it is not, normalise the new table and break it into two or more tables which are in third normal form. Strictly speaking this should never happen, but if you made any errors previously this is when they will show up and you must correct them now.

13.10.6 Task

When you have dealt with the most complex table as described above, choose the next most complex on the first RDA form and repeat the above tasks on this table. The job should get progressively easier as you merge more and more tables. This is because you need not consider any that you have already dealt with. A lot of the time the keys and the tables will be unique. You have finished when you have copied or merged every table on the set of RDA forms onto the new sheet or sheet(s) of paper.

As a final check, make sure that all of the names and key items on the tables are different. Watch out particularly for very similar table and data item names: they will cause confusion all the way through implementation so correct them now, if necessary, by giving them obviously different names.

13.10.7 Task

When you have done all of the above tasks, you should check your results against the model answer given below. As previously stop and work through how you arrived at any discrepancies to make sure that you are sure you understand the procedures.

There are often several correct choices for key items and order, and always many ways to name the tables. If your results only differ in those details do not be concerned. If they don't either you peeked at the model answer, or you are a natural at this topic, as even the same analyst will often differ in their choice of names on different occasions. In order to avoid confusion in the following units, however, you should change your solution to match the model answer. (I hope you are still using pencil!)

Relations from RDA forms

From WORK ORDER

PRODUCT
Product No.
Description

W/O LINE
Week Ending
Product No.
Quantity Ordered

From CUSTOMER ORDER

ORDER
Order Number
Customer Number
Date
Invoice No.

CUSTOMER
Customer Number
Customer Name
Customer Address

ORDER LINE
Order Number
Product No
Quantity Ordered

PRODUCT
Product No
Description
Unit Price

1) As there is a 1:1 relationship between Order and Invoice in the proposed system, one of them is redundant. We will adopt the approach of replacing Invoice Number by Order number, as the ORDER is the fundamental relation as far as the user is concerned. Remember though, no matter how familiar you become with certain relations, it is the user's priorities which should decide which you keep if one is redundant!

2) W/O LINE looks like subset of ORDER LINE with the addition of the transitory element 'Week Ending' in the key. However, the attribute 'Quantity Ordered' in this relation is the sum of all the 'Quantity Ordered' attributes in the orders in the seven days preceding the date 'Week Ending'. This is an example of using the same name to represent two attributes. The whole relation is transitory and can be physically printed at any time by selecting orders placed within any seven day period. Therefore we do not need to hold the work order in a data store, or even in the data model, something our common sense may have already told us but which has now been confirmed by the modelling process.

THE CONSOLIDATED LIST OF RELATIONS.

ORDER
Order Number
Customer Number
Date

PRODUCT
Product No.
Description
Unit Price

ORDER LINE
Order Number
Product No
Quantity Ordered

CUSTOMER
Customer Number
Customer Name
Customer Address

13.10.8   Producing a LDM from the required RDA

Once you have a full set of consolidated normalised tables, it is possible to follow a fairly mechanical set of procedures to produce a Logical Data Structure Diagram. This can then be compared to the original diagram to check both itself and the normalisation steps performed previously.

Task

Firstly you require a large sheet of paper onto which you copy the normalised relations or tables produced in Section 13.9 as Entities. In order to do this you must create a box for each relation as in a 'logical data structure' entity. A quick glance at the required logical data structure in order to see the position of entity on the diagram can help enormously at this point, but put it carefully out of sight for the rest of this unit.

Having drawn each of the boxes, label them with name of the table to which they refer, and copy into each box all of that entity's key data items and any also data items in that table which are keys for other entities (foreign keys). The primary keys should be underlined.

Next you must remove any ambiguities from the diagram by checking that all of the names are correct and that there are no entities with identical primary keys. If any instances do occur then you have either copied the normalised tables incorrectly as you converted them to entities, or your rationalisation above was incorrect. In either case you must return to the source of the error and correct it before proceeding.

Task

You must next identify the Foreign Keys within the entities by marking them with an '*' to show their purpose. Some of the foreign keys will be part of the primary keys and hence already underlined, but they should also be marked as described. If necessary go back though the tables at this point to make sure that you have not missed any items which appear as foreign keys.

The next step is create 'working entities' where necessary. You should examine all of the existing entities which have compound keys and ensure that somewhere on your diagram is an entity which has each element of that key as its sole key. Whenever you find that there is not such an entity you must create one, and at the same time you can join it to the original entity with the compound key by a one-to-many relationship.

Whenever you create a working entity check all of the non-key items in the original tables to see if the key of the new entity occurs as a data item within any of them. If it does then you must copy that item into the corresponding entity and mark it as a foreign key if you have not previously done so.

Task

Examine each of the entities and identify those which have composite keys. If the whole key for these entities is composite, check and prepare the keys by marking the relevant higher level elements as foreign keys. You may then join this entity to the entity with that data item as a primary key by a one-to-many relationship. Take care not to treat this kind of entity as if it is a compound key relation in the next tasks.

You can continue this process at this point by making <u>any</u> other relations with foreign keys details of the entity with that data item as its total primary key by joining it to them by a one-to-many relationship.

Check each entity which has a compound key. If the key has two elements in it, make that entity a detail of both the entities which have the elements as their simple primary keys by joining it to them by two one-to-many relationships.

If the entity with a compound key has a three, or more, element key, then try to identify an entity which has all the elements but one as its primary key and join them by a one-to-many relationship. Find an entity with the remaining element as its simple primary and join them by a one-to-many relationship. Otherwise you will have to join it to all of the relations with the relevant simple primary keys.

Task

You must now tidy up the final model. You do this as a final check. You should go through the model, checking that you have added any recursive relationships (ones in which a data item is a foreign key which refers to itself). After adding the correct relationships, you can make these optional, as recursive relationships must always be of this type.

If you have any tables which only contain data items which are keys, then you can probably remove that table from the model and join the relationship ends left by the removal. Such tables usually represent many-to-many relationships, but these should be resolved eventually by finding 'revealed relationships' to simplify them, as described in the section on Logical Data Structures in Chapter 5.

Finally compare the Logical Data Structure Diagram you have just generated with the original Logical Data Structure Diagram from Unit 13.5. Check on your new diagram that each of the entities is joined to at least one other entity by a relationship, and that the ends of these describe what you intend. It is very easy to get the 'many' at the wrong end if you are not quite sure of what you are doing.

Remember that you will normally only have the <u>order</u> of the relationships, except recursive relationships, as you do not have enough information to decide on the optionality of relationship by this method. Otherwise your diagrams should be identical.

Marking the foreign keys to build the new LDM diagram gives:

CUSTOMER
<u>Customer Number</u>

ORDER   PRODUCT
<u>Order Number</u>   <u>Product No.</u>
Customer Number *   Description
Date   Unit Price

ORDER LINE
Order Number *
Product No *

Comparison with the LDS generated previously shows that the entities Invoice and Packing Slip, and Payment Slip need not exist in their own right. We could deduce this from the fact that they all have a mandatory 1:1 relationship with, and hence depend for their existence on, a relationship with an Order. Apart from this the two LDSs agree.

In fact what we have generated is a model for the required <u>physical</u> data structure. If we had left in those transitory items which we removed, and we had normalised the duplicated paperwork without stating that it was redundant, we would have produced exactly the same LDS. Whilst this is strictly speaking what we should have done, it can be reassuring to allow some reality into the modelling process occasionally.

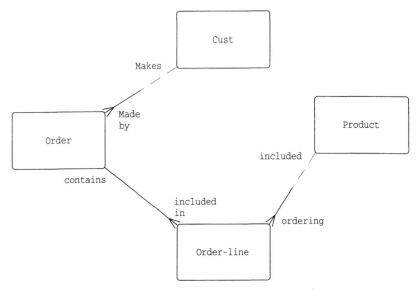

Figure 13.27

13.11 Using the Entity Life History events to check the DFM

You must now define the time element in your required Logical Data Structure as described in Chapter 11. You should therefore be familiar with their use having worked through that section, but care is needed because the Entity Life Histories are needed to provide a final independent check on the correctness of the LDS and DFM.

13.11.1 Task
The first step is to gather together all of the Entities which you have identified within

the required system. You can get this list by examining the required Logical Data Structure you produced previously. Each of the boxes on the diagram represents a required Entity. You also need a list of 'life events' which you have identified from the fact finding. Typically these will involve the creation, deletion or modification of the entities. If you cannot think of the life events in isolation try 'reverse engineering' them at this point by asking for each entity, 'What event causes it to be created?', and so on. When you have completed the previous task as set of lists produce a neatly documented form by filling in the entity/event matrix given below. Start by entering the Entity names. Turn the paper sideways and enter the events in the column headers. labelled A, B, to K.

Event-Entity Matrix Form											
Current System							Required System **Yes**				
System **Wooden Windows** Author **MJH** Date **20/12/98**							Page of				
ENTITY Function	A	B	C	D	E	F	G	H	I	J	K

13.11.2   Task

Next, identify the process that deals with each of the events which you have identified. It is probably easier to work from the Event/Entity Matrix Form, but keep the DFDs to hand in case you need to refer to them.

Take each event in turn and find the process or processes that deal with that event for each entity it affects. If you structured your DFDs efficiently then you should be able to find a single process at one level, even if it has an explosion diagram related to it, which deals with that event for a given entity. Draw a light pencil line through the lowest-level process on the DFD and also through the entry on the matrix to which it refers, to show that you have dealt with both of them.

Record the effect that each event has on an entity by noting a 'C' for creation, a 'D' for deletion and an 'M' for modification in each column on the row opposite the required Entity name. Occasionally an event may both create and modify an entity, in which case enter C/M. No other combinations should occur.

If you want to fully document the system, you should check that you have entered the reference number of the process into the 'DFD Processes' box on the corresponding Function Definition Form. You should also record the reference(s) of the event in the 'Events' on the same form. As events do not have specific references you can use the matrix entry from Event/Entity Matrix Form. For example, if you are dealing with the first entity and the third event on your form, the box on the matrix will be 'A3' (column A, row 3). You can use this throughout the subsequent documentation as a unique reference to the event.

13.11.3   Task

Finally check your work against the model Sample Event/Entity Matrix Form, and sample Entity Life History diagrams given below. Do not worry if the order of Entities and events are different in your form to the one given; the corresponding entries in the matrix should, however, be the same. Whichever way you arrived at the Entity Life History events they should be very similar to the ones given. It is a little like arithmetic: the order of working need not be identical but the answers should still be the same.

Event-Entity Matrix Form

Current System							Required System **Yes**				
System **Wooden Windows** Author **MJH** Date **20/12/98**							Page of				

ENTITY / Function	A Cust	B Order	C Order-line	D Product	E	F	G	H	I	J	K
1.1 Identify Customer	C/M										
1.2 Create new order		C									
1.3 Accept order details			C/M								
1.4 Process order		M	M								
1.5 Produce weekly work order											
2.1 Accept payments											
2.2 Process payments	M	M									
2.3 Process 4-month non-payment	M	M									
2.4 Process 8-month non-payment	M	M									
3.1 Assemble orders & deliver											
3.2 File signed delivery notes											

13.11.4 Checking the DFM using the Entity Life Histories

As a final check on the correctness of your analysis of the required system, you need to ensure that all of the Data Flow Functions are compatible with the Entity Life Histories events, produced above, and that there is a process for every event, an event for every process, and that the entities are all created, modified and deleted by at least one function in the DFDs.Producing the definitive Required Logical DFDs

Initiates the in-depth analysis and logical design of the chosen business option by producing a definitive version of the logical data flow diagrams for the required system.

When you have gone through the whole of the Event/Entity Matrix Form, and dealt with all of the ELH events, you should turn the technique around and repeat the procedure every process. You should be able to identify an event which is linked to each low-level process, or function. If you cannot identify an event for a given function, you need to ask yourself what the purpose of that function is in the new system, and if it is still required.

In the Wooden Windows system, there are two instances of functions that appear to have no effect on the data within the system, and one entity is never created or modified. Can you identify the items which are being described? Also none of the entities are ever deleted, which means that a whole process is required to remove redundant information.

13.11.5   Task

Compare your results with the model answer given below. If there are any major differences you must decide whether they are merely alternatives of acceptable answers, or whether your work needs correcting. What we have done is to remove the obviously redundant delivery processes, and add some housekeeping functions. By now you should be able to modify the required logical DFDs yourself from this information, as shown previously in Chapter 11.

Event-Entity Matrix Form											
Current System							Required System **Yes**				
System **Wooden Windows** Author **MJH** Date **20/12/98**							Page of				
ENTITY	A	B	C	D	E	F	G	H	I	J	K
	C u s t	O r d e r	O r d e r - l i n r	P r o d u c t							
Function											
1.1 Identify Customer	C/ M										
1.2 Create new order		C									
1.3 Accept order details			C/ M								
1.4 Process order		M	M								
1.5 Produce weekly work order											
2.1 Accept Payments											
2.2 Process payments	M	M									
2.3 Process 4-month non-payment	M	M									
2.4 Process 8-month non-payment	M	M									
~~3.1 Assemble orders & deliver~~											
~~3.2 File signed delivery notes~~											
3.1 Delete out of date customers and orders	D	D	D								
3.2 Add or modify products				C/ M							
3.3 Delete out of date products				D							

13.12 The requirements specification

Having completed the analysis and the logical design you must now assemble a complete Requirements Specification suitable for presentation to your management and for passing on to the implementation team who will complete the project. You may or may not be available during the implementation phase, but your aim in preparing the paperwork is to assume that you are not, and to try to ensure that all the information needed is available in the documentation without further access to yourself or the User(s).

What you include will depend upon which of the available techniques which were included in the course you have been following to get to this point. Consequently the content will depend upon you having the products generated by the route by which you arrived at this unit. If you do not have a product referred to, then you cannot include it.

13.12.1 Task

First, write a clear and concise summary of the proposed system. Make it suitable for a non-specialist, and try to keep it to one side of typed A4 paper.

Next write a simple description of each of the major parts of the proposed system, making each approximately a paragraph long, with a diagram of how these parts interact. Identify specifically any manual, as opposed to computerised, procedures. Include a very brief account to show how these parts reflect the users' requirements for the system. Put all of the above into a separate section, labelled:

Section a) Introduction

In addition to the above the specification should convey to the reader, in a clear and structured fashion:

- all the objective(s) of the proposed system,
- the functions of each of the parts of the proposed system,
- a complete definition of all the inputs to each part of the proposed system, and
- a complete definition of all the outputs from each part of the proposed system.

This requires the analyst to gather together neat copies of all of the products created during the analysis and design process and to include them in the specification with whatever extra explanatory material is required to allow the reader to find their way around the documentation. Depending on the techniques used you should include the material in a logical order such as that suggested in the headings given below.

Section b) Detail of the System Processes to include:

Process Descriptions and Diagrams (e.g. level 1, 2 etc. DFD's).

Section c) Detail of the System Data to include:

Logical Data Model.
Entity Life Histories (if produced).

Section d) Identification of all reports and outputs to include:

Screen and Report layout detail (prototypes if available).

Section e) Identification and detail of all inputs screens

Task

The final summary section of the specification should convey to the user some idea of the magnitude of the tasks and the administrative and managerial implications involved with the proposed system. As a minimum you will probably need an acceptance test plan for the complete system, and a schedule of timescales, resources and costs.

Section f) Project Control and System Management to include:

- Timescales and deadlines.
- Test procedures required.
- Manual and clerical procedures required to run the system.

Finally assemble a list of the material in the tasks above and put it at the beginning of the document labelled 'Contents list'.

13.12.2   FOOTNOTE

Congratulations! If you have worked through a set of tasks and completed them up to this Unit, then you have made your second successful pass through the analysis and design of a system. From now on every one you do will be easier. There is, however, a lot more to learn but all of the advanced techniques depend upon and assume a skill with the ones you have covered, so the more you learn - the better you will get. Speed and ability only comes with practice.

Exercise 1.7.1

Systems analysis and design (as one item) is the term used to identify certain activities performed during the development of the software for computer systems. Systems analysis, on its own, is the process of examining and learning about the current system, its problem and the user requirements, and defining an abstract solution. Systems design, on its own, is the process of turning the abstract (analysed) solution into a practical specification, suitable for implementation. Systems design itself is commonly split into logical and physical design.

Exercise 1.7.2

Systems analysis and design, as one composite activity, occur near the start of the development of a computer system, after the problem has been identified by the user, but before software production starts. Within that period, they occur should follow one another with the analysis activities first, followed by the design activities.

Exercise 1.7.3

The individual who is responsible for analysis activities, and sometimes the design as well, is called the systems analyst. That person may also be called; Project Leader, Project Manager, Chief (Software) Engineer, Chief Programmer and Chief (or Senior) Designer. The same applies to the person responsible for the design activities. They may be called the System Designer, or they may be a technically qualified analyst or a senior (or chief) programmer on a career path to analyst.

Exercise 1.7.4

There are many activities required to implement computer systems. Apart from those of analysis and design are the following (as listed in Figure 1.1).
Code Design, Coding, Code Testing, System Commissioning, User Training, System Installation, System Testing, Cutover from current system, Review, Maintenance

Exercise 1.7.5

The top-down approach is to start with the whole system and to break it down into smaller and smaller units, each of which has a defined place in the overall structure. The bottom-up approach is to assemble the finished product from a large or reproducible number of small well-defined components; often maintenance programmers have to adopt this method to 'reverse engineer' a system for which there is no documentation.

Exercise 1.7.6

The activities associated with the production of the software lie towards the end of the development of a typical system, after the analysis and design, but before the implementation of the system.

Exercise 1.7.7

The major techniques used in the development of a typical system are: Data Flow Diagrams (DFD), Logical Data Structure Diagrams (LDS), Relational Data Analysis Tables (RDA), Jackson Structure Charts (based on JSP notation).

Any three of the above would be correct for this question.

Exercise 1.7.8

Any three of the skills listed below for an analyst, and together with three relevant skills for a programmer are an acceptable answer to this question.

Systems analysts mainly deal with people! They must be able to:
Take good notes
Conceptualise computer systems
Listen patiently
Extract information without giving offence
Document the systems using agreed standards

On the other hand **programmers** deal with mainly computers! They must be able to:
Understand the documentation
Test and implement computer systems
Produce working computer code
Document the programs for maintenance teams

Exercise 1.7.9

Three document milestones in the development of a typical system, and a brief description of their purpose could be any three of the following.

Project Initiation Documents (PID) - These are anything which is produced, often by the user, to define the problem before development begins.

Systems Proposal - A report produced by the systems analyst before in-depth analysis which is used to state what the proposed system should consist of in strategic terms, and whether to start work in earnest. This is similar to a feasibility study in practice.

Business System Proposal, described later, as a convenient milestone between the end of the requirements analysis and the beginning of the logical design.

Systems Specification - A document produced by the systems analyst between the logical design and the physical design activities and similar to the requirements specification. This document marks the change in activities to software development, where the products are aimed more at the computer specialist than the user.

Functional Specification - A document produced between the physical design and coding which allows programmers to concentrate on coding possibly a small part of the application without reference to the user or the analyst.

Exercise 1.7.10

Any reasonable example which is clearly delineated as: inputs, transformations and outputs is an acceptable response to this question.

Exercise 2.13.1

The name is given to the process of learning about the user requirements is 'Fact Finding'. It is the first active task performed by the analyst at the beginning of the development of a typical system.

Exercise 2.13.2

You should have chosen interviewing and questionnaires if only because there is a lot of material for you to use for your description. Reading, researching and observing are the other relevant techniques.

Interviewing is by far the most important techniques used by the analyst at this stage in the development of a typical system. It is used when the analyst needs to be personally involved, or must gain information at first hand via direct contact with the users and clients.

The other major fact finding technique is based on the use of questionnaires. In these the user is constrained to responding to the exact questions asked, and also to answering them in a manner pre-defined by the analyst. Their use is unavoidable if there are many users scattered over a wide area, or are otherwise unavailable for personal contact with the analyst.

Exercise 2.13.3

The activity associated with the system's data is common to all types of system implementation is the 'take-on' of the current system data. It is it often overlooked as the user can believe that it will take place 'automatically'.

Exercise 2.13.4

The Analyst's skills, and the User's knowledge are required in an interview to produce the analyst's understanding of the user's requirements or problems?

Exercise 2.13.5

The three 'standard questions' which apply to almost any interview relating to computerisation are; 'what does the user not like about the current system', 'what does the user expects to gain from the new system', and 'what the user knows about computers'.

Exercise 2.13.6

The information on each area within an organisation that an analyst must identify during the interview process is the function performed by each area within the organisation, their structure and managers, and their involvement in the analysis. As soon as possible after an interview an analyst should make clear notes on what they have learned, and of any additional information that they know will be required.

Exercise 2.13.7

Analysts often overlooks the requirements for the proposed system to perform all of the current functions from the current system which are not classed as problems.

Exercise 2.13.8

Any four of the basic rules listed will, if followed, give the best chance of an interview proceeding smoothly:

- Plan the interview carefully, do try to not 'busk it'.

- Learn as much as you can about the interviewee beforehand.
- Remember to communicate at the level of the person.
- Arrange the time and place well before, and be on time.
- Select a good environment if you can.
- Listen more than talk.
- Take discreet notes as you go along.
- Try to interview only one person at a time.
- Control the interview - do not digress.
- Do not try to cover everything at one meeting.
- Avoid conflict and confrontation.
- Conclude positively with a summary of the topics covered.

Exercise 2.13.9

Gordon Bennet suggests that the the river flow data should be: carried forward, validated, authorised and edited at the Districts before it is sent to the Region.

Exercise 2.13.10

If you complete this task, save the results in a safe place and examine them from time to time to help yourself move towards gaining the skills you need to eventually get your ideal job. Identify employers who you may wish to work for, and try to predict their hiring patterns and preferences so that you can approach them at the best time and most appropriate way when you next look for a job.

Exercise 3.7.1-3.7.4

There is really no model answer that can be given as this is 'all your own work'. Compare your results with those given in the text to form a judgement of how successful you have been at complying with the work required.

Exercise 3.7.5

The modified rich picture of the river flow meter system (Figure 3.5) showing how the situation would appear if all of the work were centralised at the regional office is given below. There is nothing in the suggested root definition that need change if this were the case.

Rich Picture of Flow Meter Case Study

FLOW METER

JIM LADD (DFO)

+ FRESH DISK

EVERY 2 WEEKS

DISTRICT OFFICE

+ OLD DISK

& GRAPH FROM CHARTS

VIA POST

RFCO

CORRECTIONS NEEDED

MONTHLY AVERAGES

LOG

LIST OF READINGS

RFCO

RRT
??

Exercise 4.9.1

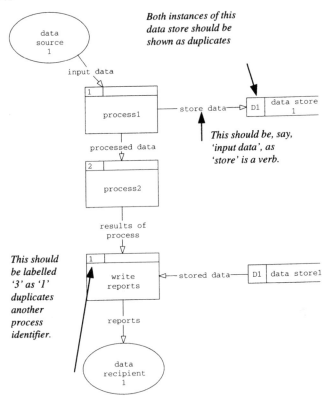

Both instances of this data store should be shown as duplicates

This should be, say, 'input data', as 'store' is a verb.

This should be labelled '3' as '1' duplicates another process identifier.

Exercise 4.9.2

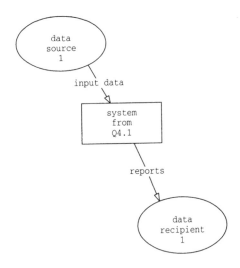

Exercise 4.9.3

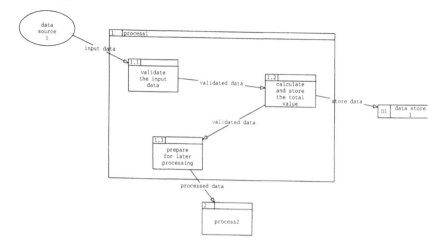

Exercise 4.9.4

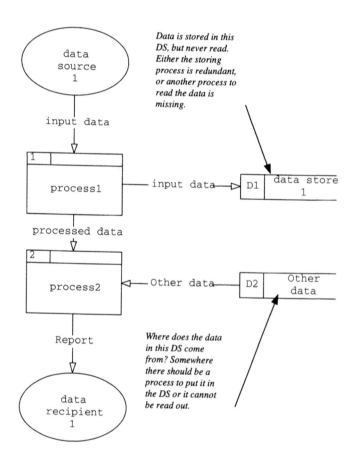

Exercise 5.8.1

Answer 5.1 i)

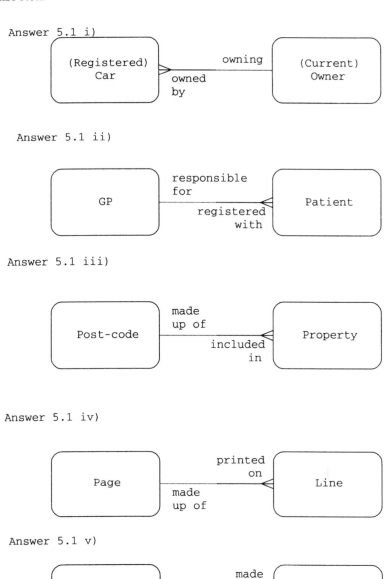

Answer 5.1 ii)

Answer 5.1 iii)

Answer 5.1 iv)

Answer 5.1 v)

Exercise 5.8.2

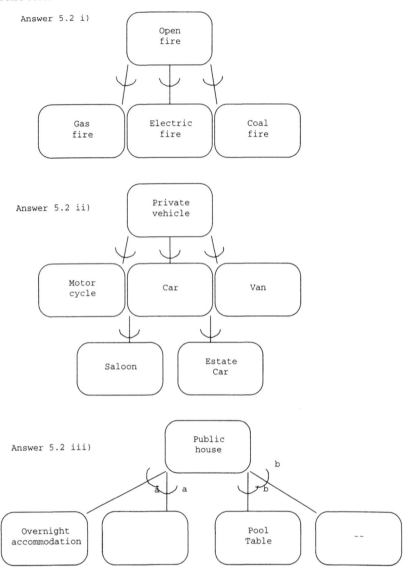

Answer 5.2 i)

Open fire

Gas fire

Electric fire

Coal fire

Answer 5.2 ii)

Private vehicle

Motor cycle

Car

Van

Saloon

Estate Car

Answer 5.2 iii)

Public house

Overnight accommodation

Pool Table

Exercise 5.8.3

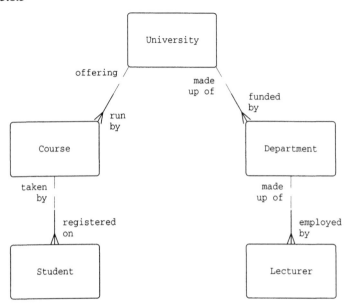

Exercise 5.8.4

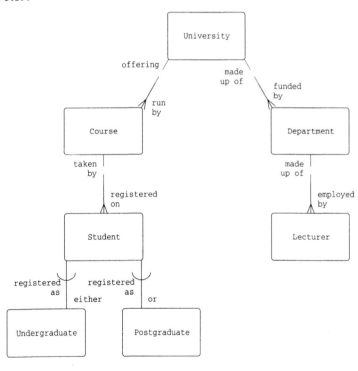

Exercise 5.8.5

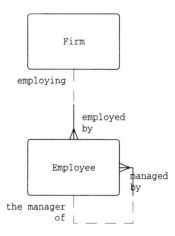

Exercise 5.8.6

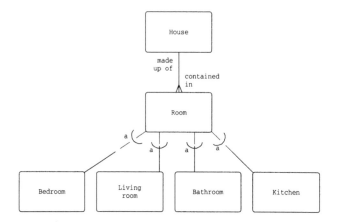

Exercise 5.8.7

The diagram shows that a house may be divided into three logical areas which must be present in some form to fulfil its purpose: a living area, a sleeping area, and a domestic area. The living area may be made up of one or more living rooms, the sleeping area may be made up of one or more bedrooms, and domestic area must contain at least one, or more, bathroom(s) and at least one, or more, kitchen(s). Obviously this is an unsatisfactory description as many more combinations are possible than are described here, but it gives more information than the previous answer which merely stated that there were four types of room in a house, and each room could only be of one type.

Exercise 6.5.1

The changes required to the system to include the weather data, as on the original report, would be as follows:

- A new data store would be required to hold the weather data for each day.
- A data entry process would be required to allow the DFO to enter this data.
- The process that prints the reports would need access to the data store.

Exercise 6.5.2

A simple proposal to suggest how all of the functions to be centralised at the regional headquarters could be as follows. Remember that, at this stage we are merely suggesting how this could be achieved. Contrast this with the answer to Q8.1, which goes into the detail of the possible effects of adopting this option. In a small system like this it is quite feasible to run these two together, but in large systems the preferred practice is to decide on the best option, and then consider how the business would be affected, otherwise resistance to change may ensure that no changes are ever implemented.

The proposed computerisation of the current system allows the Authority the opportunity to centralise the functions currently performed on the river flow data at the Districts before it is sent to the Region. At present, the river flow data is: carried forward, validated, and edited by each DFO, before being authorised by their respective DM. If the manual process of visiting the meters were to be performed at each district, possibly by a more junior person, then the data disks could be sent directly to the Regional HQ and all the above processing performed there.

Exercise 7.4.1

The modified User/Function Matrix Form is as shown next.

User/Function Relation Matrix Form											
Current System					Required System **YES**						
System **RIVER FLOW** Author **MJH**			Date **2/3/93**			Page of					
USER	A	B	C	D	E	F	G	H	I	J	K
A DISTRICT FLOW OFFICER B DISTRICT MANAGER C REGIONAL FLOW MANAGER D REGIONAL RESEARCH TEAM E REGIONAL FLOW OFFICER FUNCTION											
1 Collect river flow disk and pen chart	X										
2 Load fresh disk and pen chart paper	X										
3 Validate readings against previous reading					C						
4 Internally validate readings					C						
5 Validate readings between river flow meters					C						
6 Compare anomalous readings with weather diary					X						

7	Edit readings as necessary					C						
8	Enter new readings into system (database)					C						
9	Produce weekly reports (each month)					C						
10	Check diary and reports				X							
11	Request changes to unsatisfactory readings				X							
12	Authorise satisfactory data and reports				C							
13	Send data and reports to Regional HQ				X							
14	Read reports and store data from Districts into central database.				X C							
15	Use data for modelling						C					
16	Produce PIWFs				C							
17												
18												
Sample User/Function Matrix Form. PISAD-UF1. Version 1.												

Items 3 to 9 are now performed by the RFO, and hence 10 to 13 are probably going to be transferred to by the RFM, as he is the line manager of the person performing the prior tasks. If this is the case then functions 12, 13 and 14 will probably no longer be required, and may be able to be deleted.

Exercise 7.4.2

The context diagram will be changed by re-naming the external entity that the 'Monthly reports' go to as 'RFO' rather than the 'DM'. The other inputs and outputs to the system are not affected by re-assigning the roles between departments. This is normal. If the number or type of inputs especially, or even some outputs, were to change then the system has effectively become a fundamentally different system. So long as the inputs and output flows do not change themselves, we can consider this to be a modification.

The modified context diagram is as shown next.

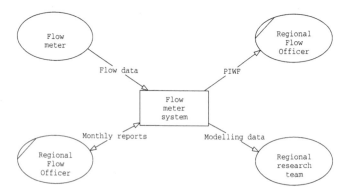

The modified Level 1 DFD is as shown next.

Exercise 7.4.3

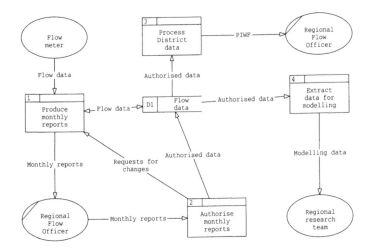

The modified explosion of rl DFD process 1 is as shown below.

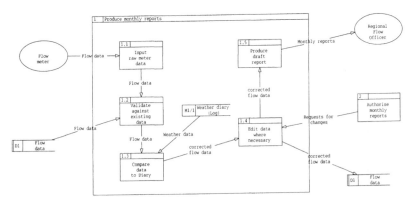

The modified explosion of rl DFD process 2 is as shown next.

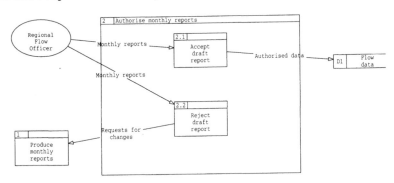

The remaining processes are not affected by these modifications.

Exercise 8.2.1

A simple proposal to suggest how the business would be affected if all of the functions were centralised at the regional headquarters could be as follows. Remember that, at this stage we are merely suggesting the possible effects of adopting this option. In a small system like this it is quite feasible to run this report together with the initial proposal document discussed in Chapter 6, but in large systems the preferred practice is to decide on the best option, and then consider how the business would be affected, otherwise resistance to change may ensure that no changes are ever implemented.

The proposed computerisation of the current system allows the Authority the opportunity to centralise the functions currently performed on the river flow data at the Districts before it is sent to the Region. At present, the river flow data is: carried forward, validated, and edited by each DFO, before being authorised by their respective DM. If the manual process of visiting the meters were to be performed at each district, possibly by a more junior person, then the data disks could be sent directly to the Regional HQ and all the above processing performed there. This would have the advantages that:

- *the raw data would be available at one central point,*
- *the data may be available more quickly at the Regional HQ,*
- *only one computer system would be required for all of the processing, and*
- *the method of processing would be guaranteed to be consistent across the Region.*

On the negative side:

- *the DFOs would effectively be made redundant,*
- *the DMs may object to the loss of a function currently within their remit, and*
- *the RFO would be obliged to authorise all of the data for the whole Region.*

It is for the Authority to decide whether to pursue the option outlined above, or continue with the implementation of the system as specified.

Exercise 9.9.1

The conversion of most of this form is just a straightforward transcription of items. However, the presence of a 'matrix' should alert us to a potential problem. The use of the repeated group of days of the week (S,M,T,) is a typical form designer's device for representing two things at once. The **position** gives us the **day of the week** (dow), and the number entered in that position gives the **quantity** (Qty) of the **Item** as in the sample from the form copied below.

Item	S	M	T	W	T	F	S	S-P
G7 Milk.	..	.4	..	.4	..	.3	..	.2-10

So the attributes should be:

Customer No.
Name
Week Ending
Address
Round No

Item } All the next section is a repeating group
S } } These are really another repeating group - Dow, Qty
M } }
T } }
W } }
T } }
F } }
S } }
£-P} This is really the 'Item Total'

Total for week
Balance B/fwd
Total
Cash Rec'd
Balance Due

Copying this forward to the table form as introduced in the text, the result of each question 9.1 to 9.4 is as shown in the columns below.

Exercise 9.9.1 cont. -9.9.4

9.1 cont. UN_NF	9.2 1NF	9.3 2NF	9.4 3NF	Notes
<u>Customer No.</u>	<u>Customer No.</u>	<u>Customer No.</u>	<u>Customer No.</u>	Table of customer
Name	Name	Name	Name	information.
Address	Address	Address	Address	
<u>Week Ending</u>	<u>Week Ending</u>			
Round No	Round No	<u>Customer No.</u>	<u>Customer No.</u>	We need both
{Item	Total for week	<u>Week Ending</u>	<u>Week Ending</u>	items to identify
{Day of week	Balance B/fwd	Round No	Round No	the bill uniquely.
quantity}	Total	Total for week	Balance B/fwd	'Total for week'
Item Total}	Cash Rec'd	Balance B/fwd	Cash Rec'd	Balance Due
Total for week	Balance Due	Total		& 'Total' can all
Balance B/fwd		Cash Rec'd		be calculated.
Total	<u>Customer No.</u>	Balance Due		
Cash Rec'd	<u>Week Ending</u>		<u>Customer No.</u>	There isonly one
Balance Due	<u>Item</u>	<u>Customer No.</u>	<u>Week Ending</u>	non-key item, so
	Item Total	<u>Week Ending</u>	<u>Item</u>	this must be in
		<u>Item</u>	Item Total	2NF and 3 NF!
	<u>Customer No.</u>	Item Total		See Note 1 below
	<u>Week Ending</u>		<u>Customer No.</u>	
	<u>Item</u>	<u>Customer No.</u>	<u>Week Ending</u>	See Note 2 below
	<u>Day of week</u>	<u>Week Ending</u>	<u>Item</u>	
	Qty	<u>Item</u>	<u>Day of week</u>	
		<u>Day of week</u>	Qty	
		Qty		

Note 1:   This group can be called the 'Item line'. There is no indication of how 'Qty' is translated into 'Item-total'. This implies that there are some attributes missing. If we knew what they were we may be able to delete the 'Item Total' and hence the whole table, but as we do not have the information there is nothing more that we can do at this stage.

Note 2:   This group can be called, say, 'Items delivered'. Whatever happens we need all of this information despite the unwieldy key.

Exercise 10.6.1

CUSTOMER
Customer No.
Name
Address

ITEM LINE
Customer No.*   }FK to
Week Ending *   }Weekly
Item   Bill
Item Total

WEEKLY BILL
Customer No.*   FK to Cust
Week Ending
Round No
Balance B/fwd
Cash Rec'd

QTY-DELIVERED
Customer No.*   }FK to
Week Ending *   }Item line
Item *   }
Day of week
Qty

Exercise 10.6.2

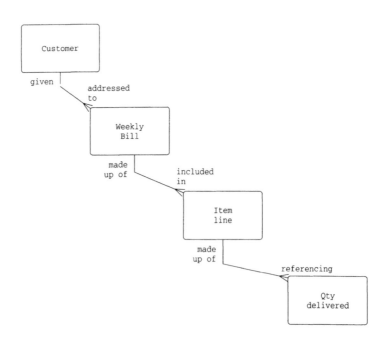

Exercise 10.6.3

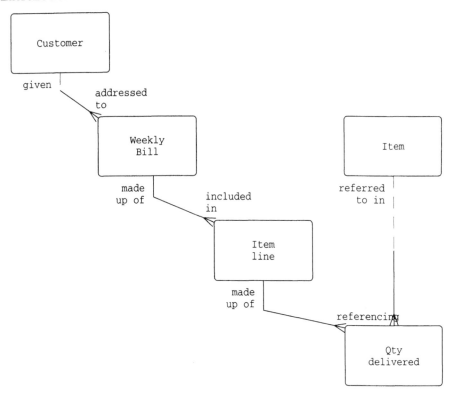

Exercise 10.6.4

- A Customer may be given many Weekly Bill(s)
- An Item may be referred to in many Qty delivered(s)
- An Item line must be included in one Weekly Bill and must be made up of many Qty delivered.
- A Qty delivered must be referencing one Item line and must be referencing one Item
- A Weekly Bill must be addressed to one Customer and must be made up of many Item line(s)

Exercise 11.5.1

A JSP-type diagram showing the structure of the train as described is as shown next.

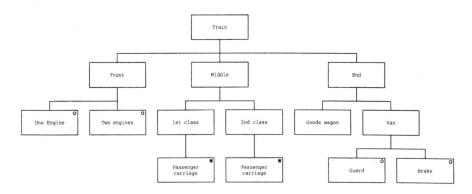

Exercise 11.5.2

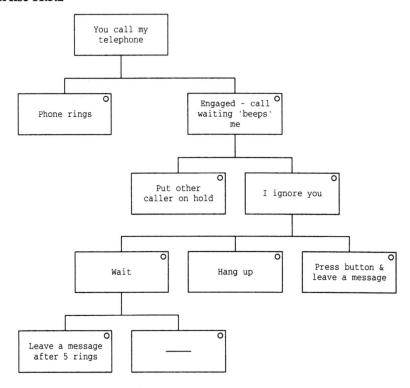

Index

233